BANNOCKBURN

BANNOCKBURN

Scotland's Greatest Battle For Independence

Angus Konstam

Aurum
Press

First published in Great Britain
2014 by Aurum Press Ltd
74—77 White Lion Street
Islington
London N1 9PF
www.aurumpress.co.uk

A catalogue record for this book is available from the British Library.

ISBN 978 1 78131 287 2

1 3 5 7 9 10 8 6 4 2
2014 2016 2018 2017 2015

Typeset in Goudy Old Style by SX Composing DTP, Rayleigh, Essex
Printed and bound by CPI Group (UK) Ltd, Croydon, CR0 4YY

Contents

Part 2   Battle of a Nation

Acknowledgements

I should begin by thanking the staff of the National Library of Scotland and the National Archives of Scotland – both in Edinburgh – and the British Library in London. Other useful havens of research were the Scottish Room of the Edinburgh Central Library and the London Library. I am also indebted to Professor Richard Oram of Stirling University and Dr Chris Brown for offering to spot the errors in my manuscript, and to steer me through the pitfalls of the subject. I should also thank Dave Patterson and Bill Gilchrist, for braving the hail, sun and snow of the battlefield.

Above all I'd like to thank my publisher Iain Macgregor of Aurum Press, and also his team, especially Lucy Warburton, Steve Gove and Charlotte Coulthard. Thank you for putting up with my idiosyncrasies, and for all your hard work and professionalism. Similarly my thanks go to my literary agent Andrew Lownie, who continues to amaze me with insight and expertise.

Bannockburn is a battle that can be interpreted in several ways, depending on how you read the sources and the ground. This book is based on my understanding of this evidence. I leave it up to you to decide if you agree with my conclusions. Finally, if there are any errors in the book, they are entirely of my own making.

Preface

Ifirst heard about Robert the Bruce thanks to my trio of widowed great-aunts. Their husbands or fiancés had all died in the Great War, and their idea of child raising involved sending their young grand-nephew books rather than toys at Christmas. I was about eight when one of them – I forget which – sent me a couple of Ladybird books, biographies of famous people. One was entitled *Captain Cook*, the other *Robert the Bruce*. The cover of the first showed a smartly dressed naval officer, watching a Union Jack being raised over a deserted beach, while the other showed a bearded man sitting in a cave watching a spider. I was intrigued. One was obviously a great leader. Who on earth was the spider watcher?

It turned out he was actually King Robert I of Scotland, who went on to win a great victory over the English at a place called Bannockburn. For an eight-year-old the story was a little bewildering. One page showed him stabbing someone in a church, and then he was crowned, while five pages later he was hiding in the hills, watching that spider. Further on in the book he was seen capturing castles by hiding his men in hay wagons, and the finale was that great victory, where his soldiers were shown using their spears to skewer charging knights. It was all enthralling stuff, and confusing enough for me to want to know more. That old widowed aunt knew how to hook a boy on history.

Two years later I visited Bannockburn as part of a school exchange trip. Kids from Edinburgh went to Orkney for a week, and then we 'peedie' islanders headed south to see the sights of the big city. We didn't just visit Edinburgh. We also went on a tour to Stirling Castle, and stopped off at the brand-new Bannockburn visitor centre on the way back. I still have the visitor's brochure from the visit, with its maps showing how the battle unfolded. I also still have a postcard showing a regal-looking statue of Robert the Bruce mounted on his war horse, gazing out across the fields where his spearmen ripped the heart out of English chivalry. It was only later – much later – that I found out the battle was really fought somewhere else, the map was probably wrong, and King Robert probably looked less imposing in the flesh than he did in bronze.

That, of course, is one of the delights of history. There's always something new to learn, something more to uncover. Our ideas about the past change with time, and so too does the way we look at the way history is presented. When we're young, we pretty much accept everything at face value, or at least we do if it's written down in a book. Then we begin questioning things, and sometimes we discover that there's more than one version of what happened in the past. After all, two people can go to the same football match, and then give such radically different versions of what went on that they could have been watching two different games. If they both supported different teams to start with, then their accounts might well reflect their partisan allegiances. History works the same way. The only difference is that if the event took place as long ago as Bannockburn, then sometimes we only have a handful of accounts, some of which were written long after the event by people who weren't even there. That's where history gets really interesting.

It becomes something of a treasure hunt, or a piece of detective work. It also involves some of the skills of the judge, weighing up evidence and trying to work out the truth from the not so true. History is a very personal journey, as everyone who embarks on a historical quest has to make their own way and reach their own decisions. Historians can be just as biased as the people whose accounts they read. Whether we like it or not, every historian has their own agenda. Some of the great historians of the past hundred years have been given labels – so and so has a political, national or ethnic bias, or is an apologist for one side or another. While we usually try to avoid this – or at least not be too blatant about it – we're all human, and so inevitably some degree of bias creeps in.

This isn't necessarily a bad thing – a strictly neutral version of any story can be very dull indeed. It might be more honest to say right at the start that any history is based on the available evidence, but written by someone with a voice, and an opinion. In Scotland, history and politics often become entangled. For some, the past is a source of inspiration for the future. For others, it becomes a salutary lesson in what mistakes to avoid. The one thing Scottish history is not is dead, fit only for scholars and schoolchildren. In Scotland, on the eve of a hard-fought referendum, history is more likely to be seen as a weapon to be wielded in a modern battle for the hearts and minds of the Scottish people.

Bannockburn was a turning point in history, for the English as well as the Scots. This medieval battle helped define the political landscape of Britain. For many Scots this seminal moment from their past has become a patriotic talisman, even though the romantic myths that surround it have all but obscured what really happened. Seven centuries later, debates on national identity and Scottish independence will inevitably be influenced by the events of 1314. While I have my own views on Scotland's future, I've tried not to let them show. After all, this book is really about Scotland's past.

The story of Robert the Bruce, the Scottish Wars of Independence and the Battle of Bannockburn has been told many times before. Both learned historians and more populist authors have recounted the tale, and the topic has attracted its fair share of cranks and axe-grinders. Much ink has been spilt over the finer points of this important battle, yet still there's disagreement over how the battle was fought, how many people took part, or even where it happened. Academics sometimes argue over the merits of the handful of sources out there, and the value of one medieval writer compared to another. Others are more than willing to overload a reader with facts, in the mistaken belief that dryness and worthiness are closely related.

As a historian I know how to sort the wheat from the chaff. As a writer, my aim is to use what we know about the past to paint as vivid a portrait of it as I can. Fortunately the subject lends itself to the task. Its historical cast includes murderous kings, scheming nobles, warlike bishops, chivalric knights, courtly sybarites, heartless taxmen and strong-willed wives. The story of Bannockburn has it all – it is a history that captures the imagination, and is a tale that deserves retelling. Please join me on a trip into that vibrant past – a journey that for me began almost half a century ago with that little Christmas present.

Prologue

Robert Clifford had met his match. As his weary and frustrated knights circled the ranks of spearmen he must have realised it. It was unthinkable that well-mounted men-at-arms could be beaten by soldiers on foot, but that was exactly what had just happened. An hour before, Clifford and his men had been moving fast across open ground, heading towards Stirling Castle. They could even see its battlements in the distance. Now his knights – the elite of King Edward's army – were being bested by mere spearmen. Clifford was one of the most important magnates in England, and a grizzled veteran of numerous battles and skirmishes. None of this was helping him now, as he stared defeat in the face.

He might have realised the significance of the moment, but despite all his experience he couldn't have been aware this was a defining moment – the turning point of the battle, the campaign and the entire war. Clifford and his men had been tested, and had been found wanting. The date was 23 June 1314, the time early afternoon, and the place Bannockburn – more specifically an area of rough pasture just north of the hamlet surrounding St Ninian's Church. The following day the same ground Clifford had recently passed through would be fought over again, as the battle reached its bloody conclusion. This, though, was the moment when the Scots learned they were just as good as the most powerful troops the English could hurl against them.

Earlier that day King Edward II's English army had been marching to relieve Stirling Castle when they came upon a Scottish force blocking their path. The vanguard of Edward's army halted in front of the Bannockburn, a stream whose wriggling course barred their advance. The Scots were waiting for them on the high ground beyond the stream, the bulk of their troops hidden by the trees which covered the ridge. In plain view was Robert the Bruce, self-styled King of Scotland, mounted on a small palfrey. The two armies had skirmished across the stream that morning, at the ford where the Stirling–Falkirk road crossed the steep-sided slopes of the Bannockburn. The fighting hadn't gone well for Edward – his men were hemmed in both by the terrain and by the Scottish infantry. He needed to find another route to Stirling.

That was where Robert Clifford came in. The forty-year-old nobleman commanded a large contingent in Edward's army, and when the king called him to his side, he was given fresh orders. Clifford and his men were to cross the Bannockburn further downstream. They would then bypass the wooded slopes and find a new way to reach Stirling Castle. A modern soldier would call this mission a 'reconnaissance in force'. Lord Clifford, though, was a knight, and his orders had a uniquely medieval twist to them. Stirling Castle was held by an English garrison, and its governor had made a promise – one that had led directly to this great battle between two royal armies. A few months before, Stirling's governor had promised that he would hold out until midsummer. If he wasn't relieved by then he would surrender the castle. There was now just one day to spare – Edward had to relieve the castle or lose it to the Scots.

Clifford's extra mission was to fulfil this obligation. Technically the castle had already been relieved when the English vanguard came within three leagues of its walls. Clifford didn't have to cut his way through to the castle gates – but it would be good to make contact with them, and reassure them that help was on its way. This venture began well enough. Clifford found a place to cross the Bannockburn, well away from the sounds of the fight raging further upstream. His mounted men-at-arms cantered and formed themselves up ready for the two-mile march to the castle. So far everything had gone to plan.

As he advanced across the flat, open alluvial plain known as the Carse of Balquhiderock, Clifford must have kept a wary eye on the wooded slopes to his left. Had the Scots seen him? Who was hidden in the trees? He would soon find out. The road to Stirling ran along the ridge, and emerged from the trees beside St Ninian's Church, where a small hamlet straddled another stream. Clifford's men crossed this burn – the Pelstream – and moved left, skirting a bog to reach the high ground beyond the church. It was then they saw the enemy. Scottish foot soldiers began filtering out of the trees near the church, and started forming up into a 'schiltron', a dense but flexible block of spearmen four or five deep. That day it proved to be a battle-winning formation.

Thomas, Earl of Moray and the nephew of the Scottish king, had been watching Clifford since his men crossed the Bannockburn. He commanded King Robert's reserve, a division of spearmen who were hidden deep in the woods overlooking the carse. He had taken no part in the skirmish near the ford – his job was to protect the Scots army from any move against his flank. While Clifford's men were certainly on the flank of Robert's army, they weren't threatening it. Instead they seemed to be marching towards Stirling. He could obey orders and stay where he was, or he could march out and meet the English. Moray chose the more active course.

When he spotted the Scots Robert Clifford had three choices. He could turn back and rejoin the main army, he could avoid the Scots and head for the castle, or he could form up his men and charge. He probably didn't even consider the first option – to retreat without even fighting would incur the wrath of the king, and he would be labelled a coward. Clifford was certainly not scared of anyone. He had already fulfilled the main part of his mission – he had been seen by the garrison, and technically he had lifted the siege. Still, to ride on to Stirling meant failure in his other duty – the reconnaissance. For that mission to succeed he needed to probe the enemy's defences, and then return to Edward to give his report. That really left him just one choice. Besides, his 300 mounted men-at-arms included some of the most experienced knights in the army. What could possibly go wrong? Clifford decided to charge.

The chronicler Sir Thomas Grey tells us what happened next. While Grey wasn't there that day, his father was. Also Sir Thomas, the elder Grey was, like Clifford, a battle-hardened veteran. He heard Clifford speak to Sir Henry Beaumont, the king's cousin, who was acting as Clifford's co-commander. Beaumont might have been a bull-headed knight, but he was so sure of himself he advocated waiting, to give the Scots a sporting chance. Sir Thomas wasn't so sure – he argued for immediate action, yelling, 'My Lord, give them what you like now – in a short while they will have everything.' If Clifford had listened to Grey the Battle of Bannockburn might have been over before it had properly begun. Instead Beaumont replied for him, shouting across to Grey, 'Flee then – flee if you're afraid.' That was enough for Grey. He kicked his spurs in, levelled his lance, and trotted off towards the enemy spearmen. Clifford now had no option but to order the rest of his knights to follow.

By now the Earl of Moray and his men were almost ready. As the English knights approached, the last of the spearmen ran into place and levelled their spears. The schiltron was a uniquely Scottish battle formation. While other fighting men, like the Flemings, adopted similar formations, what set the schiltron apart was its versatility. Essentially it involved four or five ranks of spearmen, bunched up to form a single wall of men. When the spears were levelled the schiltron presented a dense wall of spearpoints to the enemy. The schiltron could be deployed as a long line of spearmen, or occasionally its two ends could be doubled back on each other to form a ring of spears.

Like the infantry squares of Napoleon's time these spear rings were almost invulnerable to cavalry, as long as the men held their nerve. If, however, the enemy could break into the ring, then the whole thing fell apart, and it was every man for himself.

Just before the knights reached the schiltron the leading ranks of spearmen would have dug their spear butts into the ground, to help absorb the shock when man and rider hurtled into them. Most horses would shy away at the last minute, but these knights were riding destriers, big battle horses which – if excited enough – just might be convinced to smash into the enemy and ride them down. That, though, was if the enemy didn't stand their ground with levelled spears. The collision must have been breathtakingly ferocious. Sir Thomas's horse was skewered by the well-braced spears and fell to the ground, throwing its rider in front of the spearmen. A stunned Sir Thomas was pulled from his twitching horse, and spearmen hauled him into the centre of the ring. Another knight, Sir William Deyncourt, was killed outright, transfixed by a spearhead. Both knights were well ahead of their companions. The knights behind them saw the horror unfold and at the last minute pulled their horses aside. It was as if they sensed they would be unable to break through the bristling wall of spears.

Clifford and Beaumont, though, were not prepared to give up. While a frontal assault might not work, a more methodical approach should win the day. They needed to find a way into the schiltron – to encourage the Scots to break formation, or to find chinks in the schiltron's defences which could then be exploited using sword and axe. The English men-at-arms rode around the Scottish ring, and began launching coordinated assaults from several directions at once. The ring held. The air became thick with dust, and the men of both sides were now dripping with sweat. The English men-at-arms found it impossible to prise their way in, so they resorted to throwing axes at the spearmen, hoping to create a gap. The Scots knew that an opening in their ranks would be fatal, so when men died others quickly took their place.

The way to crack a schiltron was to bring up archers, just as King

Edward's father had done at the Battle of Falkirk fifteen years before. The trouble was, Clifford was on a mounted reconnaissance – the spearmen and archers he commanded had been left with the king. This meant the battle had to be won the hard way, with lance, sword, axe and knife. So the hacking and stabbing continued – the English knights launching attacks against the wall, and the Scots doing whatever they could to protect themselves. Clifford's men-at-arms threw themselves into the fray, but try as they might they couldn't break into the enemy ranks. Eventually, after an hour or so of struggle, the exhausted riders began to falter.

At that moment a fresh group of Scottish spearmen began appearing at the edge of the woods. These were the men of James Douglas, Bruce's loyal lieutenant. The English men-at-arms pulled back to regroup, giving Moray's men a chance to recover. The English withdrawal also handed the Scots the initiative. Moray ordered his schiltron to advance, and gingerly his troops stepped over the bodies of dead men and horses, moving slowly towards Clifford's horsemen. The English men-at-arms were too exhausted to continue the fight. Instead they began to break and run. This was the moment when Clifford must have realised he was beaten. His men had given their all to the fight, and still the ranks of spearmen remained unbroken. Now the same spearmen were advancing towards him. It was utterly unthinkable, but these lowly Scottish foot soldiers had won the fight.

As Clifford's men fled, either back across the carse or towards the castle, their commander must have wondered just how he could explain his defeat to King Edward. The battle had been hard-fought, but the Earl of Moray and his spearmen had clearly won a great victory. Just as important, the natural order of medieval warfare had been turned on its head. It was a long-established rule of thumb that a mounted man-at-arms would be able to defeat a soldier on foot, and in medieval armies an infantryman was largely there to make up the numbers. His role was to garrison castles, not to win battles. That was the job of the man-at-arms. That afternoon at Bannockburn men-at-arms had been beaten by common spearmen. It was nothing short of a battlefield revolution. Unfortunately for Edward the lesson went unheeded. As a result, Robert Clifford's defeat was merely a foretaste of what was to come.

Naming the Sources

Unlike journalists, historians like to name their sources. It proves they know what they're talking about, and suggests that they've not only read the sources but have fully understood what they tell us. A lot of medieval battles are poorly documented, but Bannockburn isn't one of them. Of course there are huge gaps in what the medieval writers tell us, and some were writing long after the event. Essentially though, if taken together the sources give us a pretty reasonable idea of what happened at Bannockburn.

The most famous account of the battle is found in John Barbour's *Bruce*, a narrative poem written around 1375. While it contains colour and detail, it has to be read with caution, as Barbour was writing for a much later audience, and wanted to please the king and certain nobles by emphasising the part played by their ancestors. That said, it is vibrant and colourful, and it breathes life into the kingship of Robert Bruce. For the sake of clarity, and to keep the rhythm of the original, in the excerpts used here I've used a translation of the original medieval Scots, which is too impenetrable to understand without re-reading the passage several times. I have drawn on Michael Macmillan's translation, published in 1914, which is perhaps the most elegant of all English language versions of the *Bruce*.

Then there's John Fordoun's *Chronica Gentis Scotorum* (Chronicles of the Scottish People), written around 1385. While it contains a brief description of the battle, the work was added to by Walter Bower in the mid-fifteenth century, and the result was the *Scotichronicon*. This contains new information about the battle, but of course it was written more than a century after the battle took place. Another source is *Liber Pluscardensis*, written in Pluscardine Abbey near Elgin around 1461, when William Boyce was its prior. Unfortunately that's almost all we have from the Scottish side – three accounts, all of which were written long after the event.

Fortunately some of the English sources are more contemporary. John of Trokelowe – a monk from St Albans – wrote his *Annales* around 1330, and he provides a reasonably detailed account of the battle. Then we have the chronicler Geoffrey le Baker's *Chronicon Angliae*, which he began writing in 1341, and which dealt with the reigns of Edward II and III. The *Chronicon de Lanercost* (*Lanercost Chronicle*) was penned by several hands in Lanercost Priory outside Carlisle, and has been dated to around 1346. It covers Bannockburn, and much of Edward I's campaigning as well. The anonymous chronicler of *Vita Edwardi Secundi* wrote his history of the king's reign around 1346, and it contains a fairly good description of Bannockburn.

Probably the most useful English account of Bannockburn is found in *Scalacronica*, written by Sir Thomas Grey around 1355. His father of the same name was the one who fought with Lord Clifford, and was captured on the evening of the first day's fighting. Finally Abbot Thomas Burton's *Chronica monasterii de Melsa* written around 1396 mentions the battle. While there are several other English medieval sources for the battle, including a poem composed by Laurence Minot around 1352, few of them add much to our knowledge of what took place. Obviously some of these are more useful than others. Most were written by clerics, so military matters weren't their forte. Still, taken together and read in conjunction with Scottish works like the *Bruce*, we begin to get a better understanding of what happened during those frenetic moments of battle.

PART 1

The Road to Bannockburn

1

Gubbing the English

There hasn't been a battle between Scottish and English armies for almost five hundred years. Scottish involvement in the English Civil War – now more accurately called the War of the Three Kingdoms – was about 'regime change' and 'regime preservation', not national sovereignty. Culloden and the other battles of the Jacobite Rebellions don't count either, as the protagonists were divided by politics, culture and religion. Besides, like the seventeenth-century Covenanters, the Jacobites fought for 'regime change', not for Scottish sovereignty. Most lowland Scots and certainly most Protestant ministers would have viewed Jacobites who followed 'Bonny Prince Charlie' as little more than a Highland rabble – the bogeymen their mothers had warned them about. For three of these five centuries the two nations of Scotland and England have coexisted in relative peace and harmony, as part of the United Kingdom. That of course doesn't mean we get on.

In the final chapter we will look at national identity, and the role Bannockburn played in shaping it. For the moment, let's consider the way England and Scotland have rubbed along since 1314. Bannockburn was a spectacular Scottish victory – a rare beast – but it didn't immediately result in independence, nor bring an end to the fighting. A good case can be made that the Scottish Wars of Independence weren't really about independence at all. Scotland had always been independent – it was more about re-establishing sovereignty in the face of English encroachment. This doesn't mean the Plantagenet kings of England didn't covet Scottish land – they clearly did, but thanks to Edward I they became embroiled in a war they didn't need to fight, and found hard to win. They simply had no real long-term chance to maintain control of Scotland, especially north of the Forth and Clyde.

What is fascinating about this period is the way Scottish identity evolved. By the time of Bannockburn, Robert Bruce was not simply fighting to free Scotland from English domination – he was riding a wave of patriotic sentiment that didn't seem to have existed before. Today most people can't really comprehend the way medieval society worked, with its social bonds and legal contracts of feudalism, indenture and fealty. We don't get the notions of feudal overlordship and freedom of obligation that sparked off the whole conflict. However, the battle was fought to solve medieval problems – to confirm sovereignty, to evict invaders and to unify a divided realm. Today, Bannockburn is more likely to be seen in nationalist terms, as a battle fought purely for Scottish independence. Either that or it is portrayed as a class war, where English aristocrats were beaten by Scottish workers and peasants. Both of these views would have largely been lost on Robert Bruce.

Bannockburn was a rare victory for the Scots, and the memory of it kept Scottish hopes alive that Bruce's success could be repeated. The long string of Scottish defeats that followed – Dupplin Moor, Halidon Hill, Neville's Cross, the loss of Berwick, Flodden and Pinkie Cleuch – only served to make Bannockburn seem even more special. Such battles are long in the past, and most have been forgotten, or rather most people – English or Scots – have never heard of them. Bannockburn remains the exception. While most English schoolchildren are expected to know the significance of 1066, their Scottish counterparts should know what happened seven centuries ago, in 1314.

Today Anglo-Scottish conflict is largely confined to the sports field. British football's 'Home Internationals' used to attract huge crowds, until the Football Association and the Scottish Football Association decided to abandon them in favour of more lucrative glories in Europe. The last ever game, played in June 1977 at Wembley, attracted a crowd of just over 98,000 people. Thanks to Gordon McQueen and Kenny Dalglish the final result was 2–1 to the visitors, a late consolation penalty by Mick Channon not being enough to prevent a Scottish victory. The deliriously happy Scottish fans went wild, invading the pitch and breaking the goalposts in an attempt to snatch souvenirs of this historic moment. The English newspapers saw this as an act of rampant hooliganism. For the Scots, though, it was a triumph every bit as glorious as Bannockburn.

There was still a need to confront the 'Auld Enemy', even if the footballing avenue had been closed. Therefore it is hardly surprising that the 1980s saw a revival of interest in rugby union, and in particular the Calcutta Cup. This trophy, awarded to the winner of an annual England–Scotland game, was first contested back in 1879 and has since been fought over 120 times. England has won just over half of the encounters, and has managed to hold on to the cup since 2009. While Scottish wins seem less frequent than they once were, like the more martial confrontations of old the Scots still retain the memory of their victories.

One of the best was the Calcutta Cup win of 1990, the year Scotland won the Grand Slam, the clean sweep of victories against the other contestants in the Five (now Six) Nations championship. When the game started both sides were Grand Slam contenders, but the Scots were playing at Murrayfield – their home turf. The atmosphere was electric, particularly when, rather than running onto the pitch like the English, David Sole led his team out at a slow, deliberate walk. This was a team that meant business. Then the Scots played a new anthem. 'Flower of Scotland', written by Roy Williamson in 1965, was sung at Murrayfield for the first time that afternoon.

'Flower of Scotland' is an intensely patriotic song, and one that –
more than anything else – celebrates Bruce's victory at Bannockburn.
As Ronnie Browne from folk group the Corries says, the lines 'These
days are past now,/ and in the past they must remain,/ but we can still
rise now,/ and be the nation again' mean that our history is in the past,
but we need to keep the spirit of it alive – the spirit of Bannockburn.
The line 'sent him homeward to think again' was just as appropriate
when aimed at Edward II as at an equally arrogant Will Carling and his
English team, who fully expected to win. When the final whistle blew
the score was 13–7 to Scotland. The crowd went wild – in fact there
was another pitch invasion – but this time nothing was damaged apart
from English pride. Later, the message was rubbed home by the Scots'
new chant, '1314 Bannockburn, 13–7 Murrayfield'.

This rare sporting triumph is evidence that not only is Bannockburn
embedded in the Scottish DNA, but so too is the spirit embodied in
the 'sent him homeward' line. The Scottish psyche is a complex thing,
but it embraces a degree of communal egalitarianism that no longer
seems to exist in England. The spirit embraced by Robert Burns's 'A
Man's a Man for A' That' is still alive and well. So too is a dislike of
overweening arrogance, whether exhibited by kings, rugby captains or
anyone else. In recent years this trait has been particularly marked by
English politicians and sports commentators when they speak about
the Scots. I would imagine that over the past decade the arrogance of
English sports commentators has done more to drive people into the
arms of the Scottish nationalists than any number of political speeches.

This attitude is most manifest during World Cup campaigns, when
sports presenters seem to forget there is more to the United Kingdom
than the bit south of Gretna Green. On these occasions the English
newspapers often complain about anti-English feeling among the
Scots, who – with no Scottish team involved – land up supporting
'anyone but England'. In 2010 an American friend heard a huge roar
from an Edinburgh pub. The crowd were watching the England v.
USA World Cup game, and the United States had just equalised. He

was amazed that nobody was rooting for the home team. This, I would argue, is less anti-English than anti-arrogance. A good friend of the author said recently that they plan to vote to preserve the Union in the 2014 referendum, but they'll still sing 'La Marseillaise' before an England v. France rugby game.

The conclusion then is that Bannockburn retains an important place in our collective notion of Scottish heritage for reasons as complex and deep as the Scottish psyche itself. The story of the battle appeals to several strands of that psyche: we love an underdog, we dislike strutting arrogance, and – whether we admit it or not – we like getting one over on the English. Gubbing them – beating them – is a rare but satisfying experience. The battle not only embraced all of these elements, it also showed that it doesn't pay to underestimate the Scots. Above all Bannockburn has become a patriotic talisman, to be hauled out like a sacred relic whenever we feel the need. Academic arguments that it helped forge the modern Scottish nation or sense of identity have become irrelevant. For most, the distant memory of a glorious victory is all that matters.

2

Interregnum

Two funerals, and a cancelled wedding – it reads like the gritty sequel to a box office success from the mid-1990s. This, though, was no romantic comedy. It was pure Greek tragedy – as melancholy a chapter in Scottish history as you could find – and that takes some doing. Sometimes, Scotland's national story seems to be an unending tale of misery, defeat and disaster. This made the rest seem like a golden age.

It was a time which saw a gradual slide from order into chaos. Within a decade of its abrupt start the peace and prosperity of the realm had evaporated, replaced by civil war and foreign invasion. The worst of it was, all of this could have been avoided. If those in charge of the kingdom had made better choices, or fate had dealt the players a better hand, then things might have played out differently. Instead the first of these funerals ushered in a dark new age where brutal death and wanton destruction became commonplace. This living hell lasted for almost three decades. What would finally mark its passing, a return to, or rather promise an eventual return to peace and safety, was the Battle of Bannockburn.

A prophecy fulfilled

This depressing train of events began with a banquet in Edinburgh

Castle. It was 18 March 1286, and the Scottish monarch Alexander III had just held a council meeting in the castle. He and his leading nobles had been discussing a diplomatic exchange with his brother-in-law King Edward I of England. During the banquet that followed, rumours about a grim prophecy reached the king's ears. It was said that he would die that night – or rather he would be called to answer for his sins.

Prophecies of this kind had been circulating for months. William Shakespeare drew on the tale when he wrote *Macbeth* – prophecies of divine retribution provided excellent narrative tension to a plot. However, until now these hadn't specified a date.

According to the *Lanercost Chronicle*, 'When they were come to dine, while they were eating and drinking he [Alexander], with a cheerful countenance sent a portion of fish to one of the barons, bidding him by the squire enjoy his dinner and he should know this was the Day of Judgment. He, returning thanks, made answer merrily to the king, "If this be the Day of Judgment we shall rise with full stomachs."' In other words, Alexander was unworried by the sinister prophecy. To add to the melodramatic atmosphere there was a storm raging outside – wind and rain would have been battering the walls of the castle. Other monarchs might have decided to sleep off their dinner in their royal chambers, but Alexander was newly married, and was determined to spend the night with his wife.

After being a widower for more than a decade, Alexander had married a 23-year-old French countess, Yolande of Dreux. The wedding had taken place in October 1285, and five months later the king was still infatuated by his young bride. So much so, in fact, that he decided to risk both the prophecy and the storm to be with her. The trouble was, she was in another royal castle at Kinghorn, on the far side of the Firth of Forth. As the crow flies this was only eight miles away, but by land the journey was closer to twenty miles, just over a mile of it by ferry. The *Chronicle* picks up the tale again: 'Now when after a long time the feasting was over and the evening was drawing on, he would not be withheld by the violence of the storm, nor would he hearken to the persuasions of others but made haste forthwith to Queen's Ferry.'

That was South Queensferry, where the Forth Bridges now make their spectacular crossing of the Firth of Forth. There he was warned not to make the crossing, but he ignored the advice. After landing at North Queensferry he and three squires set off on horseback, passing through the small hamlet of Inverkeithing. There, according to *Lanercost*, a local fisherman offered to put the royal party up for the night, but Alexander merely laughed. Declining, he asked for two local guides to show him the way. During the black night, however, the king and his escort became separated. The path he chose took Alexander along the top of the bluffs lining the Fife shore, while presumably his escort took a more inland route.

The Scottish king was never seen alive again. Search parties would have scoured the area, and while the accounts don't mention it, someone would have found the king's riderless horse, somewhere above the coastal bluffs. They found the body early the next morning. Alexander III, the last Celtic king of Scotland, had died of a broken neck, having presumably fallen from his horse in the darkness and tumbled down the steep tree-clad slope. Today a monument marks the spot where he died, less than a mile from his marital bed.

So began Scotland's troubles. Alexander III was generally regarded as 'a good king'. During his 24-year reign he had expanded the boundaries of his realm by gaining control of the Western Isles, defeated a Norwegian invasion, established good relations with his English neighbours, and ushered in an era of peace and prosperity. Unfortunately he was still found wanting as a medieval king, as he failed to leave behind an heir. His twenty-year-old son Alexander had died just over two years earlier, preceded by his younger brother and older sister. The main reason Alexander had married Yolande of Dreux was to produce another son, but it wasn't to be. Scotland was now without a king, and without a clear successor. The realm would pay dearly for Alexander's lack of progeny.

The guardians of Scotland

King Alexander was buried in Dunfermline Abbey on 29 March 1286, the funeral attended by Scotland's leading figures. These were the men who would determine Alexander's successor. They were probably vying for position before the prayers were concluded. Unlike the last time a Scottish king was buried, in 1249, there would be no inauguration of a successor to balance the loss. So, just four days after the funeral, these same prelates and magnates met at Scone, the site where Scotland's kings were crowned. While there was only one logical successor to Alexander, being a young Norwegian princess she was a less than ideal candidate.

After the death of his son, King Alexander had named his granddaughter Margaret as his successor. Known as the 'Maid of Norway', this toddler was the daughter of King Eric II of Norway and Alexander's daughter, also named Margaret. With the death of her Scottish mother and uncles, little Margaret was the closest thing Alexander had to an heir – at least until he married Yolande, who was now bearing his child. Neither this child nor the Norwegian toddler would be able to function as a ruler until they came of age, so Scotland would have to be governed on their behalf. That much was acknowledged by everyone. Whether Scotland's nobles wanted a child ruler, however – especially a female one – remained to be seen. For the moment though, peace prevailed, while the Queen's pregnancy ran its course.

In the meantime, Scotland needed to be governed. Six 'guardians' were elected, to supervise the day-to-day business of the country in the name of the community of the realm, and appointed 'for the government of the kingdom'. Of the six, William Fraser, Bishop of St Andrews and Robert Wishart, Bishop of Glasgow represented the Church, Alexander Comyn, Earl of Buchan and Duncan, Earl of Fife upheld the interests of the country's leading magnates, while John Comyn, Lord of Badenoch and the High Steward James Stewart sat on behalf of Scotland's barons. These were the men who would govern

Scotland, and would ultimately decide upon the succession. It was very noticeable who wasn't selected. Robert Bruce, Lord of Annandale was a rival of the Comyns and their in-laws the Balliols, and so was excluded from government. Still, Bruce and his fellow magnates swore to keep the peace, and gave their fealty to whoever 'ought to inherit'. While power-broking went on behind the scenes, the public face of the guardianship was one of accord and stability. That, though, was about to change.

By the late summer it became clear the queen wouldn't be producing an heir. The most likely reason is that she had a miscarriage, but it was also claimed the child was stillborn, or that it had all been pretence. For whatever reason, Yolande returned to France, and in 1292 she married Arthur, son of the Duke of Brittany, who succeeded to his father's title in 1305. She eventually died in 1312, having produced seven children, including two boys. She might have done the same for Alexander, had it not been for that night-time ride.

That still left the Maid of Norway. She, though, was still just a little girl, and a foreign one at that. Without a male heir to rally behind, the Scottish magnates would probably have preferred to choose a claimant from among their own ranks. That in turn meant an end to any pretence of peace and accord.

The only serious contenders were Robert Bruce and John Balliol. Both were powerful noblemen who enjoyed considerable support. A contest between the two ran the risk of dividing the Scottish nobility, and possibly even causing a civil war, as both nobles fought for the crown. Conflict looked increasingly likely by the end of the year, as Bruce besieged Buittle Castle, a Comyn stronghold in Galloway, and threatened the royal castles at Dumfries and Wigtown, held by Comyn sheriffs. Bruce was trying to consolidate his military grip on the south-western corner of Scotland, but that winter the conflict between the rivals remained low key and regional. The danger, of course, was that it could develop into civil war.

Bruce also strengthened his political hand. In September 1286 at

Turnberry on the Ayrshire coast he convened a meeting of selected nobles, who formed a pro-Bruce faction, designed to counter the power of the Comyns and Balliols. This Turnberry band included Bruce's son-in-law Patrick, Earl of Dunbar, his son Robert, Earl of Carrick, Walter Stewart, Earl of Menteith, and one of the guardians, James, the High Steward. If a civil war came, Bruce was ready. Fortunately for the rest of the realm the remaining guardians threatened to crush this potential rebellion by mustering an army, and Bruce backed down. For the moment Bruce was contained, and the fragile peace would continue.

During the next few years the guardians continued to govern, and they and the magnates still tried to find a ruler. As a female the Maid of Norway would find it almost impossible to rule on her own. She needed a husband, preferably one with the power to ensure the stability of the kingdom. Anything else would mean a return of the spectre of civil war. The guardians cast about, looking for a suitable youth, and eventually they settled on the seemingly unlikely candidate of Edward of Caernarfon, the equally young son of King Edward I of England. This offered several advantages. The English prince would be supported by his father, thereby ensuring he had the money and men he needed to hold the throne. For the guardians it meant Scotland would avoid a civil war, while the maid's father King Eric would gain not one but two useful allies. For his part King Edward felt it would safeguard his northern borders, and create a malleable kingdom beyond them. The only problem was the potential impact this alliance might have on the sovereignty of Scotland.

King Edward was away in France during the years following the death of his Scottish brother-in-law. Since May 1286 he had been campaigning in Aquitaine, where he had been keeping abreast of developments in Scotland. In fact a Scottish embassy even visited him there, to ask for his 'counsel and protection'. The English king sent them home, as he was more concerned with maintaining control of his French provinces. A Scottish delegation returned to Edward's court in the spring of 1289, where they and their Norwegian counterparts discussed the marriage arrangements. It was during this meeting and a subsequent one in Salisbury later that year that the real seeds of trouble would be sown.

The Scottish contingent included Bishops Fraser and Wishart, John Comyn (or 'the Black Comyn'), Lord of Badenoch – cousin of the Earl of Buchan, brother-in law of John Balliol – and the errant rebel Robert Bruce. The inclusion of Bruce suggests either an attempt at conciliation within Scotland, or a demand by Edward I, who wanted to make sure Scotland wasn't going to erupt in civil war. The Black Comyn would soon inherit his cousin's post as guardian. This meant the delegation included two of the surviving guardians, and the successor to a third.

The High Steward and Donald, Earl of Fife remained in Scotland. In fact, later that summer the earl was murdered while travelling through Fife, having allegedly been attacked by his own relatives. The motive for the assault is unknown, but the *Lanercost Chronicle* describes the earl as 'cruel and greedy', which suggests he might have deserved his fate. He wasn't replaced as guardian, which reduced their ranks to four active members – five once the Lord of Badenoch took office in time for the mission to Salisbury.

That November a deal was struck between the two fathers King Eric and King Edward. The young Maid of Norway would be sent to Orkney, Norway's most southerly outpost in the British Isles. If the country remained stable she could then continue on to England or Scotland. Of course both Margaret and Edward Caernarfon were too young to marry, so whatever deal was struck would have to last for several years. The English king had obtained a special papal dispensation to allow the marriage as the children were distantly related, and so there were no legal grounds standing in Edward's way. The only potential problem lay with the Scots. That's what the meeting at Salisbury was all about.

In Salisbury the Scots agreed to an arrangement where Eric would send his daughter to either Scotland or England – if the latter, then Edward would send her north. She couldn't be married without her father's permission, and Edward had a say in the appointment of her protectors, chosen by the guardians. He also had a say in who became a guardian, which would probably mean a loss of Scottish sovereignty. But for Edward these arrangements were a deal breaker. Both he and King Eric wanted to make sure their children would rule over a stable kingdom. The guardians approved the treaty because they realised that this marriage was their only chance to ensure a peaceful succession, and thereby avoid a civil war, fought with the crown of Scotland as the victory's trophy.

In March 1290 the deal reached in Salisbury was approved at a meeting in Birgham, on the Anglo-Scottish border. This was less about the marriage than about the relationship between the two kingdoms. The final version of the Treaty of Birgham, ratified in July, stated that 'The realm of Scotland shall remain separated and divided and free in itself, without subjection to the realm of England.' It went on to guarantee that the Scottish and English churches would remain distinct, as would their parliaments and judicial systems. Then it touched on royal authority. Edward Caernarfon wouldn't automatically gain control of his young bride's kingdom, but he would govern Scotland for her, helped by his Scottish advisors. If the royal couple produced an heir, then he would rule both kingdoms, just as James I and VI was to do in 1603. This would be a Union of the Crowns, three centuries before its time.

This all looked fine on paper, but inevitably Edward Caernarfon's presence in Scotland meant that his father would be the man behind the curtain, moulding Scotland to his will. Nevertheless, the deal was signed by Bishop Fraser, Bishop Wishart, James the Steward and John Comyn, Lord of Badenoch. In turn these guardians were supported by all of the leading magnates of Scotland, including Bruce and Balliol. But what had they actually agreed to? While Scotland's distinctive character would be maintained, they had effectively signed an agreement that made Scotland part of a Plantagenet empire.

While all this had been going on, seven-year-old Margaret was

torn from her family and her friends. Accompanied by a few servants
and staff, she boarded a ship in Bergen and set sail for Orkney. As a
Norwegian province the islands were the ideal place for her to wait
until her future could be decided. She would have been housed in the
Bishop's Palace in Kirkwall, where her great-grandfather had died after
his defeat at the Battle of Largs. Unfortunately the little girl never
reached Kirkwall. She died shortly after making landfall in Orkney,
on 26 September 1290. According to local tradition she landed on the
island of South Ronaldsay, which explains why the village that later
rose behind the anchorage is now called St Margaret's Hope.

The death of the Maid of Norway changed everything. Bishop Fraser
of St Andrews had sent a delegation of clerics to the islands to meet
Margaret's party, and it was probably this delegation who brought word
of the calamity to the guardians, and so to King Edward. As Margaret's
little body was transported back to Bergen, all the signatories at
Birgham were now realising that the treaty was worthless. There would
be no wedding, no formal bonding of kingdoms – all the Scots had
to look forward to was a renewal of internecine violence. The storm
clouds were already gathering: in early October Robert Bruce appeared
in Perth, accompanied by a well-armed band of supporters. He was
seeking to intimidate a Comyn-led Scottish delegation who were
holding a meeting with King Edward's representatives Bishop Antony
Bek and John de Warenne, Earl of Surrey. Civil war now seemed all
but inevitable, and Edward's Scottish 'fixers' were well aware of it.

That was when King Edward stepped in. With no legitimate
Scottish heir it was clear one would have to be found from within the
ranks of the Scottish nobility. The guardians were unable to make the
choice themselves without inviting civil war. A foreign arbitrator had
to be found – someone who could choose a monarch without being
accused of taking sides. The obvious candidate was King Edward I of
England. He already had a reputation as an international arbitrator,
having performed the role during a succession dispute relating to
the Sicilian crown. He was an experienced diplomat, and apart from

his involvement in the recent marriage negotiations he had shown no evident proprietary interest in Scotland. The guardians duly approached the English king, and he accepted the task. It was an offer they would soon regret.

3

The Great Cause

King Edward would act as an arbitrator, and would help the Scots choose a new king. He would hear the arguments of the various claimants and study the documentary evidence they brought along to support their case. Ultimately, though, it would eventually be Edward and the jurors who would decide who would be the next king of Scotland. Whoever he chose would therefore owe their position to Edward. And that was only the start. Edward planned to use the whole process to strengthen his position even more by redefining the relationship between the two crowns.

The whole process became known as 'The Great Cause'. As a history graduate in Aberdeen I once wrote a paper on the subject – my first introduction to the somewhat bewildering subject of medieval law. It would take a whole book, entailing a legal analysis of the relative worth of the many claimants, to explain the matter in full. Lawyers at that time were even more willing to wrap themselves in complexities than they are today. This would be dry stuff indeed, and so a brief summary will serve our purpose. What is much more interesting is the impact of the disputations on the relationship between England and Scotland. After 'The Great Cause' nothing would be quite the same again.

Overlordship

The hearing was convened in Norham on the English side of the River Tweed on 10 May 1291. It would last for six months, spread over a period of one and a half years. While the opening meeting was held in Norham church, sessions were also to take place in the keep of Norham Castle, at Upsettlington, a grassy meadow on the Scottish side of the river, and finally in the nearby border town of Berwick-upon-Tweed.

King Edward began his preparations even before the proceedings got under way. While he still showed no covetous designs on Scotland, he planned to use this court to settle what he considered a matter of even greater importance. He ordered his lawyers to gather whatever documentation they could to support his claim to feudal superiority over the Scottish king. He even had monks forge at least one important document – a fictitious 79-year-old record of the submission of a Scottish king to an English one. This homage meant overlordship – while whoever became king of Scotland would govern in their own right, they would have to recognise Edward as their feudal superior.

This is exactly what the French crown had insisted Edward do with regard to his lands in Aquitaine. Edward had done whatever he could to avoid this fealty – in fact it led to intermittent war between England and France. He found it humiliating – after all, he was one of the greatest and most experienced rulers in Europe. With hindsight he would have been better to make his point about overlordship without pressing the matter. Unfortunately Edward was a man who liked to make a point, and so this issue became just as divisive as it was in France. More than anything else it would set England and Scotland on the long road to Bannockburn.

The English lawyer Roger Brabazon presided at the opening of proceedings in Norham church, and his opening speech made it clear that Edward was there as the feudal overlord. Brabazon even challenged the Scots on the issue, demanding proof from any who doubted that Edward was their rightful suzerain. It was a smart move, particularly as it was followed by a three-week recess. Clearly if any candidate wished Edward to rule in their favour, he would have to recognise Edward as his overlord. When the court reconvened it met in the meadow on the Scottish side of the river – a deliberate ploy to reinforce Edward's position. A half-hearted Scottish attempt to divert the issue was swept aside, and the contenders were left with little option. They wanted the crown, which meant they needed Edward. So, one by one, the claimants agreed to recognise Edward as their superior. This agreement became known as 'The Award of Norham'.

The English-born claimants had little to lose, but for the Scottish contenders this was a major step. They might win the crown, but there was now no question of dealing with Edward as an equal, as Alexander III had done. Of the two leading contenders Robert Bruce on 5 June was the first to agree to Edward's terms. John Balliol held out for another week before he too was forced to concede. Edward had got his way. It also meant that he now had legal possession of the kingdom, albeit only until a Scottish king was crowned.

He immediately set about enforcing this by requesting that all royal castles in Scotland be handed over to him. They would be returned within two months of a decision being reached. Strangely, eight of the twenty-two royal constables in Scotland refused to hand over their castles, insisting that they held them on behalf of the people of Scotland. For the moment Edward didn't pursue the issue – he would deal with these recalcitrant governors later. The four remaining guardians resigned on 11 June and were reappointed two days later, having recognised Edward as their overlord. This time they were joined by two of Edward's appointees – Bishop Bek and the Earl of Surrey. These were Edward's 'men on the ground' in Scotland, now placed at the very heart of Scottish government. As their feudal overlord it was his right to appoint who he liked. Only then was Edward willing to continue with the hearing.

The court

Before the court began its work there was a recess for two months to give time for the claimants to prepare themselves. It also gave Roger Brabazon time to vet and approve the men who would sit in judgement on a king. The court would consist of 104 auditors, of whom 24 were English. Of the rest, 40 each were appointed by Bruce and Balliol. That showed that they were the only two serious candidates. Edward himself acted as the 105th auditor – a number decided to add gravitas to the proceedings, as it was based on the court system used in ancient Rome. The term 'auditor' hardly does these men justice – they were all important nobles, clerics and lawyers, men of substance and learning. While all this was being organised Edward went on a tour around lowland Scotland, reaching as far north as Perth. This wasn't just a royal holiday – he made sure every important Scotsman swore an oath of fealty to him. Edward was a man intent on enforcing his suzerainty.

When the court reconvened in mid-August it gathered in Berwick-upon-Tweed. In all there were fourteen contenders for the Scottish crown. One of these was Edward himself, but his case was a weak one. He registered it largely in order that, by then discounting his own claim, he could be seen to be scrupulous in his impartiality. Another late claimant was King Eric of Norway, but his claim too was lodged more as an investment for the future than as any real challenge for the crown. The remaining twelve lodged their paperwork with Brabazon, and waited for a decision. It would be a long time in coming – before the business got properly under way Edward ordered a recess, ostensibly to give the Count of Holland more time to gather his documentation. It seems more likely that Edward merely wanted time to reinforce his authority as Scotland's overlord, and to extend his grip on the country.

It wasn't until the following June that the court convened once more. There were still twelve contenders, all eager to press their case, but during the long recess the auditors had read through much of the paperwork, and now had a better idea how to proceed. Many of the claimants had little chance of winning the crown. Five were the descendants of the illegitimate offspring of William the Lion, a Scottish king who sired 'an uncounted number of bastard progeny'. A sixth was the illegitimate descendant of King Alexander II. Illegitimacy was usually a bar to succession, but these claimants all felt it worth pursuing their cause. By taking part they were effectively lodging their claim for posterity.

Of the remaining six, the cases of Florence, Count of Holland, Robert de Pinkeney and John Comyn, Lord of Badenoch were also weak, the first two tracing descent through a daughter of King David I, the other an eleventh-century Scottish king, Donald III. Like the others they were unlikely to win the crown, but they felt it important to lodge their claim. They were also in a position to negotiate deals with the other contenders, while the whole affair might raise their profile in Edward's court. Effectively that reduced the field of likely contenders to three – Robert Bruce, John Balliol and John Hastings, Baron of Abergavenny.

Of these, Hastings had the weakest claim. He was the grandson of Ada, the third daughter of David, Earl of Huntingdon, who had died in 1216. Earl David was the brother of King William 'the Lion', and the grandson of King David I. As the descendant of a third child, Hastings would be unable to claim the full kingdom – just a portion of it. If the court ruled against 'partibility' – the partition of the inheritance – then his case would crumble. While a feudal estate could be divided in this way, the same rule had never been applied to a whole kingdom. If it was, then Scotland stood to be split up between Hastings, Bruce and Balliol, as all three were descendants of Earl David.

Rather than tackle all dozen cases, Edward decided to save time by dealing with the two strongest contenders first, and then comparing the other claims against that of the winner. So, on 16 June Bruce and Balliol presented their cases to the court, a process that took a week to complete. Like Hastings' claim, their cases would stand or fall depending on the way the law was interpreted. Put simply, Bruce's case relied on succession through 'proximity', while Balliol's was based on 'primogeniture'. Bruce was closer to Alexander III than Balliol by a generation, and so claimed greater proximity of blood. While today this argument isn't a valid one, in the medieval world proximity had just as much legal merit as primogeniture – or rather it should have if the auditors were willing to accept its validity.

The Balliol claim rested on him being the grandson of the Earl of Huntingdon's eldest daughter, and the rules of primogeniture meant that the firstborn child should inherit. By contrast Bruce was Earl David's grandson, but the offspring of Huntingdon's second daughter. In theory that left the auditors with a straightforward legal decision to make between proximity and primogeniture. In fact nothing was clear-cut: both sides were busy striking deals, and probably bribing and coercing auditors, as indeed were the other contenders. Even before the hearing resumed Bruce struck a deal with the Count of Holland, agreeing to partition the kingdom between them if either should win. That gave Bruce more power in these behind-the-scenes negotiations, and kept Count Florence in the running. Meanwhile the lawyers squabbled over which legal system should take precedence – Roman law or common law. This led to another adjournment for four months, so Edward could consult some of the best lawyers in Europe.

The court opened again on 14 October. By this time it was clear that primogeniture was favoured over proximity, and common or feudal law had trumped the Roman system. Bruce made a last-ditch attempt to support proximity, a notion which was firmly supported by feudal law. This meant that he was prepared to carve Scotland into three pieces rather than concede his claim. The ruling was finally made – primogeniture was favoured over proximity. That was followed by a vote, in which sixty-seven of the Scottish auditors opted for Balliol rather than Bruce. They included almost three-quarters of the auditors Bruce had selected, who had seen which way things were going and recognised Balliol was the clear legal choice. Backing Balliol might also help their careers. After all, he now stood to become the next king of Scotland.

Robert Bruce was a spent force. He resigned his claim in favour of his son (Robert Bruce, Earl of Carrick), and left Berwick for his castle at Lochmaben, a broken and disillusioned man. It is likely his grandson Robert witnessed the final stages of this great courtroom drama. It might have brought his grandfather solace to know that one day he would claim the crown for himself. After that the remaining claimants were dealt with in quick succession. Some withdrew their claim, others had their case thrown out of court. The argument of 'partibility' was dismissed as being irrelevant when it came to entire kingdoms. In the end only Balliol remained, and so on 17 November Edward solemnly implemented the ruling of the jury in favour of him, announcing that he would duly become the new king of the entire realm. Balliol had won, but the cost was to prove high, both for his crown and his kingdom.

4

Toom Tabard

The reign of King John I began poorly, and went steadily downhill from there. John Balliol was crowned king of Scotland on St Andrews Day – 30 November 1292. For the first time in over six years Scotland had a king, albeit one of a very different hue than his predecessor. The big difference of course was that John Balliol – now King John I – had been forced to recognise Edward I as his feudal superior. Edward stamped his authority over John from the start. Even the investiture at Scone wasn't sacrosanct, as Edward's two 'men on the ground' were there, keeping a wary eye on the proceedings. Nor was John supported by a unified band of Scottish magnates – he was merely the head of the stronger of two rival factions. John needed to heal his divided kingdom, while somehow extricating himself from his feudal obligations to Edward. It would prove an impossible task.

The lesser king

King Edward did little to help John. Within days of the coronation he ordered the Scottish king to Newcastle, to spend Christmas at Edward's court. This was a feudal summons – one that was non-negotiable. To reinforce their relationship, on the day after Christmas Edward had John renew his homage, a ceremony which involved John kneeling before Edward, describing him as 'Lord Superior of the realm of Scotland' and declaring himself 'Your liegeman for the whole realm of Scotland'. As if this wasn't humiliating enough, a week later John was forced to release Edward from the constraints imposed on him by the Treaty of Birgham. All those checks imposed by the guardians against English interference in the Scottish church, the courts and the governance of the realm were thereby removed. Edward now had a free hand to do what he liked in Scotland.

When King John returned home his first priority was to establish control over his nobles. In February 1293 he called a parliament in Scone, where most magnates swore their allegiance to him. One notable exception was Robert Bruce. After 'The Great Cause' the elderly Robert – now known as 'the Contender' – had resigned his claim and his titles rather than swear allegiance to King John, and the following year his fifty-year-old son Robert, the new Earl of Carrick, did the same, while retaining the lordship of Annandale. In fact he held the earldom by courtesy of his marriage, and so was obliged to hand the title over to his son when he came of age. That meant the earl's teenage son – also named Robert – inherited the earldom, becoming the third Earl of Carrick in just over a year. It was up to this teenager – the future warrior king – to safeguard the family's land and titles in a land ruled by the Bruce's most obdurate rival. Like King John, the young Robert Bruce found himself in an extremely difficult position.

He began by delaying his oath of fealty to John for as long as he could. It was August before Bruce knelt before his king, and while this helped paper over the cracks of a divided Scotland the rift was still there. The vendetta between the Bruces and the Balliols and Comyns would continue, albeit in a less public way. A stronger king might have tried to end the feud by sharing power with the Bruces. Instead Balliol appointed his own supporters to positions of power, and naturally those outside this familial inner circle gravitated towards the Bruce camp. In modern parliamentary terms, if the Balliols and Comyns represented the government, the Bruces became the opposition.

The Bruces saw King Edward as a natural ally. After all, like several leading Scottish magnates, they held some minor lands in England, and in turn swore allegiance to Edward for them. The eldest Bruce – the contender for the succession – was Edward's constable of Carlisle Castle. On his death in 1295 this important position was inherited by his son. Just as important, if King John tried to strip the family of its lands or titles the Bruces could now appeal directly to King Edward, effectively circumventing the Scottish king. The Bruces needed Edward, and he might need them, if he ever had cause to oust John from the Scottish throne.

Meanwhile, Edward continued to undermine King John's authority. In September 1293 he called the Scottish king to London to answer legal claims that his courts had denied the successors of the Earl of Fife their lands, which were then in the keeping of the Bishop of St Andrews, a loyal Balliol supporter. When John tried to stand his ground Edward appointed his own man to administer the earldom instead of the bishop. The following year England found itself at war with France – ironically a war fought over Edward's failure to pay homage to King Philip IV for his lands in Aquitaine. This didn't stop Edward demanding that John lead a Scottish contingent south to Portsmouth, where his troops would embark for France. This involvement in a foreign war had been one of the items covered in the Treaty of Birgham. With that safety net no longer in place, Edward was able to treat Scotland as an extension of his own feudal realm.

Edward and Philip had once been allies – fellow crusaders – but the fall of Acre in 1291 had marked the end of the crusading dream. Denied all but lip service to this greater cause, both kings looked for other outlets for their energy. The issue of Edward's fealty for his lands in Aquitaine provided just such an opportunity for Philip, but a diplomatic deal was struck, designed to avert a war. Edward would relinquish his lands, Philip would then return them, and feudal honour would be satisfied. Edward played his part, but Philip reneged on the deal and held on to Aquitaine, whereupon an incensed Edward went to war to reclaim the lands that had been taken. The conflict would continue for a decade, and the reluctant Scots would be drawn into it in a way nobody could have predicted.

In Scotland, if approval ratings had existed in 1294 then King John's would have taken a dramatic tumble. His leading magnates had no desire to fight in Aquitaine, and blamed John for exposing them to this feudal demand when he released Edward from the constraints of Birgham. John was granted a breathing space when Edward cancelled the expedition in order to crush a revolt in Wales. That winter the new spirit of dissent continued to flourish. Edward's men in Scotland, Bishop Bek and the Earl of Surrey, found the mood in the Scottish court was becoming hostile. King John realised that he needed to stand up to Edward or risk losing control of his kingdom. This stiffening of resolve came too late: although he refused Edward's next summons to London, he found his own supporters at home had begun to desert him.

The English bishop and earl were there to witness a new development – one that would force the hand of both Edward and John. In the autumn of 1295 a Scottish embassy arrived in Paris to conclude an alliance between King John and King Philip. It was led by Bishop Fraser of St Andrews, but interestingly the four-strong team included two men who had been auditors for Robert Bruce 'the Contender' during 'The Great Cause'. It seemed that John was trying to present a united front abroad, although his hand was also being forced by the opposition at home.

The resulting Treaty of Paris was signed on 23 October, and marked the start of 'The Auld Alliance' – a particularly one-sided political and military partnership which would benefit the French far more than it did the Scots. The signing coincided with a similar treaty between Philip and King Eric II of Norway – who had just married Isabel, the elder sister of the young Robert, Earl of Carrick. (King Eric's first wife Margaret, the daughter of Alexander III, had died in childbirth when giving birth to the Maid of Norway.) While there was no treaty between Scotland and Norway, the result was effectively a tripartite alliance, directed against Edward. Unfortunately the deal struck by Bishop Fraser was a poor one. France could call on Scottish military support if attacked by England, but only offered vague promises of help in return. The alliance would prove disastrous, both for King John and for Scotland.

This alliance with France was only part of the Scottish diplomatic initiative. Pope Celestine V had been approached, as the Scots sought absolution for oaths (those acknowledging King Edward as their Lord Superior) made under duress. It is unclear how much of this activity was initiated by King John, but by the summer of 1295 he was being assisted by a new political group – a council of twelve, consisting of four bishops, four earls and four barons. Most historians believe these men were effectively running Scotland during this troubled period. Other magnates – most notably the Bruces – disassociated themselves from this new-found resolve, as they had no wish to support the Scottish king. The Scottish realm was as divided as ever, and it was also playing political brinkmanship with an English ruler who was one of the most respected soldiers and statesmen in Europe.

War

News of the Franco-Scottish alliance reached King Edward in early November. He wasn't amused. He had already seized Balliol lands in England, on account of the Scottish king's failure to bend his knee to his overlord. He knew of the growing hostility in Scotland, thanks to the reports of Bishop Bek and the Earl of Surrey, his men on the ground. This new development was no mere flouting of feudal obligations. It amounted to a declaration of war. Edward for one was happy to respond – the Scots needed a firm lesson in humility. From Edward's point of view the news came at the perfect moment. The Welsh revolt had been crushed, and Edward was thinking about launching a new campaign in France. Now all he had to do was to muster his army and lead it north into Scotland.

That winter both sides prepared for war. Edward felt fully justified – he was marching into Scotland as the 'Lord Superior of the realm', not as a foreign invader. King John had failed to honour his feudal obligations, and Edward was going to hold him to account. It was as simple as that. This would be a punitive expedition, with a specific objective. To the medieval mind this made perfect sense. Edward strengthened his case by issuing an eleventh-hour summons to John, demanding that he come to Newcastle, where Edward was gathering his troops. John never appeared, and so for Edward what would befall Scotland was the result of John's failings, not his own.

In fact John did respond – he sent Edward a letter, which brazenly said that Edward had 'inflicted over and over again, by naked force, grievous and intolerable injuries, slights and wrongs upon us'. It was powerful stuff – a clear message that Edward's treatment of John had gone too far, and the only honourable course left was to fight. For John, this would be a fight for 'the liberties of ourselves and our kingdom'. For Edward it was the crushing of a rebellion. This new-found Scottish assertiveness wasn't necessarily welcomed by all Scots. While most of the Scottish magnates rallied to King John's banner, Robert Bruce aligned himself with the English king.

Robert Bruce 'the Contender' had died the previous year. Having already handed over his title of Earl of Carrick to his teenage son, the Contender's son Robert had now been stripped of his own title of Lord of Annandale by King John, ironically for his failure to recognise the Scottish king as his liege lord. The lordship of Annandale was given to the 'Red Comyn', John, Lord of Badenoch. As Edward's army reached the River Tweed at Wark the two Bruces paid homage to him and joined his army. For them this was no patriotic war, but a chance to wreak vengeance on their enemies. Two other leading Scottish nobles – Patrick, Earl of March and Dunbar, and the English-born Gilbert de Umfraville, Earl of Angus – also swore allegiance to Edward.

Edward's army crossed the Tweed into Scotland, and marched downstream to Berwick. Berwick-upon-Tweed was the richest town in Scotland – the chief marketplace of the region and a centre for commerce. That all changed on 30 March 1296. The garrison was commanded by William, Lord Douglas, but he had too few men to man the town's poorly maintained walls. Instead he withdrew to the castle as the English vanguard stormed the town. Berwick fell in a matter of minutes. Edward accepted Lord Douglas's surrender, and offered him every chivalric courtesy. Then he let his men loose to pillage the town. By nightfall Berwick was a blood-soaked charnel house. It was said over 7000 townspeople were slaughtered that day – age, sex or rank were no protection against the rapacious English host.

Once this orgy of death, rape and looting had run its course Edward declared that Berwick would be an English town, a part of Northumberland. It would remain in English hands for the next two decades. Even by medieval standards this massacre was a terrible act – what today would be labelled a war crime. Edward was only paying the Scots back in kind. That winter the Scots launched a raid across the border, targeting Carlisle, which was held for Edward by Robert Bruce, the former Earl of Carrick. Unable to take the town, the Scots instead burned villages, slaughtering their inhabitants and plundering whatever they could. Just over a week after the massacre in Berwick another Scottish raiding party slipped past Edward's army towards Hexham. They matched the English for cruelty – there was even a far-fetched claim that they burned 200 schoolchildren to death inside their own school. This was medieval warfare at its worst.

By mid-April John's army was safely back in Scotland, camped around Haddington. The raids had done nothing but increase the stakes both kings were playing for. After Berwick and Hexham there could be no face-saving peace. It was now a war to the finish. John's only tangible success came when the Earl of March's wife Marjorie opened the gates of Dunbar to the Scots. She was a Comyn, and unlike her husband her loyalties lay firmly in the Balliol–Comyn camp. Dunbar lay twenty-five miles up the coast from Berwick, astride Edward's line of march. So, Edward sent an advanced guard to recapture the castle, while his main army mopped up in the Borders and then followed on behind. The scene was set for the first battle of the war.

The English force was commanded by John de Warenne, Earl of Surrey – the same man who had been sent north to keep an eye on King John. At Dunbar he proved to be as skilled a soldier as he was a diplomat. He laid siege to the town, but soon found himself caught between the garrison and King John's army, which marched east to lift the siege. On 27 April Surrey waited for the Scots to deploy, and then feigned a retreat. A portion of the undisciplined Scottish men-at-arms swept forward, only to find themselves caught in a trap. Surrey had used the low-lying meadowland of the Spott Burn to hide part of his force, who fell on the pursuing Scots. To be honest it wasn't much of a battle – most of the Scottish nobility and the remaining men-at-arms fled, leaving their English counterparts free to pursue the leaderless Scottish infantry, left behind by their feudal betters.

The Lanercost chronicler recorded a ditty penned to celebrate the incident:

> For those Scots,
> I rate them as sots,
> what a sorry shower,
> whose utter lack,
> in the attack,
> lost them at Dunbar.

It was fair comment. While King John was spirited away to safety, three earls were captured, together with over a hundred less exalted nobles. It was the beginning of the end for John. Nobles began to defect – one of the first being James the Steward, always a lukewarm supporter of the Balliol cause. Within weeks Roxburgh and Dumbarton were in Edward's hands, and as he advanced on to Linlithgow a detachment laid siege to Edinburgh Castle. It fell shortly afterwards, as did Stirling.

Scotland south of the Forth and Clyde was now firmly under Edward's control.

What had begun as a punitive action now became a farce. King John withdrew into the Mearns – the lands south of Aberdeenshire – haemorrhaging support as he went, until only his family and his closest allies remained at his side. Bereft of hope, on 2 July he met Bishop Bek in Kincardine Castle. John's attempts to blame his feudal revolt 'on evil councillors' fell on deaf ears, and so five days later he formally surrendered in the church graveyard of Stracathro, seven miles from the castle, close to the cathedral town of Brechin. It was a defining moment in Scottish history. John renounced his treaty with the French and threw himself on Edward's mercy.

The final humiliation came the following day. King John was handed over to Bishop Bek and the Earl of Surrey. His great seal was surrendered. Then his surcoat or tabard bearing the royal coat of arms was torn from his body, its shredded fragments thrown to the floor. John Balliol was a king no longer. He was merely the prisoner of his feudal lord. It was a calculated act of public humiliation and atonement choreographed by Edward's advisors, designed to reinforce the English king's authority over Scotland's crown and kingdom.

Edward celebrated his victory by holding a great feast, and then continued his journey through the north-east of Scotland. He went as far as Elgin before heading south once more, returning to Berwick in late August. As for Balliol, he and his son Edward were sent south to Hertford, to live in reasonable comfort. When rebellion flared up in Scotland again they were sent to the Tower of London, where Edward could keep better watch on them. Finally, in 1299, Balliol was allowed to leave for exile in France. For a brief while in 1302 it looked like he might stage a comeback, but nothing came of it. He ended his days on his French estates in Picardy, dying the year after his rival's triumph at Bannockburn. After his fall, the Scots called him 'Toom Tabard', or torn surcoat. There Balliol bowed out of Scottish history, a sorry figure in a sorrowful age.

5

The Wallace

Thanks to the success of *Braveheart* (1995), most people now associate William Wallace with Mel Gibson's depiction of him – a noble savage and man of the people, selflessly fighting for his nation's freedom. Leaving aside the historical inaccuracy of this deeply flawed film, such a portrayal of Wallace is nothing new. Ever since the Scottish makar or poet Blind Harry penned *The Wallace* in the late fifteenth century the poem's namesake has been idolised as a man who fought for the common good, rather than for his own betterment. In the pantheon of Scottish heroes, Wallace comes across as a romantic figure, a martyr to his country's cause. To see beyond that involves a little more historical digging.

Scotland in revolt

In the film, Wallace is a smallholder – a moderately well-off peasant, whose rebellion against the English begins when his wife is raped and executed. In fact even Blind Harry accepts that Wallace was a knight, and a member of the lesser nobility – the younger son of Alan Wallace, a minor landowner from Ayrshire, who held his lands directly from the Scottish king. Whatever his origins, Wallace was a scion of the feudal establishment, albeit not one in the same league as Robert Bruce. That gives the lie to Wallace as the man of the people, or the savage. He fought to maintain the status quo, not to overturn it.

William Wallace's exact age is unknown, but by 1297 he was an adult, noted for his strong, broad-shouldered build, his agreeable features and his height. From his actions we can tell he was also smart, focused and something of a diplomat. Blind Harry cites the burning of his home and the murder of his family as the catalyst for his rebellion, but other sources claim it began in May 1297 when he murdered William Hesilrig, Edward's sheriff in Lanark. In the account given by Sir Thomas Grey in *Scalacronica* a fight erupted during a court session – presumably one involving Wallace, who may have been there as a juror. After fleeing the scene Wallace returned with several followers and murdered the sheriff. As a fugitive from justice Wallace fled with his men into the wilds of Selkirk Forest in the Borders, where his band became a magnet for other rebels. One of the first of these was William Douglas, the man who surrendered Berwick to the English.

This was no isolated incident. It was merely one of several uncoordinated local risings against Edward's administration. In the Borders Robert, Earl of Carrick – the future king – tried to rouse the people of Annandale, but most remained loyal to the earl's father, who in turn remained loyal to King Edward. North of the Firth of Forth another rebellion flared up, led by the uncle of the eight-year-old Donald, Earl of Fife. Much further north in Moray the most serious rising of them all was gathering pace. It was incited by Andrew Murray, the son of the justiciar of Scotia. Both father and son were captured at Dunbar, but the younger Murray escaped and returned to the family seat at Avoch on the Black Isle.

Edward's stronghold in the region was Inverness Castle, which in turn was protected by an outer ring of castles, including Urquhart on the shore of Loch Ness. Moray at the time was governed by Sir Reginald Cheyne of Inverugie, the brother of the Bishop of Aberdeen. He seems to have been singularly ineffective as a regional warden, which suggests a lack of enthusiasm for Edward's rule. Certainly when Murray besieged

Urquhart, Cheyne seems to have done little to help the castle's English constable, William FitzWarin. Instead it was left to Euphemia, Countess of Ross to rescue FitzWarin, by sending a force to lift the siege. This in itself was strange as her husband William, Earl of Ross had been among those captured at Dunbar. Her aim was to earn Edward's gratitude to secure her husband's release and to demonstrate that in his absence she was in charge. It certainly worked – not only was the earl released, but Edward made William his new northern warden.

First, though, Edward had to crush these revolts, before the rebels were able to unite into a single force. Edward's guardian of Scotland, John de Warenne, Earl of Surrey, proved unable to stamp out the risings, so in June Henry Percy and Robert Clifford were sent north to help him, accompanied by a feudal levy from England's northern counties.

These two experienced commanders marched north from Carlisle, and by 7 July they were at Irvine, on the coast of Ayrshire. There they encountered a small Scottish army, led by a gaggle of bickering Scottish leaders. There was no fight – instead the Scottish magnates surrendered after a lengthy negotiation and negotiated a pardon from Edward that protected their own personal interests. In their plea for clemency they cited the demand that they serve Edward in France as the catalyst for their rebellion. Edward's requirement that his English feudal lords serve him in France had proved so unpopular it led to the defiance of two of his leading nobles. In Scotland the same demands were even more intolerable, as they meant serving overseas, in the army of a foreign king. Interestingly there was no mention of self-determination or freedom here – just the heavy-handedness of Edward's feudal demands. It was a far cry from the nationalism of *Braveheart*.

The young Robert Bruce, Earl of Carrick, was one of the many rebels who surrendered to Edward's men, as did Bishop Wishart, James the Steward, and Wallace's supporter William Douglas. South of the Clyde and Forth only Wallace himself remained at large, hiding out in Selkirk Forest. Unfortunately for Edward, de Warenne, Percy and Clifford omitted to press home their advantage. Apart from crushing the rebellion in Fife the English commanders in Scotland did nothing. They assumed the capitulation at Irvine marked the end of the rebellion. Instead it had barely begun.

Skinning the tax collector

Warenne's treasurer was Hugh de Cressingham, a man whose unenviable job of collecting Edward's taxes in Scotland had made him universally unpopular. Since the rebellion began he had been writing to Edward, complaining that de Warenne was losing control of the situation. Taxes weren't being raised, the rebellion was gaining momentum, and something needed to be done. The implication was that Cressingham was the man for the job. In fact Edward had already taken matters in hand. The Scottish magnates captured at Dunbar were freed on condition they agree to serve Edward in France. Instead, Edward planned to send them north, to deal with Andrew Murray and William Wallace.

John Comyn, Earl of Buchan and the Black Comyn – John, Lord of Badenoch – were ordered to put down Murray's rebellion. By mid-July they were in Aberdeenshire, where they mustered their men. They may have sparred with Murray, but were unable to cope with his popularity. Instead they moved to Inverness, to join forces with Sir Reginald Cheyne and the Countess of Ross. Their long-planned campaign came to nothing. Instead it was Murray who seized the initiative, capturing Aberdeen, Banff and Elgin, and cutting off the Comyns and Cheyne from their lands to the west of the River Spey. Effectively all of northeast Scotland was now in rebel hands. Screening the Inverness garrison Murray worked his way southwards through the Mearns, while Wallace moved north to join him. The two men finally met in Dundee, where they joined forces. What had begun as a series of brushfire revolts had now become a full-scale Scottish rebellion.

By then Edward was on the far side of the English Channel, trying to stave off a French invasion of his Flemish lands. John de Warenne, Earl of Surrey was ordered to join him, having been relieved of his Scottish guardianship in mid-August. His replacement was Brian FitzAlan, Lord of Bezedale, but Edward had doubts about his appointment, and the Earl of Surrey was then ordered to stay in Berwick, and to take command of the army gathered there to deal with the Scottish rebels. The victor of Dunbar was finally spurred into action. He led this army north through Edinburgh to Stirling, reaching the castle there on 10 September. Wallace and Murray were on the move too, marching from Dundee to Perth and then on to Stirling. De Warenne must have been delighted when he learned the Scots were approaching. Rather than having to deal with will-o'-the-wisp bandits, he now had the chance to crush the rebels in open battle.

When the Scots arrived they deployed below the precipitous Abbey Crag on the north bank of the River Forth. In front of them lay boggy ground, and for almost a mile the road ran along a raised causeway leading south towards Stirling Bridge. This bridge lay at the base of a horseshoe-shaped loop in the river, which made both bridge and causeway easy to hold for the Scots – all they needed to do was to block the open end of the horseshoe. To make things worse for Surrey the bridge was a wooden affair, built on stone piles, and the width of two horses. This made a frontal assault across the bridge a tricky proposition, even for a skilled commander. John de Warenne, Earl of Surrey might have been a brave and chivalric knight, but he was no Alexander the Great.

The Scots were nevertheless outnumbered and outclassed. Though the exact head count is unknown, the English not only had more men but they had mounted men-at-arms – around 500 of them. They were going to win the battle for de Warenne the only way they knew how – by launching a fearsome charge across the bridge and into the enemy ranks.

Actually, the English commander had an alternative. There was a ford further upstream, and the knights could cross there, avoiding the bottleneck of the bridge. But de Warenne and his deputy Cressingham ignored it, and at dawn on 11 September their knights led the way across the bridge. Then someone discovered de Warenne was still in his tent. The troops were recalled and the attack postponed. The same thing happened again later that morning, though this time the recall was to wait for reinforcements – a contingent of Scottish men-at-arms led by James the Steward and Malcolm, Earl of Lennox. When the Scots failed to appear de Warenne sent his men back over the bridge.

While all this was going on Wallace and Murray did nothing. If the dawn attack had been executed the English would have been able to secure their bridgehead, and then charge into the waiting Scots. The Scots' inactivity could have cost them the battle, but the English commander's late start bought Wallace and Murray the opportunity to prepare themselves. By the time de Warenne launched his third crossing they were ready. This time when the English men-at-arms galloped across the bridge the Scottish commanders let them pass, and then launched a flank attack from the side which stormed up and over the causeway. This cut the English force in two. The advance guard led by Sir Marmaduke Tweng pressed forward into the Scottish ranks in front of him, but to his rear the Scots spearmen were now between him and the bridge.

Tweng turned his men around and together they tried to cut their way to safety, but with no room to charge or fight most of the English vanguard were cut down. A few foot soldiers or Welsh archers escaped by swimming the river, but most were trapped and slaughtered. A handful of mounted knights also escaped. These included Tweng, who managed to fight his way through the cordon and across the bridge. Most of Tweng's men weren't so lucky. One of the casualties was the despised Hugh Cressingham; not only was he killed, but his skin was flayed from his body. Then, according to the *Lanercost Chronicle*, 'Of his skin William Wallace caused a broad strip to be taken from the head to the heel, to make therewith a baldrick for his sword.' It was a grisly end, even for a tax collector.

It was a major defeat, and de Warenne knew it. He paused only to place Marmaduke Tweng and a garrison in Stirling Castle before withdrawing back towards Berwick. As the English retreated, the Steward and Lennox switched sides and captured the English baggage train, and with it the supplies Tweng needed to withstand a siege. The garrison commander eventually had to surrender, as his men ran out of food. Long before this de Warenne had fled south, pursued by Wallace. Andrew Murray was one of the few Scottish casualties at the Battle of Stirling Bridge, and he eventually succumbed to his wounds in November. That left Wallace in sole command of the army. It was a rebel force no longer – the victory had transformed it into a national army.

Brought to the ring

Before his victory Wallace had been a minor rebel leader. Now he was a talisman, and while many of the Scottish nobility distrusted him or resented following someone of lower social standing, a few began drifting into his camp. Others either remained loyal to Edward or stayed out of the fight, for fear of what Edward might do to them. By the end of 1297 only the castles of Roxburgh and Edinburgh remained in English hands. It was a harsh winter, and Wallace pressed on into England, his men living off the land and looting or destroying whatever they could. Carlisle was briefly besieged, but the Scots lacked the equipment and expertise they needed to take it. Berwick fell, though, or rather the town did – the castle garrison held on, sending a swimmer across the Tweed to beg for help. Other English castles like Norham and Alnwick also remained defiant, but the population of Cumbria and Northumbria fled south, away from the Scots marauders. Wallace led his men as far south as Newcastle before they turned around and headed home, laden with English booty.

When Edward I heard about Stirling Bridge he was furious. He ordered de Warenne to stay in Scotland, and dispatched Clifford north to help him. By that time de Warenne had retreated all the way to

York. It took Edward to stiffen his resolve. The king ordered him to gather whatever force he could and drive the Scots back over the border. So, as Wallace's men withdrew, de Warenne advanced, and the castle garrisons at Berwick and Roxburgh were relieved. Meanwhile King Edward was taking steps to deal with Wallace once and for all. News of the Stirling Bridge debacle reached Edward in late September. He was in Flanders, trying to hold off King Philip's attacks. The English king made a decision. Unable to fight major campaigns in two places at once, he sent peace envoys to the French court. On 7 October an armistice was signed, and in late January this was turned into a year-long truce. Edward now had the breathing space he needed to crush the Scots.

Edward returned to England in March 1298, and by early June he was in York, which would become his centre of government. By the end of the month the king was in Roxburgh, just over the Scottish border, where his army was being mustered. He had about 25,000 foot soldiers at his disposal – Welsh and English, archers and spearmen. The core of his army were his mounted men-at-arms – about 2000 of them, including a small number of Scottish knights. As June turned into July Edward advanced into Scotland. He marched towards Edinburgh, where he hoped to meet his fleet, which was bringing up supplies. Unfortunately contrary winds had delayed them, and the English army were forced to live off the land as they marched. Still, they reached Edinburgh, and moved on to Linlithgow. By then Edward had learned that Wallace's army was only twenty miles away.

Edward's fear was that Wallace might revert to less direct tactics, and avoid a battle the English were likely to win. He needn't have worried. Wallace might have preferred to avoid a battle but the English had advanced more quickly than expected, and so the Scots now had no option but to fight. While a Scottish win might be unlikely, Wallace might be able to avoid defeat, and then escape under cover of night. On 22 July 1298 Wallace was encamped in Callendar Wood near Falkirk, with about 7000 men. Given his need to leave garrisons, Edward had about twice that number. The site of the battle is still a matter of some conjecture. There is a claim that it lay just north of Falkirk, close to where Grahamston Station stands today – a battlefield now engulfed by urban sprawl; most historians place it about four miles south of the town, just north of the village of Slamannan, overlooking the Westquarter Burn. Although the contemporary sources describe the lay of the land, they fail to provide any exact location for the battlefield.

Wherever he stood, Wallace chose a good position on rising ground, with a stream flanked by boggy terrain to his front. Behind him to the north lay the wood. It was a strong position, and Wallace augmented it by planting sharpened wooden stakes in front of his spearmen, who were grouped in four 'battles' or 'divisions' with clumps of archers placed in between. Most of the Scottish men-at-arms would have fought dismounted, alongside the spearmen. These blocks of spearmen were deployed in schiltrons – the dense formations of bristling spearpoints Clifford would encounter at Bannockburn a decade and a half later. If the men stood together they were difficult to break using cavalry. If the formation became broken, then the spearmen would be ridden down. It all depended on cohesion and morale.

Wallace did what he could to fortify his men, telling them, 'I have brought you to the ring – now dance if you can.' It was hardly a rival to the speech Shakespeare was to have Henry V give at Agincourt, but it made the point – victory that day depended on his spearmen. For his part Edward attended a field mass given by Bishop Bek, and was helped onto his horse. The previous night his men had stood to under arms, their horses beside them. During a night alarm the king's horse reared up and stepped on Edward's chest, breaking two ribs. Undeterred, Edward had his physicians bind him up, and then rode off to give battle.

The fight began when the English vanguard advanced towards the stream. The men skirted the worst of the bog to attack the Scottish right flank, while Edward sent Bishop Bek with the main body over to the right, to cross the stream in front of the Scottish left. That served to pin the Scots in place, while leaving most of their front exposed. Edward then moved his archers forward, and soon a rain of arrows began falling on the Scottish ranks. It was a slaughter. Gradually the schiltrons began to waver, which was the signal for the waiting English men-at-arms to ride in from the flanks to finish the job.

Seeing the disaster unfold, the small band of Scottish cavalry turned around and fled the field, leaving their countrymen to their fate. First the Scottish archers were ridden down, and then it was the turn of the schiltrons. The horsemen plunged into the gaps created by the English arrows, and the Scottish formations dissolved. It was every man for himself, as a pack of running Scottish infantry threw away their spears and fled for the cover of the trees. Wallace was one of the few to survive, withdrawing his spearmen into the woods and so to safety. Others were less fortunate. Although the exact numbers aren't known, at least half of Wallace's army fell on the field that day. The death toll included few leading Scottish nobles; most of those who fought that day had fled before the end.

The victorious Edward continued on to Stirling Castle, where his ribs healed, and his lieutenants took oaths of loyalty from a growing number of Scottish nobles. Food was still scarce – the Scots had burned crops and villages ahead of the English, and Edward's soldiers torched whatever was left. A fortnight later Edward headed south, leaving his administrators to govern the Scottish kingdom on his behalf. By September he was back in Carlisle, leaving the smouldering wreck of a country behind him. For his part William Wallace had been appointed guardian of Scotland after his victory at Stirling Bridge. He was now ousted from his position, leaving the Scottish magnates and prelates free to fight on, or to strike whatever deal they could with Edward.

The drama of William Wallace had played out in just over a year. While there was more to his story, including a dramatic finale, he was now relegated from leading man to a mere bit player in this Scottish tragedy.

6

Rivals and Guardians

Scotland became leaderless when William Wallace stepped down as guardian. If the fight against King Edward was going to continue then new national leaders had to be found – men who could unite the divided, broken country. So, after Falkirk, Scotland's ruling elite gathered again, and came up with a radical solution. Two replacement guardians would be appointed, representing the two factions whose feud had split the Scottish nobility for almost a decade. One was Robert Bruce, the young Earl of Carrick; the other was John Comyn, the son of the Lord of Badenoch. Bruce and the 'Red Comyn' had both joined the rebellion against Edward, while their fathers professed loyalty to the English king. These two young men represented what was effectively a wartime coalition – an alliance designed to unite the Scottish factions in a common cause.

A fragile coalition

While both Bruce and Comyn professed their loyalty to the exiled King John, Bruce had no intention of fighting to restore his family's old enemy. Both guardians were walking a political tightrope, but for Bruce the balancing act was made all the harder by his family's distrust of the Balliols. They also had to deal with Edward, whose garrisons controlled the land between Stirling and Berwick, leaving the Scots with just the lands north of the Forth and Clyde, and the south-western corner of the kingdom. Fortunately the guardians had something of a breathing space. Although Edward's armies would return, the new Scots policy of avoiding pitched battles meant that there would be no decisive victories – just the odd siege and plenty of fruitless marching across a war-ravaged land.

In August the Scottish nobles and prelates met again, this time in Peebles, some twenty miles south of Edinburgh, close to Wallace's old hiding place in Selkirk Forest. A rift between the two guardians led to a scrap between Bruce and Comyn, which proved too much for their fellow nobles. Two years before Bishop Fraser of St Andrews had died in France, and in 1298 he was succeeded by William Lamberton, formerly the Chancellor of Glasgow Cathedral. At Peebles the bishop was made a third guardian, with seniority over Bruce and Comyn. This saved the coalition, and avoided a divisive civil war at the very moment the Scots needed to stand together. The cracks had been papered over, but the rift would continue to widen.

The triumvirate's first significant victory came just before Christmas 1299, when Sir Marmaduke Tweng was forced to surrender Stirling Castle. King Edward had been unable to muster an army to come to Tweng's relief, and so the Scots were spared further destruction at Plantagenet hands. It would be the following summer before Edward marched north again, and this time his 'invasion' was a limited one, aimed at the south-west corner of Scotland. In July 1300 he besieged Caerlaverock Castle, a formidable stronghold and the power base of the Maxwells, supporters of the triumvirate. Edward's siege engines forced the surrender of the castle within a few days. Edward hanged some of the garrison, and imprisoned the rest – a stark warning that his patience was wearing thin. That, though, was the extent of Edward's campaigning that year. After marching as far as Wigtown he headed back to Carlisle, leaving the Scots free to bicker amongst themselves.

Meanwhile, diplomatic wheels had been turning. Pope Boniface

VIII issued a papal bull which declared Edward's occupation of Scotland to be illegal. Having just been entrusted with the care of the exiled John Balliol, the Holy Father was willing to look favourably on Scottish pleas. A furious Edward simply ignored the Pope's ruling. For Edward, his feudal claim of overlordship over Scotland was paramount. He forced his magnates to sign a petition supporting his claim, and then had his prelates reply to the Pope's bull, laying out the English position. They even described the Scots as 'foes of peace and sons of rebellion'. As a result the papal initiative came to nothing, and the Scots lost the support of a powerful ally.

That summer the rift between Bruce and Comyn led to the collapse of the triumvirate. In May Bruce resigned, and his place was taken by Sir Ingram de Umfraville, the man who five months earlier had recaptured Stirling Castle. Umfraville was a supporter of Robert Bruce, so in theory the status quo was maintained. In fact Comyn saw both of his fellow guardians as allies of Bruce, and refused to work with them. The Scottish ship of state remained rudderless for the best part of a year, until two events in 1301 led to a political sea change. The first was prompted by King John's release from papal authority. He went to his estates in France, where he began lobbying King Philip to support his cause. As John was now back in the political game a fourth guardian was appointed, John de Soules, a Scottish knight who had gone into exile with his king. Although the guardians had been ruling in John's name, none of them expected him to return to power. In the summer of 1301 such a return became a real possibility.

Hammering the Scots

That summer Edward mustered a fresh army, and in July he marched out of Berwick towards Selkirk. This time his aim wasn't to bring the Scots to battle – it was unlikely they would risk another defeat like Falkirk. This expedition was designed to force the Scottish nobles to submit to his authority. So, rather than advancing in one big column he split his army in two. While he marched into the Borders, his son Edward, Prince of Wales would begin the campaign in Carlisle and progress to Galloway. Between them the two forces would cover most of Scotland south of the Forth and Clyde. It was an ambitious venture, but Edward was a good planner, and everything went smoothly. All the Scots could do was nip at the English heels – they were powerless to stop the two Edwards marching wherever they wanted.

King Edward passed through Selkirk and Peebles, and then marched on Bothwell Castle. Overlooking a crossing of the River Clyde, ten miles south-east of the new bridge at Glasgow, Bothwell was one of the strongest castles in Scotland, but it fell in less than a month, thanks to Edward's skills in siegecraft. Meanwhile Prince Edward had reached Ayr, thirty miles from Bothwell. There he captured the Bruce-held castle before taking the coastal route back to Carlisle. After capturing Bothwell the king moved on to Linlithgow, where he settled down for the winter. His son joined him there in time for Christmas. That winter Edward negotiated a new truce with France, which included a temporary armistice with the Scots. For the moment the bloodletting would cease, while King Edward and King Philip performed their own diplomatic dance.

Philip IV had his own problems. The aim of Edward's expedition to Flanders had been to support his ally Count Guy, but the French army had proved too powerful for the allies. After Edward's forces withdrew, King Philip subdued the province and captured the count. The Flemish burghers didn't relish French occupation, and in 1301 they rose in revolt. The following summer King Philip sent a powerful French army to reconquer Flanders. It was led by Count Robert of Artois, who had 2500 men-at-arms at his disposal, backed up by infantry. For their part the Flemings fielded an infantry army – the spear-armed militias of cities like Bruges and Ghent. The two forces met outside Courtrai (Kortrijk) on 11 July 1302. On paper the French knights should have slaughtered the Flemings. Instead it was the militiamen who did the killing.

Led by the son and grandson of Count Guy, the Flemings used the terrain to their advantage. Then as now the fields around Courtrai were laced with irrigation ditches, and these proved deadly to the French men-at-arms. Jumping them might have been possible for knights out hunting, but not for armour-clad men encumbered by the panoply of war, and the Flemings augmented them by digging more in front of their position. Hemmed in by the ditches the French had no option but to launch a frontal attack, which was met by a bristling line of Flemish spears. Soon the ditches were clogged with dead men and horses, and sensing victory the Flemings advanced to finish off the enemy. The French survivors broke and ran.

The fight became known as the 'Battle of the Golden Spurs' on account of the hoard of such spurs taken from the French dead. Count Robert was one of the thousand French knights who died in the Flemish mud that day. This was a battle that defied military logic. It was said that a well-equipped knight on horseback was equal to ten infantrymen. Courtrai was a lesson Prince Edward – and Robert Clifford – would have done well to learn. Instead, a dozen years later they would repeat the same mistakes made by the hapless Robert of Artois.

This French disaster ended any real possibility that King John would return to Scotland. He needed French support, and that was now out of the question. Effectively, Philip wanted peace, and was willing to sacrifice John to get it. This development came too late for Robert Bruce. Alarmed by the notion that John Balliol might regain his throne, the Earl of Carrick switched sides again and offered his fealty to King Edward. That was in early 1302, before Courtrai changed the political landscape. At the time the Balliol–Comyn star was in the ascendancy, and Bruce and his ageing father had been sidelined. In 1300 the Earl of Carrick had resigned his guardianship because he felt he could no longer work alongside the Red Comyn. Any latent notions of Scottish patriotism were now discarded. The principle that the enemy of my enemy is my friend now applied. From that point on Robert Bruce – the future king of Scotland – would be the leading Scottish supporter of an English king.

The three-cornered armistice came to an end in November 1302. While Philip of France wanted peace, both King Edward and the supporters of King John were preparing for war. The Scots struck first, besieging Linlithgow and capturing Selkirk. For his part Edward organised the defences of his northern shires, and issued orders for a spring muster at Newcastle. In the meantime he launched what modern commanders might call a 'reconnaissance in force', led by Sir John Segrave. In late February Segrave was attacked near Roslin, just south of Edinburgh. The Red Comyn and Wallace's old lieutenant Simon Fraser launched a night assault on the scattered English force, and Segrave was captured. This little victory might have boosted Scottish morale, but the real fight was still to come. Edward was gathering his men around him, and preparing to march north.

Before he began, Edward negotiated a proper peace treaty with the French king. Courtrai had taken away Philip's appetite for war. This new treaty was signed in Paris in May 1303, and this time there was no Scottish clause. Courtrai had effectively ended Philip's flirtation with King John's cause, and a possible resurrection of a Franco-Scottish alliance. Even the Pope deserted the Scots, calling on the Scottish clergy to make their peace with Edward. He was embroiled in a new temporal dispute with the French king, and Edward's support was considered more important than the feudal independence of the Scottish crown. When Edward attacked, the Scots would have to fight their own battles.

It was late May when Edward unleashed his invasion, his men marching north from Roxburgh towards Edinburgh, burning everything in their path. Robert Bruce marched with him, and was there when Edward passed through Edinburgh and on to Linlithgow. The Red Comyn could do nothing to stop the advance, or even slow it down. When Edward reached Stirling he ignored the enemy-held castle and continued on across the River Forth. He then marched to Perth, which he entered on 18 June. This was a real medieval 'blitzkrieg' – a lightning campaign where Edward kept the Scots off balance, and forced them to react to his manoeuvres rather than the other way round.

At Brechin the castle held out against the English, so Edward ordered up two massive siege engines, which pounded it into submission. Its governor was Sir Thomas Maule, who raised morale by laughing off the bombardment, rubbing the battered wall after a stone missile smashed into it as if trying to rub out a dirty mark. The joke ended when he was killed by a flying shard of stone. The castle surrendered on 9 August, and Edward continued on through the north-east, capturing towns and castles as far north as Elgin and Urquhart. In fact the most northerly English garrison was established at Cromarty Castle on the Black Isle, 15 miles from Inverness and 125 miles north of Edinburgh.

By November Edward was back south in Dunfermline, where he and his army spent the winter. Prince Edward passed the winter in nearby Perth, and that Christmas both king and prince were visited by a string of Scottish magnates, eager to join the winning side. The Red Comyn remained at large in Atholl, the highland vastness north of Perth, and skirmishing continued throughout the winter. However, by then it was clear the Scottish cause was lost. The new defectors joined Edward's Scottish supporters – men like John of Strathbogie, Earl of Atholl and William, Earl of Ross – nobles whose freedom after Dunbar had been bought by their homage to Edward. Another of these winter supplicants was Richard, Earl of Ulster, Robert Bruce's father-in-law, who became a go-between when the Red Comyn asked to negotiate a surrender.

William Wallace was still at large, hiding out in Selkirk Forest. After Falkirk he spent two years on the continent, but he was now the leader of a small band of die-hards – patriots or outlaws depending on who told the story. During Edward's campaign Robert Bruce remained in Ayr, holding the west for the English king. Then in February he joined a mounted raid across the Firth of Forth, a lightning assault on

Wallace's lair. Bruce rode alongside Segrave and Robert Clifford, and together they caught Wallace completely by surprise. At Happrew near Peebles the die-hards were routed, but somehow both Wallace and Simon Fraser escaped the slaughter. From that moment on Wallace was a fugitive in his own land. Detachments of troops – both English and Scottish – guarded every town and river crossing in southern Scotland. Wallace had nowhere to run.

The surrender talks began on 19 January. The site was Kinclaven Castle on the banks of the River Tay, ten miles upstream from Perth. Unprepared to offer an unconditional surrender, Comyn instead negotiated terms, not just for himself but for Scotland. This show of bravado paid off – Edward was magnanimous, and promised to maintain the laws, customs and liberties of the realm as they had existed before the death of Alexander III. He also promised to restore the lands taken from his Scottish opponents. Comyn had read Edward well – he would need the support of these same Scottish nobles if he planned to hold on to the kingdom he had just captured. Comyn agreed to the terms, and surrendered to Edward's lieutenants. Apart from one last curtain call the long war had run its course.

That last call was the siege of Stirling Castle. For the past four years it had been held in the name of King John. It was the last bastion of Scottish resistance, and its capture would complete Edward's control of John's kingdom. In the spring of 1304 Edward set out to take it. Stirling was a difficult castle to capture – perched on top of a rocky crag, it was virtually impervious to assault. The only way to take the place was either to starve the defenders out, or to batter them into submission. Edward did both. First he invested the castle, surrounding it with troops to make sure no supplies could reach the defenders. Then he brought up his siege engines.

No fewer than thirteen great trebuchets were dragged to Stirling, and Edward ordered others to be built on site. These monsters were crewed by hundreds of sweating labourers, supervised by some of the most skilled engineers in Europe. Stores of spare beams and metal counterweights were laid in, and mounds of boulders were piled next to the machines, to use as ammunition. These machines were the technical marvels of the age, and the proud engineers even gave them names like 'Berefrey', 'Ludgar' and 'Vernay'. One shot from Ludgar demolished a whole curtain wall during the siege – proof that the machines were no mere playthings of the king. This was a serious business.

The siege began on 22 April, and would last for three months. While the trebuchets hurled rocks at the castle walls, miners tried to dig their way beneath the defences, and smaller machines lobbed incendiaries over the walls. The small garrison commanded by Sir William Oliphant took to hiding in the castle cellars, as the walls above them were gradually reduced to rubble. Finally, on 20 July, Oliphant and his men offered to capitulate. It was claimed that Edward refused to accept the offer for a while, until a boulder launched from his newest trebuchet, 'Warwolf', had struck what remained of the castle wall. Only then was Oliphant allowed to surrender. As the garrison was marched off into captivity, Edward would have had reason to feel satisfied. Scotland was conquered, and the shattered realm was at peace for the first time in decades. Edward was now the undisputed master of the British Isles.

That March Edward held a parliament in St Andrews, attended by every major Scottish nobleman and cleric. It seemed the English king had finally learned that to ensure the support of the Scots he needed to bring them into the fold. After 129 Scottish nobles repeated their oaths of fealty to Edward, the king asked Bruce and Bishop Wishart to recommend a new form of government. They proposed a ten-strong council made up of nobles, clerics and burgesses – a body that would represent Scotland in Edward's parliament. Edward agreed. While his key appointments in Scotland went to English administrators, he would rule the kingdom with the help and collusion of the Scottish nobility. They in turn needed to safeguard their own lands and titles, and for that they needed Edward as much as he needed them. It was a marriage of convenience, and while it lasted the realm would remain at peace.

By the summer of 1304 all of Scotland lay under Edward's control, but William Wallace remained at large. At the St Andrews parliament the Scottish nobles declared him an outlaw. While the nobles enjoyed Edward's magnanimity, there would be no mercy for Wallace. Edward ordered his Scottish nobles to hunt him down, but the rebel evaded capture for a whole year, lurking in the wilds of Selkirk Forest. Finally, on 3 August 1305, Wallace was captured in a house outside Glasgow. It was claimed he was taken by surprise and seized while still in his bed. His captor was a Scot – the son of the Earl of Mentieth – who dutifully handed his prisoner over to the English. Wallace was taken to London, where he stood trial in Westminster Hall.

The legitimate charge against him wasn't treason – Wallace had never sworn fealty to Edward, despite being charged with being treasonous. More accurately he was accused of murder, arson and sacrilege, the fruits of the trail of mayhem he blazed across Northumbria after Stirling Bridge. As an outlaw Wallace had no chance of acquittal – no plea, no mitigation, no mercy. On 23 August he was dragged through the streets on a hurdle before being hanged. Before he choked to death he was cut down, and his bowels were ripped out. The body was then dismembered. While his head was stuck on a spike on London Bridge, his limbs were sent north to adorn the walls of Berwick, Stirling and Perth.

There would be no *Braveheart*-style dying cry for freedom. Wallace's last moments were filled with brutality and horror. In Scotland he would be all but forgotten, at least until his memory was revived by Blind Harry in the late fifteenth century. Instead it would be the same nobleman who had hunted him down who would revive his notion of national liberty. Another brutal death and a lot more suffering would be required, however, before Robert Bruce redefined himself as the new saviour of Scotland.

7

From Murderer to Monarch

Murdering your political rival in a church wasn't the best launching pad for a bid for power. That, though, was exactly what Robert Bruce did on 10 February 1306. He and his rival John Comyn – the Red Comyn – were both in Dumfries, a busy market town in the south-west corner of Scotland. As a local magistrate Comyn was taking part in a court session, and the town was close to Bruce's lands in Annandale. The two men agreed to meet in Greyfriars Church, which formed part of the Franciscan convent founded by King John's mother Lady Devorgilla. Only one of them would walk away from the encounter.

We don't know exactly what happened – different versions tell different stories. The gist is that the two men quarrelled, much as they had done when they were both guardians. This time, though, knives were drawn, and Bruce stabbed his rival on the steps of the church altar. The Red Comyn was accompanied by his uncle Sir Robert Comyn, who drew his sword and lunged at Bruce. The blow was parried or deflected, and Sir Robert was stabbed in turn by Bruce's brother-in-law Christopher Seton. Tradition has it that when Bruce and Seton left the church, One of Bruce's companions, Roger Kirkpatrick, went back inside to check the two Comyns were dead. If not he would finish them off. The double killing was almost certainly not premeditated

– everything points to this being a heat of the moment fracas. However, at that moment Bruce's life was changed for ever.

Fall from grace

To explore the chain of events which led Bruce and Comyn to Greyfriars Church we need to go back almost two years, to Easter 1304. Bruce's father – the Lord of Annandale – died in April, leaving the 32-year-old Robert, Earl of Carrick as the head of the family. It is often said that ambition and skill can skip a generation. In any event, since the death of Robert 'The Contender' in 1295 his son had shown little interest in pursuing the family's claim to the throne. The Lord of Annandale lived the life of a country nobleman, seemingly content to maintain his lands on both sides of the border rather than fight in the political arena. The younger Robert would prove a very different animal.

The death of his father took place shortly before Stirling Castle was besieged. Robert Bruce was there – he was even thanked by Edward for supplying siege equipment. So too were most of Scotland's nobles and clerics, largely because they needed to demonstrate their new-found loyalty to their English overlord. Bruce used the opportunity to lobby for the support of some of the most important men in Scotland – men who would support his claim to the throne if the opportunity ever arose. One of these was Bishop William Lamberton of St Andrews. The pair met in Cambuskenneth Abbey, just over a mile from where the castle walls were being pounded to rubble. Like his colleague Bishop Wishart of Glasgow, Lamberton agreed to support Bruce when the time came.

That time, though, was still in the future. Robert, Earl of Carrick was still King Edward's man. Since swearing loyalty to Edward, Robert had enjoyed the tentative support and patronage of the English king. He advised Edward during the parliament at St Andrews, and became the guardian of the newborn Douglas, Earl of Mar, an appointment that involved gaining control of his lands in Aberdeenshire, and the keys of Kildrummy Castle. He was given Sir Ingram Umfraville's lands in the south-west, seized from the former guardian by Edward. However, Bruce remained something of an outsider, fully trusted neither by his fellow Scots nor by the English king. He had switched allegiances too freely and too often, and so a question mark now hung over his loyalty.

Someone who certainly didn't trust him was John Comyn. While Bruce had supported Edward during his recent campaign, the Red Comyn had fought against him. Now the fighting was over both noblemen sought to strengthen their own position, while trying to maintain good relations with the English king. It was a political tightrope walk, and Comyn proved the more adept acrobat. Exactly who proposed what is unclear – the English and Scottish sources disagree – but certainly at some stage that autumn Bruce and Comyn discussed the vacant Scottish kingship, spurred on by the news that King Edward was on his deathbed. The horse-trading for power ended when Edward recovered, and was told that Bruce was rekindling his claim to the Scottish throne. This may have been a leak, or it may have come from the Comyn camp. Whatever the source, Bruce underwent a rapid fall from grace.

In September 1305 Edward demanded that he return the Umfraville lands and hand over control of Kildrummy. His position as the guardian of the young Earl of Mar was called into question, and he was stripped of his role as sheriff of Ayr and Lanark. Edward still lacked proof that Bruce planned to make a bid for the Scottish crown, so the Earl of Carrick was kept close at hand in Westminster while the king's agents tried to dig up more evidence. It was possible that Comyn offered to furnish the proof – a letter signed by Bruce stating that the two nobles had come to an agreement over the succession, and asserting Bruce's own claim to the throne. If it existed, this would be the 'smoking gun' that would prove Bruce guilty of plotting behind Edward's back.

Edward decided to arrest Bruce, pending the arrival of this damning evidence. However, at dinner one day Edward told some of his guests that Bruce was about to be apprehended. One of those guests was Ralph,

Baron Monthermer, ward of the earldoms of Hereford and Gloucester. He was also a good friend of Robert Bruce. According to one account, that evening he sent Bruce twelve pennies and a pair of spurs. The message was clear – Bruce had been sold out by someone, and had to flee. Bruce heeded the warning: accompanied by a servant he left London in dead of night, and rode hard towards the Scottish border.

That old Ladybird book I was given as a child added to the tale by drawing on legend. The story went that Robert Bruce knew King Edward would send a mounted posse to catch him, so he devised a cunning ruse to throw his pursuers off his trail. He visited a village blacksmith, and had the man take off his horse's shoes. They were then reattached the wrong way round. The idea was to make the men-at-arms following him think the tracks were made by someone travelling the other way. The legend also had the blacksmith betray Bruce when the pursuers appeared, telling them of the ruse and pointing them in the direction of the fleeing Scottish earl. While it makes a terrific story – and an atmospheric illustration in the little children's book – the truth is this was probably a later embellishment, designed to add colour to Bruce's escape.

Bruce made directly for his family home in Carrick. There he planned his next move. Clearly he had broken his ties with Edward. While he still might be able to survive the political storm facing him, his cosy relationship with the English king had been damaged. Bruce had nobody to turn to apart from his own supporters – the men whose backing he had taken such pains to secure before his plotting was so dramatically exposed. The only other possibility was to strike a deal with his political rival John Comyn, before news of Bruce's flight reached Scotland. That was when he had the message sent to the Red Comyn, asking to meet him in Dumfries. What followed – the argument in the church, the stabbing and the brutal murder – was Bruce's 'crossing the Rubicon' moment. After that he had no option but to embark on all-out rebellion against Edward. Like it or not, Bruce was now unequivocally wedded to the Scottish patriotic cause.

The King of the May

Robert Bruce had to move fast. As the blood of John Comyn was still pooling under the altar he took the first steps towards armed rebellion. He called upon his followers and supporters, and began seizing the castles of Galloway and Ayrshire. Dumfries was one of the first to fall, closely followed by the Comyn stronghold of Dalswinton, whose castle had been built by the Red Comyn's father to control the family's lands in the south-west of Scotland. Dalswinton Castle lay six miles north of Dumfries, and it was from there that Comyn had ridden out to meet his rival in Greyfriars Church. The news of his death reached the castle only a little before a band of Bruce's retainers, who overpowered the leaderless garrison. Other castles followed – with the fall of Buittle to the south of Dumfries and Tibbers to the north, Bruce gained control of a defensive chain that stretched northwards from the Solway Firth, separating Annandale in the east from Galloway in the west.

This lightning campaign continued. Through negotiation more than force Bruce regained control of Ayr Castle on the coast of the Firth of Clyde, followed by Dunaverty on the southern tip of Kintyre, Inverkip Castle to the north of Ayr, and Rothesay Castle on Bute, a stronghold of the Stewarts. With these four castles in his hands Bruce was able to dominate the Firth of Clyde, and thereby to establish a vital sea link with his allies in the Western Isles. Within three weeks of the murder, he had effectively seized control of the south-west of Scotland.

Naturally, Edward was furious, and demanded the return of the strongholds. The English king clearly thought this was a rebellion, which could be subdued by a combination of threat and force. Bruce's reply was a dramatic act which would prove that this was no mere rebellion. This was an all-out bid for power.

For months Bruce had been wooing the Scottish nobility and clergy, hoping to convince them to support his bid for the throne. Now was the moment when all this secretive diplomacy paid off. Robert Wishart, Bishop of Glasgow, was the key figure in what happened next. The bishop had supported William Wallace's rising, and had been imprisoned for it. On his release he resumed his vocal opposition to King Edward, prompting the English king to write to Pope Boniface with a demand that Wishart be removed from office. The Pope refused to oblige, but described the bishop as 'the prime mover and instigator of all the tumult and dissension which has risen' between Edward and the Scots. It was a tough accusation, but one that had an element of truth to it.

Since his release in 1301 Wishart had encouraged the Red Comyn in his military opposition to Edward. When Comyn surrendered, the troublesome bishop was banished from Scotland. He spent two years in exile in France, but by the winter of 1305–6 he was back in Scotland, and therefore able to grasp the opportunity created by Bruce's actions. Now, within a fortnight of Comyn's murder, Bruce travelled north to Glasgow to meet Wishart in his cathedral.

This placed the bishop in an awkward position. Bruce had murdered a man in a consecrated church – an unequivocal act of sacrilege. By rights Robert Bruce should have been treated as an outcast by the Church, and Wishart should have called for the murderer to be excommunicated. Instead the bishop welcomed him into his apartments, heard his grisly confession and absolved him of his sins. Even more shockingly, he decided to reward the penitent with a kingdom. Wishart was a Scottish patriot, but his motives had as much to do with the Church as they did the need for a secular opposition to Edward. At the Treaty of Birgham Wishart and his fellow clerics had sought to safeguard the independence of the Scottish church from its counterpart in England. Now, despite the assurances made by Edward to uphold these safeguards the Scottish clergy feared they might lose their independence. Bishop Wishart saw Bruce as a leader who could help fight for ecclesiastical freedom as well as national sovereignty.

So, over a number of meetings held in Glasgow, after granting Bruce absolution the bishop and the earl discussed politics. Both knew that the murder of John Comyn had been a watershed moment for Bruce. While Bruce mightn't have wanted to launch a bid for the throne – at least not at that moment – he now had no option. The incisive mind of Bishop Wishart saw that clearly, and he understood that not only should Bruce be crowned, the coronation had to take place as soon as possible, before Edward or the Comyns could react.

Bishop Wishart organised everything. The coronation would take place in Scone at the end of March. Wishart made sure the Scottish clergy were well represented – Bishop Lamberton of St Andrews was there, as were David de Moravia, Bishop of Moray and a gaggle of minor clerics. The magnates were less united. Bruce's leading supporters were present – the earls of Atholl, Lennox, Mar and Menteith – as were over a hundred lesser nobles. Absent from the proceedings, however, were any supporters of the Comyns.

That was perfectly understandable. The coronation represented the seizure of power by the Bruce faction. After the murder in Dumfries, the Comyns and their supporters were Bruce's implacable enemies. Bruce was usurping the crown and rebelling against King Edward, his feudal overlord. Previous rebellions against Edward's authority had been carried out in the name of King John – 'Toom Tabard'. John was still very much alive and still recognised by most Scots as their rightful king. Far from being designed to unite a divided realm, this coronation was merely the opening move in a new civil war. This time though the allegiances had switched – the Comyn faction was on the side of Edward, while Bruce's party espoused the cause of Scottish independence.

The inauguration was held on 23 March 1306. Unfortunately the coronation ceremony had to wait. Traditionally the Scottish king was crowned by the Earl of Fife, but the teenage nobleman was in England, under Edward's guardianship. Instead his aunt Isabella was to perform the ceremony. Since, however, her husband John, Earl of Buchan was a Comyn – the cousin of the Red Comyn – and therefore Bruce's enemy, it took time for the Countess of Buchan to slip away and travel to Scone, and she arrived a day too late. But Bishop Wishart refused to let that spoil the event. He simply organised a second inauguration for the following day – 25 March – and this time Bruce was properly crowned as Robert I, king of Scotland.

So, Scotland had a new king – and an old one. Naturally the Balliols and the Comyns remained loyal to King John, while Bruce and his adherents attempted to pretend they represented the whole realm, not just one small but powerful faction. Today, Bruce's action would be seen as a coup, and would probably be deplored by the international community. In 1306 his coronation was seen as what it was – a bid for power by a man who had the odds stacked against him. Bishop Wishart did what he could. He or Bruce dug out a royal banner of Scotland, which flew behind the new king as he sat on the throne. But though Bruce might look the part, he was a king in name only. Even his new teenage wife Elizabeth understood this: when she described their new position as the 'King and Queen of the May', she was only partly speaking in jest.

It goes without saying that King Edward wasn't particularly impressed. It was claimed that when his fury abated he vowed never to rest in the same place for more than two nights until he had defeated Bruce and his men. According to my old Ladybird book, he made his vow while placing his hand on a golden-threaded bag containing a pair of swans – the symbol of constancy and truth. Whatever really happened, it was clear that Edward planned to deal with Bruce, and to extinguish with him the last embers of Scottish rebellion. So, just eleven days after King Robert's coronation, Edward appointed a hard-bitten young nobleman as his new commander in Scotland. His job was to hunt down the self-appointed Scottish king and to bring him to Edward, dead or alive.

8

The King in the Heather

The man King Edward chose to hunt down Robert Bruce in the spring of 1306 was Aymer de Valence. A nobleman with royal blood, his father being the stepbrother of Edward's father King Henry, he also had familial links with the Comyns, as his sister Joan was the widow of the Red Comyn. This meant he had a personal stake in the apprehension of Bruce. A tall and sallow man in his mid-thirties, de Valence was heir to the earldom of Pembroke – a title he would accede to two years later, in the spring of 1308. During the recent campaign in Flanders he had proved himself a natural soldier, a gifted leader and a skilled diplomat. In short, he was the ideal man for the job.

King Edward's revenge

De Valence raised a small force of men-at-arms, archers and crossbowmen – about 2000 men in total, of whom no more than fifty were mounted men-at-arms. He marched north from Berwick, and headed through Dunbar and Edinburgh towards Perth. Edward had already told him to destroy or burn the property of Bruce's supporters as he advanced into Scotland, and de Valence's men did exactly that. On reaching Perth, de Valence learned that Bruce and his followers had flown, and were now operating in the north-east. Still, this gave Edward's commander the chance to consolidate his hold on southern and central Scotland, and to cut Bruce off from his power base in the south-west.

On 8 June an English detachment captured Bishop Wishart at Cupar, where he was encouraging the besiegers of the royal castle. Edward was delighted, and his pleasure increased when Bishop Lamberton surrendered to de Valence. The two bishops were sent south in chains, to be incarcerated in Hampshire. Bruce was now denied the services of the two men who could best add legitimacy to his claim to the throne. Wishart was unrepentant, and so he languished in an English prison until after Bannockburn. By contrast Lamberton protested he had been forced to support Bruce, and while he remained in England, he was treated less harshly than his fellow cleric. He finally returned to Scotland in 1312, following an exchange of prisoners. While de Valence was in Perth, Bruce was campaigning in the Mearns and Aberdeenshire, threatening the lands of several leading nobles in the region who refused to support him. Prominent among them were John Comyn, the Earl of Buchan and William, Earl of Ross – both of whom appear to have been less adventurous than their wives. Then there was Gilbert de Umfraville, Earl of Angus, who was in no hurry to risk his lands and title. Malise, Earl of Strathearn was another potential threat, but Bruce invaded Strathearn and captured the earl. He was briefly imprisoned, until he reluctantly offered Bruce his support. All this campaigning achieved little – the expected volunteers failed to flock to the royal standard, and Bruce's opponents were closing in.

In early June Bruce decided to head south again, to deal with de Valence in Perth, and on 19 June he arrived before its gates. He demanded that de Valence come out and fight, but the gates remained firmly closed, and so that afternoon Bruce withdrew to Methven, six miles to the north-west. There he set up camp in a nearby wood, and his men settled in for the evening. De Valence had every intention of fighting, but only on his terms. After Bruce's departure he led his men out of the town and followed the Scots to Methven. Bruce's men were scattered – foraging for supplies and firewood, cooking meals, and generally making themselves comfortable in their encampment. De Valence's attack came as a complete surprise. While Bruce's leading supporters mounted and fought back, the rest of de Valence's men swept through the encampment, slashing and killing as they went.

The so-called Battle of Methven was over in a matter of minutes. Bruce escaped, but many of his men were not so fortunate. Most were killed or captured. One of the prisoners was de Valence's friend Thomas Randolph, who was released on condition that he switch sides. Fleeing into the Highlands, pursued by de Valence, Bruce and his companions reached Loch Tay, where they were forced to fight again as the English caught up with them. Bruce suffered another defeat, but once more he evaded capture and the flight continued. His only chance now was to escape to the west coast, and seek the protection of his friends and allies in the Western Isles.

The fugitives travelled down Glen Dochart, beneath the looming peaks of Beinn Cheathaich and Meall a Churain, and turned into Strath Fillan. By the start of July they reached the spot where the village of Tyndrum now stands. There, in the narrow pass between the mountains, they found their path blocked by Highlanders. These were the men of John Macdougall of Argyll, a supporter of the Comyns. In the fight that followed, Bruce's outnumbered force was defeated for a third time in as many weeks. This proved too much for the so-called royal army. After fleeing back down the glen they stopped to count their losses. Bruce had less than 200 men with him now – too small a force to guarantee the safety of either the king or his family. So Bruce made the decision to split up.

The women in his party were sent back to the east on the remaining horses, escorted by the Earl of Atholl. Meanwhile Bruce and his much-diminished band continued their escape to the west. The women were heading for Kildrummy Castle in Aberdeenshire, which was held by Robert's brother Neil. Then they learned that de Valence and

Prince Edward were advancing into Aberdeenshire, so it was decided Kildrummy wasn't such a secure refuge after all. Instead they decided to travel north to the Moray Firth. From there they hoped to find a boat to take them to Orkney, which was then governed by Norway. Having married the late King Eric, Bruce's sister Isabel was still living in Norway. She would offer the Bruce women sanctuary. Unfortunately they only got as far as Tain, twenty-five miles north of Inverness. There they were captured by the Earl of Ross, who slaughtered the escort and sent the women to Prince Edward in Aberdeenshire.

These female prisoners didn't fare well in English hands. Edward shipped them south to Berwick, where Isabella, Countess of Buchan was imprisoned in a wooden cage, attached to the battlements of Berwick Castle. It was exposed to the elements – the only shelter to be had was in a small privy, which as modesty dictated lay inside the castle wall. Bruce's younger sister Mary was given an identical cage mounted on the walls of Roxburgh Castle, while a third cage was prepared on the battlements of the Tower of London. Its lodger was to be Bruce's 12-year-old daughter Marjory, but Edward took pity on her, and she was banished to a nunnery instead. Bruce's elder sister Christina was also sent to a convent, after watching her husband Christopher Seton – captured at Loch Doon in Ayrshire, where he was guarding the local Bruce estates – hanged, drawn and quartered. As for Bruce's wife Elizabeth, as the daughter of the powerful Earl of Ulster she was spared a cage – instead she was placed under house arrest in Yorkshire. Isabella and Mary would remain trapped in their tiny cages for four long, harrowing years.

Meanwhile, in late July Prince Edward reached Kildrummy Castle, still held by Bruce's brother Neil, and promptly laid siege to it. The siege lasted until early September, until the castle blacksmith, a man called Osborne, set fire to the stronghold's dwindling store of grain. Faced with starvation, the garrison had no option but to surrender. Osborne had presumably sabotaged the grain stocks in order to gain a reward from Prince Edward. Instead – it is claimed – he was paid back by having molten gold poured down his throat. The prisoners were killed, and Neil Bruce was sent south as a prisoner. At Berwick he too was hanged, drawn and quartered. Two months later John, Earl of Atholl was hanged for treason in London – the gallows being built especially high in honour of his elevated social status – and his decapitated head stuck on a pole on London Bridge. King Edward was determined to show no mercy to Robert Bruce, his family and his supporters. Come what may, this was a rebellion that had to be crushed.

Appointment with a spider

After saying farewell to the women, Bruce and his remaining men moved south to Loch Lomond, where they were welcomed by the Macdonalds. Any enemy of the Macdougals was their friend, and so they spirited Bruce to safety. The fugitives were transported by boat down Loch Long to the mouth of the Clyde, and then on to the Isle of Bute. Their final destination was meant to be Dunaverty Castle on the southern tip of Kintyre. While the castle was still held for Bruce, it was about to be besieged so he only stayed there briefly before moving on, courtesy of the Macdonald galleys. Dunaverty fell to the English in late September 1306.

By that time Bruce was either on little Rathlin Island, twenty-five miles west of Dunaverty, off the coast of Ulster, or elsewhere in the Macdonalds' island heartland. While English ships searched the coast of the Scottish mainland, Bruce was safe in his island retreat, weathering the storms of winter and laying plans for a counter-attack in the spring. Bruce's local ally was Angus Og Macdonald, head of the Macdonalds and Lord of Islay. The Macdonalds lent Bruce galleys and men, and together the king and the Highland leader plotted their campaign. It would involve two attacks against the English-held mainland – a main assault on Bruce's home county of Ayrshire, and a diversionary attack on Galloway, a region where the Comyns and their allies held the reins of power.

During the winter the castles captured by Bruce in the south-west had fallen to the English or their Scottish allies, and so Bruce felt he had to prove to the local population that he remained a rallying point for patriotic resistance. The only problem was that while the Macdonald galleys gave Bruce and his men the ability to strike wherever they liked, he had virtually no idea how strong the English garrisons of Ayrshire and Galloway might be. Bruce was about to commit the cardinal military sin of launching an amphibious attack without conducting a proper reconnaissance first.

The diversionary force was led by Sir Reginald Crawford, accompanied by Malcolm MacQuillan, Lord of Kintyre, and Bruce's youngest brothers Alexander and Thomas, both of whom were in their early twenties. They sailed into Loch Ryan on 9 February, landing near Stranraer. There they encountered Dungal Macdouall, an ally of the Comyns. The attackers were defeated, and while some managed to flee to their ships the rest were either killed or captured. Only two galleys escaped. Macdouall sent the head of MacQuillan to King Edward in Carlisle, accompanied by his prisoners. Thomas Bruce had been badly wounded in the fight, but this didn't prevent him being bound and led to Carlisle, nor did it help him escape his fate. Both he and his scholarly brother were hanged, as was Sir Reginald. Soon three more severed heads adorned the battlements of Carlisle's walls.

In Ayrshire Bruce's main assault fared little better. He sent a scout ahead to spy out the land, and to light a bonfire if the coast was clear. The man was apprehended, and mistaking a camp fire on the shore as his signal, Bruce led his thirty-three galleys towards the beach at Turnberry, next to what is now a world-famous golf course. Unfortunately for Bruce the local village contained an English garrison, as did nearby Turnberry Castle. Although he and his men managed to surprise and defeat the village garrison, Henry Percy, Baron of Alnwick and 300 men had little trouble holding the castle. Denied a beachhead, Bruce had to decide whether to withdraw to his ships or bypass the castle and take his chances in the hinterland. He chose the latter, and slipped away into the hills, accompanied by a small band of followers. Not only had this main attack achieved little, overall the operation had proved an unmitigated disaster. Since claiming the throne, Bruce had lost three of his four brothers – a personal cost that must have seemed prohibitively high to a king on the run.

While an increasingly frail King Edward waited for more news in Carlisle, his men searched the countryside. Robert, King of Scots was now little more than a fugitive, hiding in the rugged hinterland of his native Carrick, hoping that his luck might change. During this time in the Carrick hills Bruce learned of the imprisonment of his sisters, wife and daughter, and the death of his brother Neil. This was the moment when, as legend has it, a disconsolate Bruce sought refuge in a cave and had his encounter with a spider. As the story goes, he watched the spider try to spin its web, but it kept failing. Bruce vowed that if the spider succeeded, then so would he. On its seventh attempt the web held, and the fugitive king took heart. While the tale is fanciful legend, it remains an important part of the Bruce myth. In any event, after that, things began to improve.

Bruce strikes back

Slowly, men began straggling into the hills, seeking to join Bruce's band. Soon he had a sizeable force behind him – one large enough to begin hitting back. He moved south into northern Galloway, setting up camp in Glen Trool. In March 1307, when his scouts encountered a much larger English force led by Sir Robert Clifford, Bruce and his men kept the English cavalry at bay as they withdrew back into the hills. While John Barbour's epic poem *The Bruce*, written in 1375, makes much of this 'battle', in fact it was little more than a skirmish, and not a major first victory as is often claimed. Still, it was a victory, in that Bruce and his band managed to get the better of de Valence and his men, and then successfully break contact. For almost two months the increasingly frustrated English had no idea where they had gone.

In early May Bruce reappeared near Kilmarnock in Ayrshire, about fifteen miles from the coast at Irvine and eighteen miles south of Glasgow. He had been in the hills to the south of Ayr, gathering more recruits, and now he was heading to fresh recruiting grounds in the north of the county. Aymer de Valence marched from Ayr to intercept him, and found Bruce waiting beneath a rocky crag called Loudon Hill. There, on 10 May, Bruce scored his first genuine victory. Bruce had about 600 men under his command, and they formed a schiltron near the base of the crag. De Valence's cavalry were hemmed in by a boggy stream to the south, and by a series of ditches dug by Bruce's men to hamper the English horses. When they charged they were channelled by the ditches, and the bunched-up riders could make no impression on the ring of spearmen. Eventually de Valence sounded the recall, and withdrew back to Ayr.

While this was only a small defensive victory, it was a start. King Edward was furious that an English force had retreated from a band of Scots spearmen. Equally, the small victory at Loudon marked a turning of a corner. Bruce had shown that the English could be defeated, and that he was determined to fight for his crown. He was still little more than a fugitive, or at best a rebel leader, but he now had a reputation as someone who could win. All this might well have counted for nothing – the bulk of the English army in Scotland was concentrated in the south-west, and even after Loudon it seemed just a matter of time before Bruce and his men were caught, beaten and captured. What really transformed the situation was the long-expected death of King Edward.

In the summer of 1307 the English king was sixty-eight, and for a number of years his health had been in steady decline. Since the previous autumn he had based himself in Carlisle, or in the nearby Priory of Lanercost. Once dubbed 'Longshanks' on account of his height and long legs, now he was stooped and feeble, and towards the end he was carried around on a litter. Still, his mind was active enough, and while he had become too ill to campaign himself, he was able to organise the mustering of a fresh army, destined to be sent north to reinforce de Valence and to flood the south-west of Scotland with so many troops that Bruce's capture would be inevitable.

Edward died at Burgh-on-Sands on the afternoon of 7 July 1307. He had been visiting his army, which was then moving towards the Scottish border. While many historians have dubbed Edward I a just and able king, others – particularly Scottish ones – have pointed out his obsession with feudal control and the subjugation of the Scottish kingdom. In truth, much of the troubles facing Scotland – and England – at the time of his death were the result of his policies. News of the king's death was kept quiet for eleven days, until Prince Edward of Caernarfon arrived in Carlisle. There he was offered homage by the assembled magnates and the waiting troops. It has been claimed that on his deathbed Edward begged his leading nobles and clergy to keep an eye on his son, whom he knew lacked his father's resolve. Just how poor a leader the future king was would soon become apparent.

There was no question surrounding the succession – Prince Edward acceded to the throne the moment his father died. However, it would be seven months before his coronation; in the meantime his father's army was gathered on the Scottish border, and he was expected to lead them into battle. First he took his father's body to York, where it was handed over to the highly capable Archbishop William Greenfield. He would transport the late king's body to Westminster while his son returned to the army gathered north of Carlisle. At the end of July Edward marched over the border and advanced on Dumfries. He spent ten days in the town, receiving the renewed homage of the nobles of the south-west who weren't adherents of Bruce. Then he marched on to Cumnock, forty miles away, and a few miles from the site of Bruce's recent victory at Loudon Hill.

He reached the village in mid-August, and his army remained there for just over a week. It was as far as Edward would go. No contact had been made with Bruce's rebels – hardly surprising as the Scottish king lacked the men to take on the full might of Prince Edward's army.

By the start of September Edward was back in Carlisle, and from there he rode south to Westminster to oversee the final arrangements for his father's funeral, which was held in Westminster Abbey on 27 October. After that, Edward immersed himself in court life, and the company of his favourite Piers Gaveston. It would be three long years before he returned to Scotland. In effect, Edward had given Robert Bruce a breathing space, just when he needed it most. The Scottish king would make good use of this vital reprieve.

9

King Hobbe's War

In England, Bruce's hasty coronation was generally viewed with derision: he was dubbed 'King Hobbe', which roughly equates to 'King of the Fools'. As his successes mounted, though, many English nobles began to feel a sneaking admiration for the troublesome rebel, or had begun to doubt the moral validity of Edward's war. Most of them knew him socially – in 1302 Bruce's wedding to Elizabeth de Burgh had taken place near Chelmsford, just about as far from Scotland as you can get with dry feet. Many of these same English nobles had danced at his wedding. Robert Bruce was no upstart like William Wallace. He was one of them, or at least he had been until he claimed the Scottish crown. In the chronicle known as the *Vita Edwardi Secundi*, written two decades later, Bruce is described as 'Aeneas, fleeing alone from the captivity of Troy'. The author of the chronicle omitted to remind the reader that the legendary Aeneas had gone on to found Rome.

Naturally this growing respect for Bruce was tinged with alarm, particularly as he began to take the fight to the enemy. The death of King Edward I, and the failure of his son to make use of his military superiority, meant that Bruce was able to think beyond the everyday – the need to survive. As his numbers grew he became capable of launching more significant raids, and controlling larger areas, which in turn boosted his popularity and his following. For the first time since his defeat at Methven he was able to look at the strategic picture, and plan a campaign designed to bring a large portion of Scotland under his sway.

Blood feud

Bruce made his move as soon as Prince Edward returned to Carlisle. His plan was to fight a winter campaign as far from the major English garrisons as he could. This meant moving his small force from the south-west of Scotland across the line of the Forth and Clyde, to reach the safety of the Highlands. There he could march north to Moray, and take on the Scottish nobles in the north-east who were either Comyns or their supporters. He realised that the murder of the Red Comyn had left the family without a strong cohesive leader. It would be a good six to eight months before Edward – soon to be King Edward II – returned to Scotland. Bruce made the most of this precious respite.

First, though, Bruce had unfinished business with Dungal Macdouall. The string of castles he had won on the fringes of Galloway had all been recaptured, and he lacked the strength to assault them. Instead he bypassed them and spread out through Galloway, burning and plundering Macdouall's lands, causing as much havoc as he could. Macdouall avoided battle, and called on the English to help him. By the time troops could march up from Carlisle Bruce and his men were gone, having slipped back into the Carrick hills.

Only then, in late September, did Bruce march his men north as planned. Like King Edward, Aymer de Valence had quit Scotland for the winter, and so there was no powerful force barring Bruce's way. Evading the enemy garrisons at Bothwell and Dumbarton, he probably reached the River Clyde near its mouth, and using Macdonald galleys he crossed the Firth of Clyde.

His appearance in Kintyre forced the Macdougalls to agree to a winter truce, which meant he was safe from interference from them while he campaigned further north. The same galleys then whisked Bruce and his men through the Sound of Jura and the Firth of Lorn, and on into Loch Linnhe. This great sea loch marks the start of the Great Glen (or Glen More), the geological fault line that splits the Highlands in two and provides a link between Scotland's west coast and the Moray Firth. The impressive castle of Inverlochy dominated the head of the loch, barring Bruce's way up the Great Glen. Built by the Black Comyn three decades earlier to guard this southern gateway to the lands of the Lord of Badenoch, it was too strong to attack. But it fell that October thanks to the defection of part of its garrison. The Great Glen now lay open to Bruce.

The small army continued up the glen, through Loch Lochy and Loch Oich, to reach the southern tip of Loch Ness. This is where the small town of Fort Augustus stands today, but in 1307 the only habitation was a small hamlet called Kiliwhimin. Halfway up the western shore of Loch Ness stood Urquhart Castle, held by Gilbert of Glencarnie for the Comyns. Problems with the water supply made the castle indefensible, so it was abandoned, and after burning it Bruce pressed on towards Inverness. The castle there was also taken without much trouble, and it too was razed to the ground. That left Bruce on the edge of undefended Moray, a county he would use as his base. In two months he had traversed half of Scotland, and was poised to strike at the Comyn heartland.

He advanced as far as Nairn, burning its castle before turning back through Inverness to deal with William, Earl of Ross, whose lands lay beyond the town, across the Beauly Firth. Lacking the strength to fight for his estates, William preferred to use diplomacy to protect his earldom. Before Christmas he signed a truce with his new king, agreeing to a cessation of hostilities until the following Whitsun – 2 June 1308. This secured Bruce's rear, allowing him to move east into the north-eastern corner of Scotland. There was no hostile magnate in Moray, as the earldom had been vacant since 1147. Instead the region was administered by Reginald Cheyne, who was in England when

Bruce appeared. Thus there was nobody to oppose Bruce's occupation of the region, and his recruitment of local troops.

So began a confusing campaign of marches and counter-marches, as Bruce and his small force struck at Comyn targets throughout the north-east. This was no war of national liberation, this was a brutal civil war – a blood feud and a long-awaited reckoning between the Bruce and Comyn factions. First, Bruce laid siege to the royal castle at Elgin. Like his father at Urquhart, the younger Gilbert of Glencarnie had no stomach for battle, and agreed a truce. The king then marched on the region's other royal castle at Banff. As Bruce prepared to lay siege to the place he fell ill. Barbour claimed the sickness was brought on by Bruce spending so many nights lying outside in the cold; whatever its cause, for a time it looked as if the illness would claim him. It was at that moment that John Comyn, Earl of Buchan appeared, and Bruce's men withdrew, dragging their leader with them on a makeshift sled.

With his elder brother incapacitated, Edward Bruce took charge of the small army, withdrawing through the snow towards Strathbogie (now Huntly), twenty miles to the south-west. The Comyns caught up with him at Slioch, two miles to the east of the town. An inconclusive Christmas Day skirmish followed, with both sides shooting arrows at each other, but Buchan decided not to launch a costly assault on Bruce's camp. He went off to gather reinforcements, but when he returned a week later the Bruces had gone. The Comyns had missed their chance to defeat Robert Bruce when he was at his most vulnerable. For Prince Edward it would have been the perfect Christmas present.

We can't be sure, but Edward Bruce probably spent the next few weeks in the family's lands in the Garioch, to the west of Aberdeen. From there he launched more raids towards Elgin, and burned Cheyne's nearby castle at Duffus, as well as the Comyn stronghold at Balvenie in Speyside. Edward even harried the lands of the Earl of Ross to dissuade him from breaking his treaty. It was a busy few months, and all this time Robert's health was slowly improving. Then, in early May, the Earl of Buchan made his move. The earl learned that Bruce was encamped outside the Aberdeenshire village of Inverurie, and planned to launch a surprise attack. He had been reinforced by a contingent of English knights, and Barbour described his small army as being 'well-arrayed'.

At dawn on 23 May Comyn's lieutenant David of Brechin led a mounted assault to seize the little bridge over the River Urie, before Buchan himself attacked Inverurie from the north. When Bruce learned of this he buckled on his armour, claiming that the earl's attack would cure him more readily than any medicine. Bruce advanced towards Buchan, who deployed next to Barra Hill, to the north-east of Inverurie. As Bruce made his move the Comyn levies spied the king – a man they were told was unable to rise from his sickbed. Panic ensued, and Buchan's spearmen began to drift away. Left to their own devices, Comyn's men-at-arms followed suit and fled. It was claimed the rout continued as far as Fyvie, seven miles to the north. For his part the Earl of Buchan didn't stop running until he reached London, leaving Bruce the undisputed master of the north-east.

Carving out a kingdom

It was now almost midsummer 1308, and still no English army marched north from Berwick or Carlisle. This gave Bruce a chance to finish off his civil war. The Earl of Buchan's flight left his lands completely unprotected, and Bruce took full advantage. He moved through the Comyn heartland of Buchan, burning, looting and plundering as he went. Even John Barbour, an almost sycophantic admirer of Bruce, described the 'Harrying of Buchan' as an act which would be lamented for the next fifty years. By its end the region was nothing more than a smouldering landscape of death and destruction. Then Bruce moved on to Aberdeen, whose capture gave him a port, and with it a maritime link with the rest of Europe. This meant income through trade, and the chance to import weapons from the continent.

While Bruce was campaigning in the north-east, his able lieutenant James Douglas was equally active in the south-west. When Bruce marched north, Douglas had been left behind to safeguard Bruce's interests in Carrick and Galloway. He spent the winter skirmishing with the English garrisons in the area, and in early April he recaptured Douglas Castle in Lanarkshire after massacring the bulk of the garrison as they attended church. After that the taking of the castle was easy. While he knew he would be unable to hold the place, Douglas destroyed whatever stores he couldn't take away with him, and left the bodies of the dead in the castle kitchens, amid the detritus of food and drink tipped onto the stone floor. The castle overhead was then razed. This ghoulish mess was dubbed 'The Douglas Larder'.

By the time Robert Bruce had won his victory at Inverurie his brother Edward had travelled south to reinforce Douglas, and together they launched a fresh attack on Galloway. During June they repeated the king's assault on Buchan, harrying the Macdouall lands and defeating the defenders on the banks of the River Dee near Buittle. By the end of July Dungal Macdouall and his ally Ingram de Umfraville were driven from the region. This was only a temporary victory though – the English still held the castles that underpinned their control over the area. Macdouall would return as Edward II's governor in Dumfries, while de Umfraville continued as Edward's overall governor in the south-west. Bruce and his supporters could harry the area, but they couldn't conquer it.

Meanwhile, Bruce left Aberdeenshire and led his army back through the Highlands to deal with the Macdougalls. Alexander Macdougall was too ill to fight, and remained on his sickbed in his stronghold of Dunstaffnage, beside the modern town of Oban. Instead it was his son John of Lorne who took the field against Bruce; John had defeated Bruce once in Strath Fillan two years before, and had every hope of doing so again. He arrayed his men across the Pass of Brander, beneath the steep slopes of Ben Cruachan. The pass guarded the land route to Dunstaffnage and was an ideal place to ambush Bruce. Unfortunately for the Macdougalls Bruce realised that too. Instead of meekly walking into the ambush, he set up a trap of his own.

As Bruce approached the head of Loch Awe he detached a force of men led by James Douglas, fresh from his exploits in the south-west. This band climbed the slopes of Ben Cruachan, and as Bruce's main force approached the Macdougall killing ground Douglas launched his men down the mountain. The ambushers were scattered, and the route to Dunstaffnage was clear. The battle probably took place in mid-August, and Bruce went on to besiege and capture the Macdougall stronghold before the end of the summer. While Alexander Macdougall swore allegiance to Bruce, his son John fled south to England, and ended his days in English service. This little campaign meant that Bruce had now extended his control into Argyll, a significant boost to his growing portfolio of Scottish territory. For the first time since his coronation, Bruce could lay some claim to being a king with a kingdom.

The four pillars

Edward II needed to take immediate action to regain control of these lost portions of Scotland. Unfortunately he had more serious problems – namely a simmering dispute with his English nobles, the prospect of armed rebellion, a shortage of funds and an unhappy marriage. In the summer of 1308 he ordered an army to muster at Carlisle, but disbanded it before it ever set foot in Scotland due to his lack of money. It was left to his Scottish wardens to keep Bruce in check, and without men and resources they could do little to stem the tide of Scottish success. So, when King Philip IV of France offered to broker a truce between England and Scotland, Edward willingly agreed. It would buy him the time he needed to strengthen his hand, both in England and in Scotland. In retrospect it was one of his poorest decisions – and this from a king who seemed to specialise in doing the wrong thing.

The deal was that Bruce should give up all the gains he had made since late July 1308. He had no intention of doing so, and the truce which lasted most of 1309 allowed the Scottish king to strengthen his hold even further. In March 1309 Bruce held a parliament in St

Andrews. The main item on the agenda was the public declaration of support for the king by his leading clerics and nobles, based on 'the four pillars of inheritance, virtue, election and conquest'. While the nobles' written declaration hasn't survived, we still have that signed by the clergy, which was designed to remove any lingering doubt over the legitimacy of Bruce's right to the crown. It was a propaganda exercise worthy of Bishop Wishart, even though Glasgow's prelate was still languishing in a well-guarded English castle.

Equally important was an exchange of letters from Philip IV of France. They were addressed to Robert, king of Scots – an indication that Bruce's position was now recognised by the French court. All of this helped to give his regime a greater degree of legitimacy. It was an important diplomatic watershed, as it marked a change in attitude, both at home and abroad. By the spring of 1309, only the English, or the most die-hard supporters of the Balliols refused to accept that Robert Bruce was now the undisputed king of Scotland. His realm though was still fragmented. The English and their Scottish allies held all of the major castles south of the Forth and Clyde, as well as Perth, Dundee and Stirling. While the truce with England might have helped Robert improve his grip on his kingdom, it also prevented him from expanding its boundaries.

That summer, Edward declared that as Bruce had failed to return the castles he'd captured since the previous July, he had therefore broken the terms of the truce. Attempts to take the offensive came to nothing – troops to be mustered never appeared, nor did reinforcements begged from Ireland. The only action Edward's English garrison carried out was the relief of Rutherglen Castle near Glasgow, after Bruce besieged it in December 1309. The relief force was led by Edward's new commander in Scotland, the teenage Gilbert de Clare, Earl of Gloucester. King Edward had sacked Aymer de Valence, and his replacement, John of Brittany, Earl of Richmond had proved completely ineffective. Gloucester's appointment was designed to breathe new life into the war effort.

Instead, Edward's local commanders in Berwick and Carlisle

negotiated an extension of the truce until mid-January, and then until the middle of the following summer. This meant that it would be June 1310 before the fighting resumed. By that time Robert Bruce – King Robert – had made peace with many of his former enemies such as William, Earl of Ross and John, Earl of Lennox. Others drifted into the fold. Robert's nephew Thomas Randolph had been captured at Methven in 1306, and had duly offered his allegiance to Edward I. He was captured again in 1308, and eventually elected to support Robert. In 1312 he was rewarded with the vacant earldom of Moray, and became one of Bruce's staunchest supporters.

Another important adherent was James Stewart, the High Steward. Although he died in 1309, his declaration for Robert ensured the loyalty of his teenage son and successor Walter, and their kinsman John of Mentieth, the man who had captured William Wallace and who held Dumbarton Castle in the name of Edward. After 1310 the castle flew King Robert's standard. The fragmented nobility of Scotland was gradually beginning to heal itself and rally together under Robert's leadership. It was just in time. After several false starts, King Edward was finally preparing to launch his long-awaited expedition to reconquer Scotland.

By September a large army had gathered in Berwick, and on 16 September 1310 Edward led his men across the border at Wark. Unusually he chose to head inland, rather than hug the coast where his supply ships could keep pace with his advance. Instead he marched on Roxburgh, and then plodded through Selkirk Forest to reach Biggar on 29 September. Any hope that Robert would meet him in battle soon evaporated. The Scots avoided open combat – instead they indulged in what the *Lanercost Chronicle* describes as 'secret warfare'. This meant using Fabian tactics, withdrawing ahead of the English advance, and guerrilla tactics, employed to harass Edward's lines of supply. Edward then marched through Lanarkshire to the Clyde, and continued downstream through Glasgow to reach Renfrew. All the while Bruce kept his distance.

Edward though, was marching through a desert. The countryside had been denuded and burned by Bruce, who adopted a 'scorched earth' policy. There was widespread famine in the Clyde valley, and so in October Edward marched east again to Linlithgow, where supplies were slightly more plentiful. Still, James Douglas's raiding parties stripped the land of provisions, and so Edward continued to Berwick, which he reached at the start of November. The English king and his court would remain in the town for six months, before returning to Westminster the following summer, in 1311. There a political row with his nobles boiled over into out-and-out rebellion, and Edward's lieutenants in Scotland were effectively left to their own devices.

While Edward was still in Berwick Robert launched the first of a number of raids into the northern counties of England. These were to serve two main purposes, sapping the morale of the very English counties who supplied the bulk of Edward's troops for his Scottish campaigns and bringing much-needed revenue into Robert's coffers. His first raid into Northumberland lasted just over a fortnight, and yielded a small fortune through extortion, or rather protection money. Robert promised to spare Northumberland for another year, in return for a substantial cash payment. He would return when the deadline expired, to extort yet more money, and in the summer of 1312 was to lead a major foray into Cumberland, sacking the lands around Carlisle – including Lanercost Priory – before moving across the moors to Durham. There Robert extracted another large protection payment before heading back over the border.

This new policy of cross-border raiding was only one element of Robert's strategy. The other was to continue expanding the areas of Scotland under his control by capturing English-held castles. Lacking the siege train needed to take on the largest of these castles – at least by conventional means – he resorted to besieging such strongholds without assaulting them, hoping to starve the defenders out, or else making opportunistic attacks on these castles, seizing them by *coup de main*. The morale of many of these garrisons was low. After all, if King

Edward let the Scots raid as far south as Durham, what chance had he of supporting his own isolated strongholds in Scotland? Following Bruce's capture of the royal castles in the north, only Dundee and Perth remained in English hands north of the Forth.

So, between his raids into England, Robert laid siege to Dundee in January 1312, and after three months the castle's commander William Montfitchet surrendered to the Scots – a similar arrangement to the one Edward Bruce later negotiated with the garrison at Stirling. Dundee was strategically important as a port which served as a staging post for supplies bound for Perth, twenty miles further up the River Tay. With Dundee in Scottish hands Perth became vulnerable, although it would be early 1313 before Robert finally invested the town. Instead he was fully occupied leading his raids into northern England and in the reduction of other smaller Scottish strongholds. On 6 December the Scots launched their most audacious attack yet – an assault on the walls of Berwick. Rope ladders were used to scale the walls, but a barking dog alerted the garrison and the Scots were repulsed.

In January 1313 it was the turn of Perth. Robert feigned a withdrawal to lure the garrison into complacency, before returning to lead an assault on the town walls. The town fell when the Scots successfully captured a section of the walls. In the *Bruce*, Barbour gives some credit for the victory to the Earl of Atholl, a man who had only just switched sides. The former earl, John, had been captured at Methven in 1306 and then hanged in London. His son David remained in English custody, and fought for Edward before offering his allegiance to Robert in late 1312. He was duly appointed Constable of Scotland. The commander of the Perth garrison was none other than William Oliphant, the soldier who had held Stirling against Edward I eight years before and had been released by the English king on condition that he fight for him. While most of the garrison were killed Oliphant survived, although his subsequent fate is unknown.

Bruce then turned his attention to the south-west. Ayr and Loch Doon had fallen to the Scots during the last few months of 1311, but the large strongholds of Dumfries, Caerlaverock and Lochmaben remained in English hands. So too did the chain of smaller satellite castles Bruce had first captured back in 1306. Dumfries was held by Dungal Macdouall, and the royal castle was besieged at the same time as Perth. Bruce was present when it surrendered in early February, and agreed to spare his old enemy, despite his involvement in the death of the two younger Bruce brothers. Caerlaverock, Dalswinton, Lochmaben and Buittle fell soon after. By the spring of 1313, the south-west of Scotland was securely in Robert Bruce's hands.

In May Robert ventured into the Irish Sea, using Macdonald galleys to attack the Isle of Man, also held by Dungal Macdouall. Robert captured Castle Rushen in June – the second major stronghold taken from the Macdouall chief that year. While such successes didn't bring back his brothers Alexander and Thomas, it must have been particularly rewarding to have captured all of Macdouall's lands. The unfortunate Macdouall went into temporary exile in Ireland before eventually finding his way to King Edward's court. After razing the castle, Bruce returned to Scotland to supervise the consolidation of his new-won land.

The English still held several important castles south of the Forth and Clyde, from Stirling, Linlithgow and Bothwell in the centre and west to Edinburgh, Dunbar, Roxburgh, Jedburgh and Berwick in the east and south. By the autumn of 1313 Bruce had effectively won his civil war, but these castles split his kingdom, denying him safe access between the lands north of the Forth and Clyde, and those in the south-west. They also served as secure waypoints which Edward's army – when it came – could use when it marched into Scotland. From Stirling it could strike north into the Mearns and Aberdeenshire, or south towards Galloway and Carrick. Only by controlling these castles could Robert safeguard his grip on his kingdom – and the Scottish crown.

10

In the Shadow of Longshanks

When Edward I died, his last words concerned his son, Edward Caernarfon, Prince of Wales. In his royal pavilion pitched at Burgh-on-Sands he had motioned his senior advisors to his bedside, and bid them keep a watchful eye on his errant son. The prince himself, though, wasn't there – he was still in the south of England, smarting from a dressing down his father had given him five months before, and the exile of his best friend on his father's orders.

Despite his many faults, Edward I would be a hard act to follow. A forceful and charismatic man, his abilities as a soldier and statesman had transformed the fortunes of the Plantagenet dynasty.

Now he was dead, and as messengers sped south to inform his son, the leaders of the English army gathered around his pavilion must have wondered just what the future might hold.

For Prince Edward was a very different man from his father. The 22-year-old heir to the throne lacked his father's determination and obstinacy. He had displayed bad judgement in his choice of friends and advisors – the reason for his last row with his father – and he showed little interest in the kingly arts of war and diplomacy. The prince couldn't match his father when it came to martial ability, despite his minor successes in Scotland. The late king's senior nobles and commanders must nevertheless have hoped that once he bore the crown their young king would grow into his new role. Few of them could have imagined just how badly dashed these hopes were to be.

The favourite

The scene was a crowded Westminster Abbey, while throngs of Londoners waited outside for a glimpse of their new king. In fact, so dense were the crowds in the streets outside the abbey that many were killed and injured when a wall collapsed under the weight of the people clambering on top of it to get a better view. Inside the abbey the great magnates and their families had gathered to witness the coronation of their 23-year-old king. It was the morning of 23 February 1308, over seven months since the death of King Edward 'Longshanks' and almost four months since his state funeral, held in the same building. Today the newly finished marble tomb of the father would serve as a backdrop to the ceremony which would honour his son.

These occasions were wrapped in a web of ceremonial pomp and circumstance, of feudal etiquette and reign-affirming symbolism – pageantry that, six and a half centuries later, was still very much in evidence during the televised coronation of Queen Elizabeth II. In 1308, feudal hierarchy was of far greater importance to England's magnates than it was to be in the twentieth century. The protocol of the time-honoured ceremony was as much an affirmation of their own social standing as that of the king. Still, this was also a time of celebration – for most of the guests it was their first chance to see the king's new bride, the twelve-year-old princess who was the only surviving daughter of King Philip IV of France. Isabella had married Edward in Boulogne the month before, and now entered the abbey beside her new husband.

Edward was barefoot to symbolise Christian penitence, but the royal couple trod on a bed of cut flowers as they walked down the aisle towards the dais. Royal family members and leading magnates followed, carrying the symbols of kingship – sword, sceptre and coronation robe.

In their midst was a young Gascon knight, Piers Gaveston, who wore a jewel-encrusted robe of royal purple – a costume fit for a king – and in an overturning of convention and protocol he carried Edward's crown, the ceremonial object which formed the centrepiece of the ceremony. You can almost hear the murmurs of discontent in the abbey seven centuries later.

Piers Gaveston had first appeared at court as a teenager. A year older than Prince Edward, he was placed in the royal household by the king around 1300. A young French-born knight aspirant with impeccable manners, good conversation and a proven record of military abilities, Gaveston must have seemed a good companion for the sixteen-year-old royal heir. Instead Gaveston seemed to dominate the prince, who appeared to dote on the older boy. While it has been claimed the two youngsters had a physical relationship, there is no clear evidence of this – it is just as likely to have been a platonic bond, and that Edward treated Gaveston as the elder brother he never had.

By 1305 King Edward had become aware of Gaveston's unhealthy influence over the royal heir. When his treasurer told the king of the stream of presents and money frittered on the prince's favourite, the king banished Gaveston from his household. He was readmitted the following year, after a campaign of pleading from the prince, and was formally knighted with other worthy men-at-arms on the eve of Edward's invasion of Scotland in the wake of Robert Bruce's coronation. Shortly before, Prince Edward had tried to award Gaveston his own title of Count of Ponthieu. This was stupid – the prince's mother Queen Eleanor had come from Ponthieu, and the king saw the transfer of the title as a move that was grossly disrespectful to her memory. After a blazing row Prince Edward was dismissed from the royal presence. A few months later, when Gaveston evaded military service, King Edward gleefully exiled him from his kingdom.

Almost the first thing Prince Edward did after learning of his father's death was to recall Piers Gaveston to his side. To make up for the Ponthieu title, he awarded Gaveston the earldom of Cornwall.

The title had long been associated with the royal family and was usually held by someone of royal blood. Now a prestigious earldom belonged to the royal favourite – an elevation to the peerage that shocked the nobility of England. This though was only the start. Gaveston would become the king's regent – the man who ruled the kingdom when Edward was abroad. As Edward's chronicler put it, 'Yesterday's exile and outcast has been made governor and keeper of the land.' While many of England's leading magnates were horrified by the rapid social promotion of this *arriviste*, it was the coronation that demonstrated just how high Gaveston had flown. The central role he played at the ceremony was a public affirmation of his close bond with the king. Then, at the banquet which followed, Gaveston sat beside the king, and the two young men ignored both Edward's young queen, and the assembled nobles and clerics. The whole event was a calculated slap in the face for the establishment, whose status depended on maintaining the rigid pyramidal structure of feudal society. Edward would soon discover that his obsession with Gaveston had alienated the very nobles whose support he needed to rule his kingdom.

The public outburst of discontent came in April 1308, when Edward held his first parliament. Led by Henry, Earl of Lincoln, his leading nobles demanded that Gaveston be exiled and stripped of his earldom. The magnates' armed retainers surrounded Westminster to add weight to the demand. When called in to mediate, Robert Winchelsea, Archbishop of Canterbury sided with the nobles, and Edward was forced to back down. To compensate for the loss of his title the king's favourite was sent to Ireland as the King's Lieutenant, and was given gifts of royal land to replace the earldom that had been taken from him. For Edward, this exile was seen as a temporary arrangement – he seemed unable to grasp the widespread hatred felt for Gaveston by England's nobles and clerics. The lack of common sense shown by Edward during this scandal didn't bode well for the future.

A troublesome prince

Edward's first appearance in our story was as a five-year-old boy, thrust into the limelight in the summer of 1289 when someone proposed a dynastic union between his family and that of a Norwegian king. The marriage between young Edward of Caernarfon and the six-year-old Margaret, Maid of Norway had been the best solution anyone could find to the vexing problem of the Scottish succession. What might have been is mere speculation – the Norwegian princess died in September the following year, before she and her child groom ever met. It would be another seventeen years before Edward was betrothed again, by which time he had become the king of England, and the inheritor of his father's bittersweet legacy.

In an ideal world Edward would never have become king. At his birth he had six surviving siblings – five sisters and his ten-year-old brother Alphonso. This older brother died four months after Edward's birth, leaving him the sole surviving male Plantagenet heir. Then in 1290 his mother died, and his heartbroken father seemed to spurn his son. Still, the young prince had his uses. He was named Edward Caernarfon because he was born in the Welsh fortress town during a royal visit to inspect work on its new castle. In 1301 this regional association was strengthened when Edward was named Prince of Wales – a title designed to consolidate King Edward's grip on the Welsh Kingdom. Even before his tenth birthday, the last Plantagenet heir was being thrust onto the political stage.

Described as a strong, handsome and athletic youth, Edward should have been the apple of his father's eye. Instead he proved to be a sad disappointment. As a child Edward was schooled in the kingly arts of warfare and statecraft, but his father – a natural soldier and statesman – would have set the bar impossibly high. Meanwhile the youngster seemed more interested in thatching roofs – a skill seen as far beneath the dignity of a royal prince. Nevertheless, when he was twelve years old Edward was left in England as regent when his father went to war in Flanders. This was part of the problem – the king was an absentee father, and his son had no male role model to aspire to. As a teenager Prince Edward was increasingly called upon to perform the duties of a royal prince, but he continued to show little aptitude for such matters. Instead he seemed inordinately fond of extravagance and frivolity – two things his father had little time for.

Edward accompanied his father on his Scottish campaigns of 1300 and 1301, but while he proved an accomplished musician and huntsman, his military prowess was unremarkable. It was probably to instil some degree of martial professionalism in his son that King Edward selected Piers Gaveston as a suitable companion for the prince. During the 1301 campaign, Prince Edward was entrusted with an independent command. Accompanied by Gaveston he marched through the south-west of Scotland, but failed to bring the enemy to battle. As Gaveston's hold over the prince increased, Edward became increasingly estranged from his father, and when they met the two argued. The underlying cause for this acrimony was the prince's association with Gaveston.

The prince did better during the campaign following Robert Bruce's coronation, but he lacked his father's ruthless streak and his single-minded determination. For the younger Edward, campaigning was merely something to endure before returning to the comforts of the court. For his father it was the bread and butter of kingship. Their final row, over the prince's wish to name Gaveston Count of Ponthieu, ended in violence – according to the *Lanercost Chronicle* King Edward pulled his son around by the hair, and tore handfuls of it out before physically expelling him from his court. It was the last time father and son were to see each other before King Edward died.

Breaking point

When the king named Piers Gaveston his Lieutenant in Ireland he stripped the title from Richard, Earl of Ulster, a powerful nobleman whose support Edward would need if he were to defeat the Scottish king. In July, though, he reached an agreement with his nobles, curbing the powers of his royal officials in return for their agreement that Gaveston could return. Within the month Gaveston was back in court, and the earldom of Cornwall was returned to him. This *rapprochement* didn't last long. While Gaveston could be charming and well-mannered, he was also arrogant, and soon managed to offend many of those who had voted for his return. Anger mounted, and by the spring of 1310 there were fresh demands for Gaveston's exile.

A petition from the nobles claimed that Edward had been guided by evil counsellors, and added that he had lost Scotland through his negligence. This was heady stuff, yet there was more. It recommended that a council be appointed to guide the king. The nobles added that if Edward failed to heed them then they would not have him as their king. In other words, Edward had two choices – dismiss Gaveston or face an outright rebellion. He had no real option. On 10 March a council of twenty-one 'Ordainers' were elected from the leading nobles and clerics to 'help' Edward govern his kingdom. Effectively these men now ran the country.

It must have been almost a relief for Edward to travel north to campaign in Scotland that autumn. Back in Westminster the Ordainers continued to draw up reforms – another reason why the king and his royal favourite spent the winter in Berwick. When he returned to London in the early summer of 1311 he found the Ordainers were set to publish their Ordinances for reform, and at a specially convened parliament that August Edward was presented with their demands. Most concerned fiscal matters and taxation, the limitation of royal power, safeguards for the position of the nobility and an assertion of the right of the nobility to select the king's advisors. Then came the damning part dealing with Piers Gaveston. It catalogued his offences and demanded that he be sent into exile. Edward had no choice but to comply.

Piers Gaveston was exiled to Flanders in November 1311, but by January 1312 he was recalled, by order of the king. Edward had been pushed too far, and while he would accede to most of the nobles' demands, his association with Gaveston was non-negotiable. Gaveston landed in Yorkshire and was reunited with his wife and his king. The reaction of the nobility was predictable. The Ordainers rose in rebellion, and while Edward returned south Gaveston took refuge in Scarborough Castle. One of the rebels was the gifted Aymer de Valence, Earl of Pembroke, Edward's former governor in Scotland. He promptly laid siege to Scarborough, and by mid-May he had forced the castle's surrender. Gaveston was taken prisoner and transported south to Deddington in Oxfordshire, while the Ordainers negotiated with the king. Some of them, though, had a more permanent solution in mind.

On 9 June, de Valence left Deddington to visit his wife, while his prisoner remained securely lodged in the village rectory. When Guy de Beauchamp, Earl of Warwick learned of Pembroke's departure he rode to Deddington at the head of an armed posse and surrounded the building. Gaveston was taken prisoner and marched out of the village. He was taken the twenty-four miles to Warwick Castle, while de Beauchamp called for his fellow Ordainers. The Earl of Pembroke's protests for clemency were ignored. Instead a court was set up, chaired by the king's cousin Thomas, Earl of Lancaster, and Gaveston was found guilty. On 19 June 1312 he was dragged to a nearby hill and killed. Though dressed up as civic justice, this brutal act was little more than murder. King Edward was utterly distraught, and even more determined to oppose the men he saw as a pack of murderers.

Edward refused to have any further dealings with Lancaster, Warwick and the others. Pembroke – who felt used by Warwick – and another moderate, John de Warenne, Earl of Surrey both felt Lancaster had gone too far, and offered their loyalty to the king. The enmity between Edward and his cousin now threatened to tear England apart. This volatile situation simmered for almost eighteen months – only diplomatic intervention by the French king and the papacy helped avert a civil war. Eventually a peace of sorts was agreed, brokered by Gilbert de Clare, Earl of Gloucester. On 14 October 1313 in a parliament held in Westminster King Edward pardoned Lancaster,

Warwick, Hereford, Arundel and the other nobles associated with
Gaveston's murder. In return demands to implement the Ordinances
were shelved. The peace of the realm had been preserved, but deep
mistrust remained, particularly between Edward and his murderous
cousin.

Parliament also agreed to the funding of a new campaign in Scotland.
As Robert Bruce had feared, the plight of the garrisons in Scotland had
helped unite the English nobility behind the king's banner, now their
very public differences had been set aside. Edward was also granted a
substantial loan from the papacy, secured against his lands in Gascony.
This money would be used to raise and equip an army, designed to
crush the upstart Scottish king, and to recover King Edward's tarnished
reputation. A victory over the Scots would greatly strengthen Edward's
position in England, and the reconquest of Scotland would provide
him with the chance to reward the nobles who had stood by him during
his recent troubles. In short, it was hoped that the Scottish campaign
of 1314 would transform Edward's fortunes, and allow him to emerge
from the lingering shadow of Edward 'Longshanks'.

11

The March on Stirling

A glance at a modern map will show just how important Stirling Castle was. It lay on the dividing line between northern and southern Scotland – a line marked by the course of the River Forth in the east and the Clyde to the west. Stirling lay near the headwaters of the Forth, while to the west a band of high ground which encompassed the Fintry Hills, the Campsie Fells and the Kilpatrick Hills spanned the twenty-five miles between Stirling and Dumbarton, where another castle standing on top of a volcanic crag loomed over the River Clyde. Save for the small pass at Strathblane there was no way through these hills, and even that was unsuitable for the long string of wagons and carts that accompanied a medieval army on the march. If you wanted to move an army from one part of Scotland to the other, then you needed to hold Stirling.

The importance of Stirling is even more apparent when you look at a medieval map. In 1250 the monk Matthew Paris drew up a map of Britain, which survived the intervening centuries and is now housed in the British Library. At first glance it seems hopelessly inaccurate, as the north of Scotland curves away into the North Sea, so that Orkney ends up somewhere to the east of Aberdeen. However, on closer inspection the map shows much of what a medieval strategist wanted to know. The Scottish border is marked by Hadrian's Wall, and beyond it lie the rivers and towns that would dictate the way a campaign would be fought. Two large estuaries or firths almost cut Scotland in two. In between lies a town and a bridge. That town was Stirling. Looking at the map Edward II would have been familiar with, it is easy to see why Stirling Castle was described as the key to Scotland.

Four castles

However important Stirling Castle might be strategically to Robert, it was also difficult to capture, which meant that taking it would probably be a long drawn-out affair. There was also no guarantee King Edward would continue to sit idly by while Bruce laid siege to this vital stronghold. Besides, it was just one of several important Scottish castles that still remained in English hands. Their capture would be Bruce's next priority. The strongholds themselves were relatively unimportant to Bruce. What was important was to deny the castles to the enemy rather than simply occupying them. The castles could be recaptured all too easily by an invading English army. That meant it was probably safer to slight a castle – breach its walls to make it indefensible – than to garrison it.

What was important for Robert was control of the kingdom. Ownership of a castle meant control of any surrounding town and countryside. Even if the castle was destroyed, King Robert could still use the neighbouring town as an administrative centre for the region. Everyday life could return to normal, while the raising of tithes and taxes could provide the infrastructure he needed to raise troops. Still, this stratagem of capturing castles was a tricky one to accomplish. Lacking the siege equipment needed to batter such castles into submission, and given that many of them were well enough provisioned to withstand a long siege, Robert's most effective option remained the use of stealth.

Linlithgow fell by trickery in September 1313. According to Barbour a farmer named Matthew Binnock jammed his hay wagon in the castle gateway, and out of it sprang eight well-armed Scottish soldiers. After overpowering the gate guards they held the gateway until the rest of their company raced forward to join them. Together they captured the castle, slew the garrison and burned the castle keep. Roxburgh was captured in February 1314 thanks to a more elaborate ruse. James Douglas and his men dressed in black cloaks and crawled forward on their hands and knees, pretending to be grazing livestock. As it was Shrove Tuesday, most of the garrison were feasting, and the handful of remaining guards didn't realise the threat until too late. Douglas's men were able to reach the walls, swarm over them and seize the castle.

Three weeks later it was the turn of Edinburgh Castle. Having offered his allegiance to King Robert, Thomas Randolph had been rewarded with the earldom of Moray, and sufficient trust to lead a detachment of Bruce's men. He and his soldiers laid siege to the castle, but he lacked the strength to do anything more. The castle stood at the summit of a precipitous rocky crag, with only one means of approach along the mile-long ridge that ran from its gates down through the town. The Earl of Moray's men manned the siege works which spanned the ridge, and they were quartered in the town. It must have been a dispiriting task, as the castle was virtually impregnable and its cellars were well stocked. No doubt the siege would drag on until the English arrived to drive the Scots away. Then the earl's luck changed.

According to Barbour's account a local man called William Francis approached Randolph, and told him he was the son of the former castle's keeper. In his youth he had visited a young woman in the town. As the gates were locked and guarded at night he found a route down the north face of the crag instead. He returned the same way before morning, and none of the garrison ever learned of his nocturnal sorties. Francis offered to lead the earl and his men up the crag by the same route. So, while a diversionary assault was stage-managed in front of the main gates, the earl, the keeper's son and thirty men began the long and dangerous climb.

Unlike the young lover, these men were fully armed, and equipped with the tools they needed to scale the wall at the top – ropes, grappling hooks and ladders. The night of 14 March had been chosen because it was particularly dark, but that also made the climb fraught with danger. One slip and the sentries would be alerted. According to Barbour a sentry did indeed hear something, and threw a stone down the crag to see if it hit anyone. The assault party remained frozen, and eventually the sentry went on his way. At last they reached the top, just as the assault on the main gate was at its height. Moray and his men scrambled up the wall and reached the battlements. At that moment they were spotted and a sharp fight ensued, but the Scots had surprise and numbers on their side, and the defenders were driven back. Thanks to William Francis the Scots were inside the castle.

Moray then led the way to the main gate, and after cutting their way through the defenders the great wooden gates were swung open. The rest of the Scots raced through the gateway, and the surviving defenders were overwhelmed. Edinburgh Castle was now in Scottish hands. Like Linlithgow and Roxburgh before it, Edinburgh was slighted sufficiently to make it indefensible. Ruined or not, it still gave Robert control of Midlothian, allowing him to install his own magistrates and local officials and begin to integrate the county into his kingdom, much as he was already doing in West Lothian.

Dunbar and Berwick to the east, Jedburgh to the south and Bothwell to the west were still garrisoned by English troops, but for the moment the Scottish king felt he could ignore all of these. The most important English-held castle in Scotland was Stirling.

Edward Bruce laid siege to Stirling Castle at Easter 1314, but the defences were too strong for him to achieve anything, while it seemed there was no chance to take the castle by stealth or trickery. His only option was to starve the garrison into submission, and the castle cellars were once more well stocked. Bruce and his men faced a long and dispiriting siege which would only end when the garrison ran out of food. So Robert handed over control of the siege to his brother Edward and busied himself elsewhere, seeing to the raising of taxes and troops.

It was then that the castle's Scottish governor, Sir Philip Moubray, offered Edward Bruce what must have seemed like an olive branch. He proposed a deal. Sir Thomas Grey recorded its terms in the *Scalacronica*. Moubray would surrender the castle 'Unless he should be relieved – that is unless the English army came within three leagues of the said castle within eight days of St. John's Day in the summer next to come.' St John's Day was midsummer – 24 June. Three leagues equated to nine miles, so a relief force only had to march within sight of the castle, within eight days of midsummer, to honour the agreement.

It was an offer Edward accepted with alacrity. A similar arrangement had led to the capture of Dundee two years before. However, if he had thought it through, he might have been a little more reluctant to agree to Moubray's terms. Edward II was bound to try and relieve Stirling before the deadline expired, so Robert and his brother Edward would have to stop him. That of course meant fighting a battle – something Robert had avoided whenever he could. Everything he had achieved so far had come by adopting less direct tactics. Now he would have to fight in the open field – or lose the key to Scotland.

King Edward's invasion

For his part Edward II also realised he would have to fight. He had tried to raise armies to invade Scotland for the last few years, but the feud with the Ordainers and the Piers Gaveston row had prevented him from taking the field. Still, by the end of 1313 the king and his nobles had set aside their differences – at least in public – and money had been set aside to fund a new expedition into Scotland. For the first time since the autumn of 1307, King Edward looked set to follow in his father's footsteps.

In November Edward set the whole thing in motion. First he wrote to his garrison commanders in Scotland, telling them he would be marching north the following summer. One of those he contacted was Philip de Moubray, who when he struck his deal with Edward Bruce was therefore well aware that the king of England would be coming to his rescue. King Edward also issued demands to eight earls and eighty-seven lesser nobles, demanding they and their retinues muster in Berwick and be ready to march by 10 June. These nobles and their men would constitute the core of the army – the contingent of mounted men-at-arms. In March 1314 King Edward ordered the raising of the levies in Wales and England's northern counties. This was expected to yield a force of 25,000 infantry – 9000 of them coming from Wales. Of these, up to 3000 would be archers.

Given the size of any army Bruce might be able to raise, this force should have been more than adequate. However, Edward went even further. Another 4000 Irish troops were to be hired, and shipped over in time to join the expedition. In addition, invitations were issued in France and elsewhere on the continent, offering to pay any knights and their retainers who were willing to ride alongside the chivalric cream of England. Aymer de Valence, Earl of Pembroke was named as Edward's Lieutenant in Scotland, and by March he was fully occupied hiring the hundreds of wagons the expedition would need, and finding enough provisions to feed the largest army Edward had ever mustered. He also prepared a string of encampments on the English bank of the River Tweed, stretching from Berwick to Wark.

On 27 May King Edward was on his way north from York. He had already planned a Scottish invasion that summer, but Philip de Moubray's deadline added a degree of haste to the proceedings. Obviously thinking about the confrontation that lay ahead, two days later he demanded the supply of yet more infantry, as 'the Scots are striving to assemble great numbers of foot in strong and marshy places, extremely hard for cavalry to penetrate, between us and our castle of Stirling'. There was too little time for many of these fresh troops to reach Berwick before 10 June, so Edward delayed his departure for a week and spent his time awarding Scottish lands to the magnates who answered his summons. First, though, these English nobles had to defeat the Scots.

The expedition finally crossed the border on 17 June, fording the River Tweed between Wark and Norham. Rather than follow the coast, Edward planned to march up the north bank of the Tweed and then turn north into Lauderdale. Behind the men-at-arms marched the infantry, and behind them came a long line of carts and wagons, stocked with supplies, weapons and siege equipment. It was claimed this wagon train stretched for seven leagues – officially twenty-one miles, but the phrase was often used to mean 'a very long way'. The army was the largest force raised in England for sixteen years – since Edward I's Falkirk campaign of 1298.

While King Edward must have taken pleasure in marching at the head of this great army, his enjoyment was soured a little by the knowledge that his invasion force could have been even larger.

Although the Earl of Pembroke was joined by Humphrey, Earl of Hereford and Gilbert, Earl of Gloucester, as well as Hugh Despenser and Roger Clifford, conspicuous by their absence were the realm's other senior magnates. The earls of Lancaster and Warwick who had masterminded the execution of Piers Gaveston refused to answer their king's summons. Their followers, the earls of Arundel and Surrey, also failed to appear in Berwick. Instead they offered feeble legal excuses for their absence. They sent the minimum number of retainers they could, to avoid claims that they'd defied the king. The scars of the Gaveston affair evidently still ran deep; these magnates had no desire to strengthen the hand of a king they regarded as their enemy.

Still, the mounted nobles, knights and their retainers who rode in the van of Edward's army were numerous enough to deal with the Scots. According to the chronicler of the *Vita Edwardi Secundi* this great army 'was quite sufficient to penetrate the whole of Scotland'. On 18 June the army followed the old Roman road as it climbed into the Lammermuir Hills, and that evening its vanguard camped on Soutra Hill, with the Lothians spread out below them. The next morning they marched the fifteen miles to Edinburgh, the vanguard reaching the town before nightfall. There the army waited two days for the wagon train to catch them up, and to recover from their exertions.

The men must have been grumbling. According to a cleric who chronicled the march, 'Brief were the halts for sleep, briefer still for food – hence horses, horsemen and infantry were worn out with toil and hunger.' This was something of an exaggeration. The men marched an average of fifteen miles a day – a comfortable enough pace for a medieval army. Besides, as they descended from the Lammermuirs the troops could see the sails of Edward's supply ships as they worked their way into the Firth of Forth, and continued on to Leith, the small port that served Edinburgh. When they reached the town, they would not only get a chance to rest, but they would be well fed too.

King Robert had been kept informed of Edward's progress, and was well aware that the English would appear before Stirling within a few days. He was as ready for them as he would ever be. The Scottish army had been gathered outside Stirling for months, and while some of the men would have drifted off to visit their families, the majority knew about the deadline, and of Edward's approach. Robert had used the time wisely. As well as mustering a fair-sized army he set about making sure the men knew how to use their weapons. Companies were drilled in the use of spears, and in the forming of schiltrons. These Scottish soldiers weren't full-time soldiers – most were modest farmers and townspeople – but they were leavened with some of Bruce's more experienced veterans, and they had been well trained in the use of their weapons. Only time would tell if this preparation was enough.

It was thirty-five miles from Edinburgh to Stirling. On 22 June the English army broke camp and resumed their march. Given their earlier pace they should have halted at Linlithgow, sixteen miles west of Edinburgh, but the deadline was fast approaching, and so King Edward ordered the men continue for another eight miles, until they reached Falkirk. They were now just ten miles from Stirling, but the infantry would have been tired after their forced march. It was a weary army that settled down in their encampment that night. With the enemy so close it was almost certain that battle would be joined the following day, if the Scots didn't slink back into the hills. For many it would have been a restless night.

PART 2

BATTLE FOR A NATION

12

Raising an Army

O ver the years, historians have disagreed about almost everything to do with Bannockburn. The list of disputed matters includes where the battle was fought, what the terrain looked like, what the participants were armed with, how they fought, what happened and when it happened. Strangely, one of the few areas where there seems to be general agreement is over how many people took part, and what kinds of troops were involved.

A question of numbers

This wasn't always the case. John Barbour's epic poem *Bruce* describes the English host as follows:

> The King, as counselled by his men, arrayed his folk in battles
> ten,
> Ten thousand were in every band, who thought that they would
> firmly stand,
> And in the struggle stoutly fight, undaunted by the foemen's
> might.

Clearly this total of 100,000 is nonsense – a poetic artifice designed to portray a mighty army. By contrast King Robert's army is given a much smaller total:

> When all were mustered round the king, I trow that those who
>   weapons bore,
> Were thirty thousand men and more, not counting peasants in
>   whose care,
> The carts with food and armour were.

We can pretty quickly dismiss the totals. At a time when medieval battles rarely involved more than 20,000 men a side, Barbour's numbers are equivalent to a battle the size of Blenheim or Waterloo. Even the Battle of Towton, fought in 1461 – and dubbed the largest battle fought on British soil – involved no more than around 50,000 men. What is more interesting is Barbour's ratio of the two forces, with the English outnumbering the Scots by a little more than three to one. The *Vita Edwardi Secundi* beefs up the Scottish numbers by a quarter, to 40,000 men.

The figures given by the late fourteenth-century cleric and poet seem to have been taken at face value until a century ago, when J.E. Morris published a study of the battle to commemorate its 600th anniversary. He scaled the numbers down to something more logical: 17,500 English, including 2500 cavalry, with the Scots mustering around a third of that – 6500 or thereabouts, including 500 cavalry. One suspects that he arrived at his totals by simply quartering the numbers given by Barbour. Surprisingly this seemed to work – subsequent research into the raising of both armies tends to agree with his figures. Since then the general numbers and ratios have fluctuated slightly, but most historians favour a similar figure.

Of course there are exceptions to the rule. One recent study of the battle argues that the Scottish army was much larger, as that would be a better reflection of the estimated Scottish population of the time. This ignores the fact that parts of Scotland were still under English

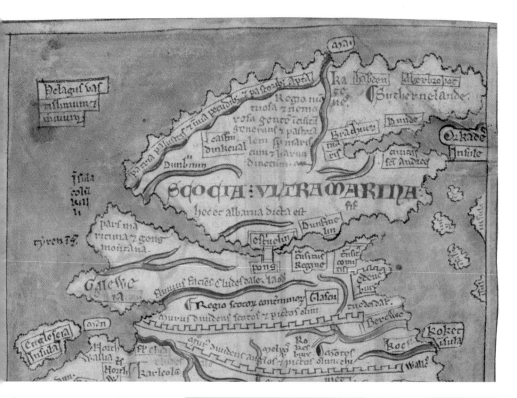

Fourteenth century Scotland, a detail from a map drawn by the English cleric Matthew Paris. © *British Library Board/ Robana/TopFoto*

Sir James Douglas, pictured leading the spearmen of a Scottish shiltron at Bannockburn. © *Andrew Hillhouse*

The Battle of Bannockburn,
with Stirling acting as a backdrop.
a fifteenth century illustration
from John Fordun's *Scotichronicon*.

Courtesy of the Master and Fellows of
Corpus Christi College, Cambridge. CCC
MS 171, f. 265r

A modern
depiction of
Bannockburn,
showing the
climax of the
battle on
24 June 1314.
© *Andrew Hillhouse*

King John of
Scotland,
paying homage
to King
Edward I in
Newcastle,
December 1292.
© *British Library
Board, Royal MS
20. C. VII, f 28*

The most likely site of the ford over the Bannockburn, across which Sir Henry de Bohun charged on 23 June 1314. © *Dave Patterson/Bill Gilchrist*

A panorama of the carse, looking eastwards from the site of the English camp towards the Dryfield. © *Dave Patterson/Bill Gilchrist*

The Carse of Balquhiderock close to the Pelstream burn, looking towards the south.
© Dave Patterson/Bill Gilchrist

above: A late seventeenth century depiction of Stirling Castle and the town, viewed from the south. Painting by Johannes Vorsterman.

© Stirling: in the Time of the Stuarts, Vorsterman, Johannes (1643-99)/Smith Art Gallery and Museum, Stirling, Scotland/The Bridgeman Art Library

left: This decorated sedilia arch in Westminster Abbey c.1300 is thought to depict King Edward I.

© Angelo Hornak/Alamy

above: The Great Seal of King Robert I, King of Scots, an important emblem of royal authority.

© *Classic Image/Alamy*

right: Aymer de Valence, Earl of Pembroke (c.1275-1324), from his tomb n Westminster Abbey.

© *Michael Jenner/Alamy*

The statue of King Robert I at Stirling Castle, with the Wallace Monument in the background.
© UIG via Getty Images

control, that the army seems to have been a predominantly lowland force, and that only men of a certain worth in terms of money or land were recruited. This was no 'peasant army'. Another historian argued for even smaller totals for both armies, but this seems unlikely given the ground the battle was fought over and the way it was fought.

The most convincing arguments are those based on what we know of Plantagenet and Scottish armies during this period. This evidence tends to agree with the general notion that the armies consisted of something akin to the numbers given by Morris a century ago. Until someone produces conclusive evidence to the contrary, we can assume that Edward's and Robert's armies consisted of roughly 17,500 and 6500 men respectively. That is still about half as many men again as Scotland's other well-known battle – Culloden, fought in 1746.

As for the way these armies were organised, once again we should start with Barbour's claim that the English divided their army into ten 'battles', while the Scots had four such formations. A battle was a medieval term given to a division of the army, and almost always there were three of these – the vanguard, the main body and the rearguard. Barbour has the Scottish army 'arrayed in battles four their armed host'. He lists their commanders as Thomas Randolph, Earl of Moray, Sir Edward Bruce, Walter Stewart, assisted by Sir James Douglas, and finally King Robert himself.

This equates to the contemporary three-battle arrangement, with a very unusual extra battle added to the array. Many modern historians claim this is how the Scottish spearmen were organised, but other sources tell a very different story. They give the Scots only three battles, commanded by King Robert, his brother Edward, and the Earl of Moray. The fourth battle is almost certainly literary invention, designed to pander to the subsequent rise of Douglas's influence and the social rise of the Stewarts. So we can discount Barbour's claim, and give the Scots the standard organisation of the period in three divisions of battles – a vanguard, a main body and a rearguard.

In fact two more divisions were mentioned by Barbour as his poem unfolded. One was the Scottish cavalry, which formed its own division, and the last was the 'small folk' – the 'peasants in whose care, the carts with food and armour were'. These camp followers or non-combatants would have numbered anything up to 3000 people – men, women and children. While it would be wrong to include them in the military line-up, they did have a role to play in the final stages of the battle, if we believe Barbour's version of the battle. He is the only source that mentions the intervention of this rag-tag band – and for that matter the Scottish cavalry. Although we can be reasonably sure about the general composition of the Scottish army, Edward's host poses more of a problem. Barbour's ten battles or divisions make little sense, unless it referred to some other type of organisation.

If we assume for a moment that Edward's forces conformed to the usual organisation of a medieval army, then like the Scots they would have been grouped into three or four battles. Like the Scottish army the English force consisted of three basic troop types: mounted men-at-arms, spearmen and archers. In Bruce's army the spearmen predominated – there were probably no more than 500 cavalry and a similar number of archers in the whole force. Barbour has already told us the cavalry formed their own division, so we have to assume the archers were attached to one or more of the infantry battles when the situation required.

In the English army the number of each troop type was much larger. It might therefore make more sense if each of Barbour's ten divisions was actually a component of a larger battle – one composing a selection of cavalry, spearmen and men-at-arms. Three battles would account for most of these units, while a final large formation of cavalry might be directly attached to the king, as a reserve or bodyguard. We will never know for sure, but this ties in with the way other medieval armies were organised. In battle the smaller divisions would have been divided into their component troop types for the duration of the engagement. This gave the English a degree of flexibility – the ability to call up composite bodies of spearmen, cavalry and archers as the situation demanded, or to deploy units of one troop type or another to conform to a particular plan of battle.

The problem was of course that the very size of the English army made it less manoeuvrable than its Scottish counterpart. This would become all too evident once battle was joined. At Bannockburn this problem was amplified by the cramped space the English army was deployed in, and its leaders' inability to move the various troop types around in order to deal with the Scottish threat. That, and the seeming lack of initiative shown by the English king and his commanders, was the real reason why Bannockburn turned out to be such a fiasco. Put more simply, it was the Scots who enjoyed an edge in the way their troops were controlled on the battlefield, and in the tactical skill of their commanders.

Men-at-arms

Despite the claims of some, the building blocks of both armies – the mounted men-at-arms, the spearmen and the archers – were essentially the same on either side. The men looked similar, wherever they came from. What differences there were – and such differences became apparent during the battle – were due to the way the troops operated, and what was expected of them. Of course there may have been other troops present at Bannockburn – a smattering of crossbowmen, engineers and non-combatants – but the sources remain silent about them, and they didn't appear in sufficient quantities to make a difference. By understanding what these troops were capable of we get a better understanding of how they fought during the battle.

The most important troop type in an early fourteenth-century army was the mounted man-at-arms. These weren't necessarily knights, although some were. The term man-at-arms covered anyone who was mounted on a war horse and equipped with a full set of arms and armour. The arms usually meant a long spear or lance, a sword and sometimes an axe. Armour consisted of a mail shirt or surcoat, a mail hood – a bit like a balaclava, only made from metal rings – leather or mail gloves, and a helm or helmet. The helm in vogue at the time was a bascinet – an open-faced and often pointed helmet, with an attached faceguard or 'aventail'. Some of the wealthier knights or men-at-arms would have plate metal pieces, protecting vital places like elbows and shoulders. In almost all cases this 'kit' was supplied by the man-at-arms himself.

Most men-at-arms had two or more horses – a palfrey used to ride around on, and at least one larger and more powerful charger – a destrier – which was saved for use during battle. Again these were usually paid for by the owner, and if a horse was killed in action a claim for reimbursement could usually be lodged with the royal exchequer. While men-at-arms could be mounted throughout a battle, they could be called upon to fight on foot, but this was extremely rare, at least in England. If they fought dismounted they would need a groom nearby to act as a horse holder. It appears that apart from those serving with Keith, most of the Scottish men-at-arms fought on foot during the battle, serving alongside the spearmen, where they probably functioned as junior leaders. Most of the men-at-arms in the English and Scottish armies would be members of the nobility – anyone from a great earl to a minor baron – or more likely men from the nobles' own retinue.

'Knight' is often used as a blanket term to cover all mounted men-at-arms. In fact knights were simply part of the feudal hierarchy. Before a campaign the king would demand a quota of knights and men-at-arms from each of his nobles, and normally the obligation was for these men to serve the king for a set period – usually forty days. Beyond that, or if they performed garrison duties, then the men – or rather their feudal lord – would be paid for their service. In Scotland most held their property thanks to the king and owed their allegiance to him, rather than any intermediary great lord. A knight was merely a holder of a certain rank, and his social standing was usually marked by the wearing of a surcoat and horse barding, bearing the knight's coat of arms. Much has been made of the difference between English and Scottish men-at-arms. It has long been claimed that the Scots were inferior in both equipment and horseflesh. All the evidence, though, suggests that there was no difference between them. After all, many had served alongside each other before, even if at Bannockburn they found themselves on opposite sides. The evidence for this stems largely from one throwaway word in Barbour's *Bruce*, which calls the Scottish cavalry 'licht'. While this could mean 'light' it could also mean 'agile'. The fact they were also described as being fully armed is a clue that the word referred to the manoeuvrability of their small all-mounted formation, rather than the way these Scottish horsemen were equipped. Fully armed meant they were fully armoured. In both armies, then, these men were the most powerful troops on the battlefield.

Spearmen

At Bannockburn, most of the men in both armies fought on foot, and were primarily armed with a spear. The Scots had about 5500 spearmen on the field, while the English total must have been around 12–13,000. Again, much has been made of the deep formation of Scottish spearmen known as the schiltron. In fact, in Barbour's *Bruce* the term is also used on one occasion to refer to the English army, deployed in a vast schiltron. This suggests he was using the word to refer to a general disposition of forces, not to some special Scottish formation. Spearmen fought shoulder to shoulder, several ranks deep, and this was as true for the English spearmen as it was for the Scots. The only difference was probably one of training – the English spearmen had been freshly raised from the northern counties of England and Wales, while the Scots had spent several weeks encamped near the battlefield, honing their skills for the coming fight.

If used correctly – as the Scottish spearmen were at Bannockburn – these troops could win a battle. However, in the 'rock, scissors and paper' game of medieval warfare spearmen were the rock – the stolid and largely defensive building block of the battlefield, whose job was primarily to contain the enemy, and to hold ground. This isn't to say spearmen couldn't be used offensively – they often were – but they were best suited to less aggressive tactics. That is one of the reasons why King Robert's dawn attack on the second day at Bannockburn came as such a surprise to the English. Launching an all-out attack with an army of spearmen was a novel tactic – and one that worked.

Another misconception about Bannockburn is that the Scottish spearmen were all of hearty peasant stock. Some historians have almost claimed that the battle took on aspects of a class war, with lowly serfs defeating the aristocratic elite of England. In fact the spearmen of both England and Scotland were not only armed and equipped the same way – they both came from the same social background. Military service was based on landholding and wealth. The spearmen called upon to serve in the two rival armies were men with a stake in society – skilled tradesmen, craftsmen and farmers. They were required to supply their own arms and armour – something a penniless serf couldn't do. Their equipment usually consisted of a helmet, a padded jerkin, stout gloves, a spear and a knife or axe. More fortunate soldiers or veterans might even have brought along a mail shirt, or mail-reinforced gauntlets.

Much has also been made of the spears carried by the spearmen in the two armies. There is a long-held belief that the Scots favoured longer spears than their English counterparts, but while there is some evidence for this, none of it can be tied directly to Bannockburn. A typical spear of the period had an iron point about eight inches long, which broadened out to its widest about two-thirds of the way towards its base. The head ended in a socket which was fitted onto a long wooden haft about two inches thick. The length of the haft has caused problems for historians largely because, while the metal heads have survived the centuries, the wood has not. Some inventories mention spears around ten or twelve feet long, but others could be longer – as much as fourteen feet overall. If the Scots had longer spears than their English counterparts, then they wouldn't have been longer than that.

Incidentally, in the *Bruce* Barbour mentions that a Highland contingent formed part of the king's 'battle' – troops belonging to Angus Og, and men from Argyll and Kintyre. Everyone else in the Scottish army – according to Barbour – hailed from the lowlands, a term that applied as much to Moray and Aberdeenshire as it did to Midlothian or Ayrshire. There is no indication that Highlanders were armed and equipped any differently from their lowland comrades. They certainly didn't look like the woad-painted kilted savages of *Braveheart*. In fact, evidence from the tomb effigies of medieval Highland leaders suggest they kept abreast of the latest military fashions, and dressed and equipped themselves accordingly.

Archers

One of the great 'what-if' questions asked of Bannockburn is what might have happened if King Edward had made better use of his archers. After all, archers had proved highly effective at Falkirk in 1298, and would do so again against the Scots at the battles of Dupplin Moor (1332) and Halidon Hill (1333). A mere thirteen years after that was the Battle of Crécy, when the English longbow reigned supreme. The problem here is that in the early fourteenth century archers on the battlefield were something of a novelty. While they had certainly been used before, they were seen as skirmish troops, good for little apart from harassing the enemy. In previous centuries crossbows had been the preferred missile weapon, and bows were usually seen as weapons more suited for hunting than fighting. However, the thirteenth century saw a greater use of a military bow – the 'great bow' – and these are the weapons that would have been used at Bannockburn.

It was only during the reign of Edward III that the English were fully to embrace archery, and it was this era that saw the development of the longbow. That though was less of a weapon than a matter of training – a lethal combination of weapon and skilled soldier. While in the right hands the English longbow became a fearsome weapon, and would remain in use for more than two centuries, longbowmen

weren't around during 1314. Both sides were equipped with great bows
– weapons which were effective – but without extensive training these
lacked the greater power and penetration of the longbow. At Falkirk,
archers had been used to shoot at the static Scottish schiltrons, while
cavalry waited in the wings. These archers weren't trained in firing
massed volleys of arrows, the kind that darkened the sky as they flew.
This was lower-key archery, although it could still prove effective as
long as the archers had the space to deploy, and were protected from
the enemy.

These were the three main building blocks used by both armies.
Much has been written on the way the troops were organised into units.
A lot of it is supposition – we simply don't know how the troops were
organised at Bannockburn, at least below the level of the 'battle' or
division. But we do know rank structures existed – there is mention in
the records of corporals and also *vintenars*, a name based on the French
word for twenty – and these would equate to modern-day squad and
platoon leaders. Further up the chain the company (run by *Centenars*)
existed, as did the rough equivalent of the battalion (commanded by
Millenars). While the exact structure remains unclear, and would have
been influenced by feudal and social obligations, the point remains –
the troops who fought at Bannockburn were organised in a way that
made the most of their fighting potential, using a military hierarchy
which a soldier might be able to understand today.

13

Field of Battle

Over the past century the battlefield of Bannockburn has moved around the area like a cat in search of a sun-warmed place to sleep. If Edinburgh-born crime writer Sir Arthur Conan Doyle had ever written a Sherlock Holmes story about it he might have called it 'The Case of the Moving Battlefield'. Much of this is due to the way historians have interpreted the various sources. The battlefield moves slightly with every fresh interpretation of what actually happened over those two blood-soaked days. Another problem is the way the landscape has changed over the intervening centuries. While some have argued that the exact location of the battlefield may never be known, the development of battlefield and landscape archaeology, new scientific techniques and a willingness to preserve what remains on the ground have all encouraged a new look at an old problem.

The terrain

The landscape in the area of Bannockburn may have changed considerably over the past 700 years, but it can still tell us a lot about how the battle was fought, and how the lie of the land affected the outcome. The battle was named after the Bannockburn, a stream that runs to the south and south-east of Stirling Castle. It actually loops in a curve, working its way around the high ground of Gillies Hill just over two miles south of the castle before curving back like a drawn bow to enter the low-lying Carse of Balquhiderock. From there the burn flows into the River Forth. A carse is an area of very low-lying alluvial land bordering a river, and in the case of the Balquhiderock and the area known as The Polles to the east this carseland stretches for almost two miles, from the river to the low ridge known as the Dryfield, which lies immediately to the north of the Bannockburn.

For much of its length below Gillies Hill and the Dryfield the burn flows between steep-sided tree-lined banks, creating a natural ravine that prevented formed bodies of troops from crossing it unless they used a ford. The stream emerges from this ravine as it enters the carse. The carse itself is often covered in little standing pools of water, particularly in winter, and it becomes prohibitively boggy close to the river. Another small burn – the Pelstream – runs eastwards across the top of the carse, before the Bannockburn loops northwards to join it just over a mile from the River Forth. Effectively these two burns mark the boundaries of the triangular-shaped Carse of Balquhiderock – the third side of the triangle being the eastern spur of Gillies Hill known as the Dryfield. Further to the east of the triangle the ground closer to the Forth was too boggy to permit the movement of troops. However the carse itself was dry enough – otherwise the English wouldn't have pitched their camp there.

An old Roman road runs from Falkirk north to Stirling, and in 1314 this was the main medieval route into Stirling from the south. It crossed the Bannockburn at a place now known as Milton Ford, and climbed the slopes of the Dryfield between the ridge and Gillies Hill. To the left of the road but north of the burn lay an area of bog, but above it the higher ground was firm and wooded. The spot where it disappeared into the trees – near today's battlefield visitor centre – was known as 'The Entry'.

Much of the western side of the Dryfield was covered in trees in 1314, but these probably petered out on its eastern slope facing the carse. At the time of the battle fields of wheat and barley were planted at the base of the slope. The medieval road emerged from the trees just in front of a group of buildings clustered around the small church of St Ninian's. This was where the road also crossed the Pelstream, and from there it was just over a mile into the town of Stirling, clustered at the foot of the castle crag. To the right of the road beyond the stream lay Livilands Bog, which was impassable to formed troops.

The area to the west of the road was known as the New Park, a hunting preserve of open parkland and trees. It occupied the high ground as far as the slopes of Gillies Hill, a mile west of the church. Immediately to the south of the ford the ground was reasonably flat and open, but three miles further south the road passed the Torwood, another wooded area in a largely open rural landscape. The English army approaching Stirling from Falkirk would thus pass through the Torwood, and then find itself free of obstacles until it reached the Bannockburn. There the obvious crossing place was at the ford, as the ravine extended for the best part of a mile in either direction. The only other crossing point was where the burn flowed through the carseland. Another small ford existed just beyond the eastern end of the ravine, where a small road known locally as 'The Way' led north along the edge of the Dryfield to St Ninian's Church.

This position on the Dryfield was a strong one. The ravine to its south made it difficult to assault across the Bannockburn, and so an attacker would be funnelled into the ground beyond the ford, or else would debouch onto the carse, which in winter was less than ideal ground for cavalry. To the north of the burn, hidden in the trees of the New Park, the Scottish army stood waiting for the English. The message was clear – if the English intended to reach Stirling, they would have a fight on their hands, and the Scots were ready for them.

Locating the battlefield

Tradition has it that the Battle of Bannockburn was fought near the

Bore Stone, a near-circular rock on the top of Brock's Brae, about half a mile north of the ford over the Bannockburn. According to mid-nineteenth-century antiquarians, King Robert planted his standard next to this small circular boulder. This is where the new Battle of Bannockburn Visitor Centre stands today. Close beside it towers the magnificent equestrian statue of a grim-faced King Robert created by Charles d'Orville Pilkington Jackson, and between the two stands a rather less aesthetically pleasing saltire-bedecked Rotunda. This is the heart of today's Bannockburn 'visitor experience', and an essential place for battlefield tourists to begin their search for the site. Unfortunately, for more than a century historians have argued that the battle was actually fought some way to the north-east. Just where, though, is still a fiercely contested question.

As late as 1924, the deeply respected military historian Sir Charles Oman wrote an account of Bannockburn in his great tome *Art of War in the Middle Ages* that didn't really bear scrutiny. Oman claimed that King Robert's army deployed on the north bank of the Bannockburn, somewhere near the Bore Stone. In his interpretation the ground between the burn and the Bore Stone was covered by the marshy ground of Milton Bog – a natural barrier to cavalry. The single way through it was by the medieval road. To Bruce's left the only other crossing place was well to the west of the main ford, where a track passed between the carse and the Dryfield, leading towards St Ninian's. This is where – according to Oman – Bruce dug a field of pits, which acted a bit like a minefield, a means of stopping cavalry from crossing the burn and assaulting Bruce's army in the flank. It was a very neat and military explanation.

Oman's version fitted the traditional location of the battlefield. Unfortunately it didn't sit so well with the various sources – the contemporary or near-contemporary accounts of what actually happened. Still, this version was extremely influential – after all, he was one of the most renowned military experts of his day. Its influence was still felt in the 1960s, when the National Trust for

Scotland built its old visitor centre next to the Bore Stone. Strangely, two other accounts of the battle appeared a decade before Oman, but were largely ignored. Written by Mackay Mackenzie and the Reverend Thomas Miller, they argued that the battle actually took place somewhere else – Mackenzie arguing the case for the Carse, and Miller advocating the Dryfield. Actually, Mackenzie's carse was one beyond the Carse of Balquhiderock, but his argument was plain – the battle was fought on carseland, not on the slopes of the Dryfield. A low-key argument rumbled on into the 1930s, but nobody took the debate too seriously. In the minds of the general public, Oman's version still reigned supreme.

In 1959 Sir Philip Christison – a retired general and holder of the Military Cross – published a scholarly paper which reinforced the location of the battle in the Carse. Six years later Geoffrey Barrow published his definitive biography of Robert Bruce, and moved the battlefield back to the Dryfield again, this time centred on the rise where Bannockburn High School stands today. The one consistent thing about these studies was that they disagreed with the traditional explanation – they all placed the site somewhere between half a mile and a mile and a half from the Bore Stone. Since then historians – both popular and academic – have swithered between these two locations – the Dryfield and the Carse.

The next big development came in 2001, when Stirling Council decided they needed to pin down the moving battlefield. After all, in 1314 this whole area had been a largely natural landscape, save the possible cluster at St Ninian's and the odd scattered cottage where the town of Bannockburn now stands. By the start of the new millennium the area had been extensively built on, with St Ninian's and the neighbouring communities of Bannockburn and Whins of Milton serving as a sprawling southern suburb of Stirling. For the purposes of urban planning, the council wanted to be assured that any new housing developments weren't sited on top of the medieval battlefield. They commissioned a report by historians Fiona Watson and Maggie

Anderson, who were unable to give a definitive answer but suggested two sites – the Carse near Millhall, a small road running beneath the modern railway, or the Dryfield near the high school. Of the two they argue that the Dryfield site was the more likely.

Since then the amateur historian William Scott has argued vehemently for the Carse location, placing the centre of the fighting as far to the east as Mackay Mackenzie did a century ago. His argument rests on the description of the battle in a contemporary Welsh manuscript as being the Battle of the Polls – the battle among the pools. That appears to be a reference to the Carse, where occasional pools of standing water remain a problem for local farmers. However, 'polls' more commonly meant 'streams', and appears in other lowland Scottish names such as Pollock and Polmont – areas where the connection to streams is more apparent.

Other recent books on Bannockburn have opted for one of the two locations suggested by Watson and Anderson, or the more distant mid-Carse location advocated by Mackenzie and Scott. In the report for Stirling Council, one phrase stands out: 'If there has been no agreement on the location of the second day of the battle to date, it is highly unlikely there will ever be.' While this may be true, for the sake of safeguarding our heritage let's hope the authors are wrong.

Perhaps the only way the moving battlefield will be pinned down is through archaeology. There should have been mass burial pits on the battlefield, but these have never been located. Interestingly, although the Dryfield has been extensively built over, no medieval remains were uncovered during all these decades of construction. There has also been a scarcity of relevant archaeological finds, although a spearhead and parts of a dagger of the right date have been discovered near the visitor centre. Other digs have been organised in various locations around the area, but the soil conditions aren't ideal, and so far no crucial evidence has been unearthed. Work also needs to be done on landscape archaeology – reconstructing the historical terrain, so we know how the area looked at the time of the battle.

If archaeology fails us then we are left with one other option – looking at the original medieval sources. In theory they all tell different versions of the same story. Most of them provide us with clues which can help us tie down the location of different phases of the fighting. Strangely the best way to do this is to start by ignoring these important clues. The first job is to see how they recount the flow of the battle, to get a clear picture of what happened. That will then let us look at these topographical clues again, to see which of the likely battlefield sites ticks all the boxes. After discounting the sites that don't fit the evidence, what we'll be left with is – with luck – the site of the battle. While this process isn't perfect, without archaeological evidence it's the best tool we've got.

Modifying the battlefield

Before the battle, King Robert had spent enough time in the area to know how to make the most of the terrain. He realised that his position on the Dryfield to the north of the Bannockburn was a strong one, as it limited an attacker's options. Edward could either try a frontal assault across the ford – a tactic that hadn't worked well at Stirling Bridge – or he could try to bypass it. That in turn meant entering the Carse. If that happened, all Bruce needed to do was to turn his army around through ninety degrees, so that it faced the Carse rather than the burn. Still, to improve his defensive position even further he decided to add some man-made obstacles.

In Geoffrey le Baker's *Chronicon*, written in 1344, the chronicler describes what Bruce did:

> The Scots selected the battlefield for the greatest possibility of victory, dug extended ditches three feet deep and three feet wide from the right to the left flanks of the army, filling them with a brittle plait of twigs, reeds and sticks, that is a trellis, and covering them with grass and weeds. The infantry might be

aware of a safe passage through these, but heavy cavalry would not be able to pass over them.

Effectively this was the medieval equivalent of an anti-tank minefield. Infantry could negotiate the obstacle, but mounted men-at-arms could not. Interestingly, Baker has Bruce's men dig these across his whole front, not just in one spot as Oman suggested. Oman also calls them pits rather than trenches or ditches. Oman's pits are taken from Barbour, ignoring the mention in the *Chronicon*. These defensive ditches were the type of obstacle that had served the Flemings well at Courtrai in 1302. Now Bruce planned to use the same *machina plena malis* – a contrivance full of evils. That was just how Walter Bower described them in his continuation of John Fordoun's *Scotichronicon*: 'A contrivance full of evils is fashioned for the feet of horses, trenches set with stakes so they cannot pass without tumbles.'

The passage in Barbour's *Bruce* that mentions pits is translated as follows:

> He told his men to hollow out pitfalls, three feet round about,
> Where men would sink up to the knees, much like the honey
>   cells the bees make in their comb.

The dimensions are the same as those given in the *Chronicon*, but the reference to honey cells reinforces Oman's pits rather than Baker's ditches. This is further confirmed by the original medieval Scots:

> He gert men mony potties ma, off a fute-breid round, and all
>   tha,
> War dep up till a mannys kne, Sa thyk that mai mychtliknyt
>   be,
> Till a wax cayme that beis mais.

The word 'potties' looks a lot like pits rather than ditches, and 'wax cayme' is undoubtedly a wax comb. That means there is sufficient benefit of doubt here – these traps could either be ditches or pits.

The question remains – just where were these ditches or pits dug? While historians argue over the location of the second day's fighting, most agree that apart from Clifford's reconnaissance in force, the main skirmish was found near the ford where the old Roman road crosses the Bannockburn. The American historian Kelly DeVries suggested the ditches were dug on the south bank of the burn, which doesn't make a great deal of tactical sense, given that the banks of the stream in the area were impassable to mounted men-at-arms. The only way across was at the ford. BBC Television's *Two Men in a Trench* team of Neil Oliver and Tony Pollard dug where DeVries suggested, but found no evidence of ditches. While ditches or pits might have been dug around the secondary crossing place downstream from the ford, no evidence of this has been found.

A more likely spot is on the north side of the burn, above the ford at The Entry, where the road climbs the slope towards St Ninian's. If Bruce's men were deployed there on the first day of the battle, then the traps would lie across the most likely path taken by the attackers. Unfortunately the traces of these ditches are unlikely ever to be found. The spot is now covered by new housing rather than trees, and so any archaeological evidence has almost certainly been lost. Strangely the ditches or pits barely came into play during the battle, or at least they had no major impact on what happened. Perhaps they were dug in the wrong place, or the English spotted them and were able to bypass most of them. Just as likely, while they might have existed, their presence was then used by chroniclers like Geoffrey le Baker to excuse the poor showing of the English men-at-arms. Like many aspects of the battle, there are still questions to answer about Bruce's *machina plena malis*.

14

Clash of Vanguards

On Sunday 23 June, a weary English army stirred itself and prepared to set off. The forced march of the day before would have pushed many of the men to the point of exhaustion, and now after an all too brief rest they were not only on their way again, but were expected to fight the enemy at the end of it. Miles to the north, meanwhile, the Scottish army heard mass before the men reformed in their battles, and waited for the onslaught.

The duel

When Edward's army was in Edinburgh, Bruce's men were encamped in the Torwood, the patch of ancient woodland between Falkirk and Stirling. On 22 June he pulled his men back across the Bannockburn, and established an encampment in the New Park, just outside Stirling. As Barbour put it: 'With all his troops for war arrayed, and camped them in the woodland shade.' It was probably on this evening that Bruce gave the order for his defensive traps to be dug. While their location is unknown, it would have made excellent tactical sense for them to be laid across the road beyond the ford, at The Entry. This ties in with a throwaway line in Sir Thomas Grey's *Scalacronica*, which we will look at in a moment.

The following day – 23 June 1314 – was a Sunday, and the English like the Scots would have heard mass that morning. The *Vita Edwardi Secundi* mentions the English troops approaching a wood, where they saw the Scots straggling through the trees. These trees were in the New Park, not the Torwood, as the rest of the account shows, going on to describe that evening's skirmish. When the English vanguard passed through the Torwood the Scots were long gone. That said, King Robert did send out a strong patrol to see how far away the English army was. James Douglas and Robert Keith led the reconnaissance 'with well-armed horsemen in their train', but it seems that they avoided contact with the English.

However, they did return to the Scottish king, and told him just how large and impressive the English army was. As Barbour puts it:

> The English host soon met their sight, a mighty mass of armour bright,
> Reflecting back the sunbeam's glance, from burnished buckler, shield and lance,
> So many 'broidered banners flew, varied in emblem, shape or hue,
> So many knights on gallant steeds, sat glittering in their martial weeds,
> Such huge battalions deep and wide, covered the ground in power and pride.

According to Barbour, Bruce very wisely asked his scouts to keep the size of the enemy host from the rest of the Scottish army, for fear of sapping morale. Instead he asked them to put the word around that the enemy were 'in poor array'.

It was mid-afternoon now. King Edward would have been marching with the main body of his army, while ahead of him was the vanguard, commanded by Gilbert de Clare, Earl of Gloucester. We don't know the exact size of Gloucester's vanguard, but it probably contained around a third of the total strength of the army, less the king's escort of cavalry, so around 5000 infantry and 500–600 men-at-arms. In other words, the English advance guard was only a little smaller than the whole of the Scottish army.

It was around this time that, as the *Scalacronica* recounts, an encounter took place somewhere between Falkirk and Stirling. Sir Philip Moubray, the commander of Stirling's castle garrison, had left the castle, circled around Bruce's army and ridden down the Falkirk road to meet the king. Sir Thomas Grey takes up the story, after reaffirming that King Edward was there to relieve the castle:

> The said King of England came thither for that reason, where the said constable Philip met him at three leagues from the castle, on Sunday the vigil of Saint John, and told him that there was no occasion for him to approach any nearer, for he considered himself relieved. Then he told him how the enemy had blocked the narrow roads in the forest.

This last phrase could be merely a reference to the Scottish encampment in the New Park. It might also be a reference to obstacles like felled trees inside the wood, or possibly be a description of Bruce's defensive traps.

Unfortunately for the Earl of Gloucester, it seems Moubray's circuitous ride around the Scottish army meant that he didn't encounter the English vanguard before he met King Edward. While the vanguard might have expected the Scots to be lurking somewhere between them and Stirling, they thus failed to hear Moubray's warning that they were encamped in the New Park. It also highlights that the vanguard was now well ahead of the main army. In fact, from what happened next it looks as if its cavalry contingent had outpaced the infantry, and while Moubray was reporting to the king, Gloucester and his fellow mounted men-at-arms were approaching the southern bank of the Bannockburn.

First though, they stopped. They were evidently still some way short of the burn, but close enough to gain some idea of the lie of the land. The 23-year-old Earl of Gloucester probably knew something about the terrain in front of him; in 1306 he had served in Scotland alongside Edward II, and he returned to Scotland in 1308 and 1309. On this last occasion the teenage nobleman had commanded troops in the area, so he had passed over this ground before. So too had his co-commander Humphrey de Bohun, Earl of Hereford, who was around forty at the time of the battle. Hereford had served in Scotland during several campaigns, and also knew the local lie of the land. This experience should have worked to their advantage, but the two men loathed each other, and unnecessary communication between them would have been unlikely.

The sources are a little unclear about when Lord Clifford was detached to conduct a reconnaissance in force. The *Lanercost Chronicle* seems to muddle the two clashes on 23 June, and lumps them together. The *Scalacronica* is a little clearer, and implies that the action described in our Prologue took place after the rest of the English vanguard approached the Bannockburn. However, Lord Clifford began his reconnaissance before the clash at the ford. Whenever the order was given is largely immaterial. In any event, around 300 men-at-arms were detached from the English army, and were sent on a flank march to ride around the Scots and make contact with the garrison at Stirling.

When the English vanguard reached the edge of the gully above the ford, Gloucester and Hereford would have realised there was only one way to cross the burn, and it involved wading through the ford. If we agree with the evidence of William Roy's military map of 1750, the ford appears to be about 200 yards to the east of the modern bridge where the A872 crosses the burn. Of course there is no guarantee that this was where the ford was in 1314. However, the spot is certainly shallow enough for one, and traces of a track leading to the river can be seen which match the Roy map. Standing a few hundred yards south of the ford, it is difficult to see what the terrain looks like on the far bank. Then as now, trees probably hid the north bank of the burn from view, until you were actually standing at its edge. This then is probably where the Earl of Gloucester first sighted the Scottish army.

It was late in the afternoon – 3 or 4 p.m. Still, that didn't deter Gloucester and his men. Below them lay the ford, while across the burn was open ground, and the road leading up the slope and into the trees at The Entry. In amongst these trees they saw Scottish soldiers. According to the *Vita Edwardi Secundi* these men were on the move, and the presumption was that they were in retreat. It is possible too that this was a feigned flight, to draw the English across the burn, so that Bruce's men could cut them off and chop them up – just as Wallace's men had done at Stirling Bridge sixteen years before.

What followed next was either a noble chivalric duel or an act of rank impetuosity. One of the nobles accompanying Gloucester and the other senior figures of the vanguard was Sir Henry de Bohun, the nephew of Humphrey de Bohun, Earl of Hereford. By this time Scottish troops were forming up on the open ground, and at their front Sir Henry spied the distinctive mounted figure of King Robert. This was an opportunity that seemed too good to miss. Sir Henry spurred his horse down the slope and splashed across the ford.

According to Barbour others followed him, but the impetuous de Bohun was 'a bowshot length' in front of the others. Given the effective range of a bow of the period, that was around 200 yards. A charging war horse running at a canter could cover that distance in around thirty seconds, possibly a little longer if the ford slowed the horse down. Bruce had very little time to react, and nor did his nobles, who might otherwise have moved to intercept the charging English knight. Bruce was at a disadvantage – de Bohun was almost certainly riding a powerful destrier, while King Robert was mounted on a smaller palfrey, a horse used for riding rather than for fighting. He barely had time to wheel around to face the threat, let alone do anything else.

Here Barbour takes up the story:

Now when Sir Henry was aware, that the good king would
    meet him there,
He to the combat spurred amain, assured that he would quickly
    gain,
Great glory, and would work his will, upon a foeman horsed so
    ill.

Together to the charge they came, but bold Sir Henry missed
    his aim,
The king high in his stirrups stood, wielding his war axe hard
    and good,
And struck Sir Henry with such force, that nothing could resist
    its course,

But downwards in its sheer descent, through hat and helm and
    head it went,
The battle axe in two was smashed, the knight down to the
    ground was dashed,
Deprived by death of all his might – that was the first stroke in
    the fight.

In other words, Bruce was armed with nothing other than an axe, but he waited calmly for de Bohun to reach him, pulled his horse aside at the last minute, and cleaved the English knight in two with a single stroke. It was the stuff of legend – an iconic moment in the life of Bruce, and of the Battle of Bannockburn. Part of the romance here is the chivalric ideal of a single combat, but the moment has also captured the imagination of people over the centuries because Bruce was the poorly armed and poorly mounted underdog here. Bruce moreover emerges as a hero, and as an inspiration to his men. In more modern parlance his performance was the epitome of 'cool'. This of course was the opening blow of the Battle of Bannockburn. Over the next few days a lot more gallant men-at-arms and common

foot soldiers would share the fate of the impetuous Sir Henry de
Bohun.

Skirmish by the ford

What followed is confused slightly by the sources. The death of de
Bohun raised a great cheer from the Scottish ranks and incensed the
English men-at-arms, who according to Barbour were already following
Sir Henry down to the ford. In the *Scalacronica*, this attack is described
as an impetuous one, without much evidence of thought or discipline:

> The young troops would by no means stop, but held their
> way. The advanced guard, whereof the Earl of Gloucester had
> command, entered the road within the park, where they were
> immediately received roughly by the Scots, who had occupied
> the passage. Here Peris de Mountforth, knight, was slain with
> the axe of Robert de Brus, as was reported.

In fact Sir Thomas Grey got the name wrong, as it was de Bohun who
was killed by Bruce's axe.

Obviously there was too little room for hundreds of mounted men-
at-arms to cross the ford at the same time, and even once they reached
the far bank the ground was constricted by a marsh on one side and a
spur of the Dryfield on the other. The road disappeared into the trees
ahead of them, where the Scottish spearmen of King Robert's schiltron
had emerged from cover and were ready for them. As *Scalacronica*
suggests, this charge went badly for the men-at-arms. The inference
is that they lacked cohesion and discipline, while the Scots had both
in ample measure. In the scrum the Earl of Gloucester was unhorsed –
presumably when his mount was speared – and de Bohun's squire was
killed as he tried to protect his liege lord's body. Barbour describes an
even more one-sided affray, with the English bested fairly quickly, and
then withdrawing over the ford. As he put it:

The Scottish warriors glad to see, the Englishmen before them
   flee,
Upon their rear made fierce attacks, in haste the English turned
   their backs,
And some of them were over ta'en, and by their fierce pursuers
   slain,
But in the flight not many fell, their horses carried them so
   well,
They fled away with nought but shame, back to the place from
   whence they came.

The English men-at-arms withdrew over the ford and regrouped
beyond the southern edge of the Bannockburn. This was an interesting
psychological moment in the battle, as what appears to have been one
Scottish schiltron – around 1500 men – had managed to form quickly
enough to thwart a mounted charge. With the attackers outnumbered
and unable to break through the spearmen, the Scottish advantage in
numbers prevailed, and the Englishmen were forced back after what
appears to be a short but hard-fought skirmish. This though, was all it
was. It wasn't a battle, or even a choreographed part of one. It was a
brief clash between two small groups of troops, which achieved nothing
apart from demonstrating the superior discipline of Bruce's spearmen.

Another little mystery about this skirmish concerns the *machina
plena malis*. There is no mention of them. Surely they would have been
placed to stop exactly the type of cavalry charge launched by de Bohun
and his colleagues. The inference is, of course, that they were either
dug somewhere else, on the flanks of The Entry, or that the Scots
spearmen formed up in front of them. This latter notion makes sense,
in that if the English were to attack in the same direction the following
day, then they would have no knowledge of these defensive traps. By
fighting in front of them, Bruce and his men would have prevented the
English from discovering their location, and therefore saving them for
the 'main event' rather than a small skirmish. According to Barbour

the traps were dug across the army's front. This suggests they might also have been dug at the eastern end of the ravine, exactly where Sir Charles Oman placed them. However, their presence played no part in the battle.

After the skirmish, while the Earl of Gloucester mounted his spare horse, he ordered his men to remain where they were. At some time King Edward would have appeared, leading the main body, and Gloucester's infantry. The king and his senior commanders would have discussed what to do next, although the chances are they'd already selected their camp site for the night. Meanwhile, Barbour claimed that over on the north bank of the Bannockburn Bruce's men chided their king for risking his life in the duel with Sir Henry de Bohun, whose body presumably still lay in front of them. Apparently the Scottish king didn't answer, but merely mourned the loss of his battleaxe, which had shattered when he struck that one almighty blow. This display of sangfroid merely added to his image as a fearless commander – and in more modern terms enhanced his 'cool' status.

15

Beyond the Bannockburn

While the Earl of Gloucester's men were skirmishing with King Robert's troops at the ford, Robert Clifford's reconnaissance in force was under way on the far side of the Dryfield. This move served several purposes. First of all, it helped determine where the left flank of the Scottish line was. As Bruce's men were largely hidden by the trees of the New Park and the Dryfield, someone needed to figure out how far their encampment extended. It also allowed King Edward to claim he'd made contact with the garrison at Stirling Castle. This meant the siege would be properly lifted, rather than just fulfilling the terms of the pledge made by the castle governor. Finally, if the Scots should try to break contact with the Earl of Gloucester and withdraw towards Stirling, Clifford's men would be waiting for them.

The reconnaissance

The dramatic events surrounding Lord Robert Clifford's reconnaissance have been recounted in the Prologue. That allows us to concentrate on setting his action in its perspective, and showing how it tied in with what followed. The key to understanding the episode's importance is the word 'reconnaissance'. Clifford wasn't supposed to become embroiled in an engagement with the Scots if he could avoid it. His real job was to probe the left flank of the Scottish position, not charge into it. Another unstated aim of the mission might have been to confirm that the Carse of Balquhiderock was empty of Scottish troops, as the English army would have to make camp somewhere in the area, where there was water and a reasonable degree of security.

First, though, he had to cross the Bannockburn. Obviously this crossing took place somewhere to the east of the gully through which the burn ran as it passed the Dryfield. The obvious place was where the track or small road known as The Way, leading northwards towards St Ninian's Church a little over a mile to the north-west, crossed the burn immediately beyond the end of the gully. On the left of the track the slope of the Dryfield rose fairly steeply to the tree line at the top of the ridge, while to the right lay the carse. Interestingly there is no mention that when Clifford's horsemen crossed the burn they encountered Bruce's defensive traps. Either Clifford anticipated this trick and crossed the burn well to the east of any ditches or pits, or else they weren't emplaced near this obvious crossing point. The likelihood is that they were concentrated around The Entry.

Two sources mention the way Clifford and his men-at-arms carried out their mission, and surprisingly they both use the same phrase. The *Lanercost Chronicle* claims: 'Upon information that there were Scots in the wood, the king's advance guard, commanded by Lord de Clifford, began to make a circuit of the wood, to prevent the Scots escaping by flight.' The *Scalacronica* tells much the same story. While the advance guard were occupied near the ford, 'Robert, Lord de Clifford and Henry de Beaumont, with three hundred men-at-arms, made a circuit upon the other side of the wood towards the castle, keeping the open ground.' This is all very straightforward, and the use of the word 'circuit' emphasises the reconnaissance element of Clifford's assignment.

The mention of the possibility that the Scots might withdraw from the area is an important one. In almost every case the Scots had tried to avoid open battle, if they thought the odds were unfavourable. There was no reason to expect that this wouldn't happen at Bannockburn too – in fact the odds were high that Bruce would try to do just that. If his troops tried to withdraw then it was hoped that Clifford's men could pin them long enough for the rest of the English army to bring the retreating Scots to battle. Given what happened that afternoon it was just as well Clifford's men-at-arms weren't confronted by the whole of King Robert's army.

The battle that followed somewhere beyond St Ninian's Church is described in the *Scalacronica*, which also includes an account of that conversation between Clifford's deputy, Sir Henry Beaumont, and the chronicler's father Sir Thomas Grey:

Thomas Randolph, Earl of Moray, Robert de Brus' nephew, who was leader of the Scottish advanced guard of the English on the other side of the wood, thought that he must have his share, and issuing from the wood with his division marched across the open ground towards the two afore-named lords [Clifford and Beaumont]. Sir Henry de Beaumont called to his men: 'Let us wait a while – let them come on – give them room!' 'Sir', said Sir Thomas Gray, 'I doubt that whatever you give them now, they will have all too soon.' 'Very well', exclaimed the said Henry – 'If you are afraid be off!' 'Sir', answered the said Thomas, 'it is not from fear that I shall fly this day'. With that he launched himself directly at the enemy.

Grey continued to recount the fate of his father:

So saying he spurred in between him and Sir William Deyncourt, and charged into the thick of the enemy. William was killed, Thomas was taken prisoner, his horse being killed on the pikes, and he himself carried off with them on foot when they marched off, having utterly routed the squadron of the said two lords. Some of whom fled to the castle, others to the king's army.

The *Lanercost Chronicle* tells a similar tale, but here the story becomes muddled, as if the whole of the English vanguard was involved, rather than just a detached force of cavalry: 'The Scots did not interfere until they [the English] were far ahead of the main body, when they showed themselves, and cutting off the king's advanced guard, from the middle and rear columns, they charged and killed some of them, and put the rest to flight.'

That brought to an end the fighting on the first day of the battle – Sunday 23 June 1314. Both engagements were little more than skirmishes. The fight at the ford had possibly involved less than a hundred English men-at-arms – and had been essentially a rash and intemperate charge. The Earl of Gloucester reined in his men, and while he managed to extricate them, he either spent the rest of the afternoon facing the Scots from the south bank of the burn or – more likely – marched off to the chosen camp site on the Carse. While his men were greatly outnumbered in the fight, they probably faced only King Robert's own battle – less than a quarter of the Scottish army. In the larger fight beyond St Ninian's Church, Clifford commanded anything from 300 to 800 men-at-arms depending on which source you believe, but an average figure of 500 men is probably closer to the mark. Barbour implies that the Earl of Moray marched out of the woods to meet him with only part of his full battle, a force of spearmen 'of his own leading' – in other words tenants, retainers, relatives and old soldiers loyal to him– not his full battle.

Despite the ferocity of the fighting, neither of these actions resulted in many casualties. If we presume that Clifford lost less than fifty men-at-arms during his assault on Moray's schiltron, and Gloucester a similar number or even less, then such casualties would do little to reduce the fighting potential of the English army. Even if half of Clifford's men fled towards Stirling Castle after the fight, the English still had an extremely powerful body of mounted men-at-arms to draw upon the following day. The real damage was in the psychological impact these two reverses had on the morale of the army. In both actions the men-at-arms had been bested by Scottish spearmen, which flew in the face of conventional military thinking. English arrogance had led to a blind assumption that the men-at-arms would prevail whatever the odds stacked against them. The realisation that this wasn't necessarily going to work would have come as something of a shock to the English cavalry and their commanders.

It is interesting to speculate what a more experienced commander might have achieved in the same circumstances. If Aymer de Valence, Earl of Pembroke had been in command of the vanguard things might have been different. Even if Humphrey de Bohun, Earl of Hereford had been in overall command of this advance guard he might have been able to restrain the impetuosity of his nephew and his young men-at-arms. Either earl might have tried to outflank Robert's defensive position, or waited until he could launch a combined assault on it using archers and spearmen as well as mounted troops. If Robert Clifford had attacked Moray sooner, before he had a chance to deploy his small schiltron into a circle, then the Scottish formation might have been broken. These of course are the vagaries of warfare. The bets had been laid and the dice had been rolled.

The camp in the carse

It was now later in the afternoon, and probably too late in the day for Edward to consider launching a major attack. Instead he would have consulted his senior commanders – men like the earls of Pembroke, Gloucester and Hereford – as well as others with even greater local knowledge, such as Sir Ingram de Umfraville, the cousin of the Earl of Angus. The decision was made to make camp. The only question was where to site it. The army contained about 2500 men-at-arms, and most of them would have two or more horses. Then there was the vast baggage train, with yet more horses and oxen, as well as meat transported 'on the hoof'. This meant the encampment had to be close to a stream, the closest of which was the Bannockburn.

This decided, the next question was on which side of the burn to establish the camp. The advantage of the southern side was that it provided additional security in the event of a surprise attack. However, the English had little fear of that – in previous campaigns the Scots had either stolen away and avoided battle, or had meekly waited for the English to attack them. The advantage of the north side of the Bannockburn was that the carse there had the space to house the encampment, it was protected on three sides, and it placed the army closer to Stirling Castle. If battle was joined the following morning there would be no waterway to cross, and the army would be ready to deploy, facing the enemy without hindrance. It could then launch its attack secure in the knowledge that both flanks were protected by streams – the Bannockburn to the south and the Pelstream to the north.

The decision was made. The army swung to the right and followed the southern bank of the Bannockburn as it looped and wriggled its way through the gully. Beyond this was the smaller ford where the track or small road ran along the edge of the Dryfield. The army could have crossed there, but the spot was uncomfortably close to the Dryfield's southern end, and the Scots lurking hidden in the woods that ran along the top of the ridge. While the sources don't mention it, the logical place to cross would have been a little further downstream, perhaps beyond where the burn loops its way around a spear-shaped wedge of land, pointing directly towards the highest part of the carse.

The process of leading the army from the main road south of the ford to this crossing point would have taken an hour or so – the distance was less than one and a half miles, but troops had to be given their instructions, wagons had to be moved off the road, and any logjam of men, horses and wagons had to be sorted out. Today the town of Bannockburn is built over this spot, and a marvellous circular-arched bridge designed by Thomas Telford spans the gully. Further on, a bridge built in the early sixteenth century also crossed the Bannockburn, since replaced by a less charming modern road crossing. Beyond that the railway crosses the burn by way of an iron bridge, but in 1314 neither the town nor these bridges existed. Only a cluster of houses – hardly a hamlet – stood there. The army had to make its way onto the carse without the aid of modern roads and bridges – just timbers and doors looted from these local cottages.

The Plantagenet army had made camp like this many times before while on campaign in Scotland, Wales, France and Flanders. The secret was to have a logical plan, so that the various battles didn't become intermingled, the men and animals had access to water, and the perimeter was secure from attack. In this case the Pelstream and the Bannockburn protected the northern and southern flanks of the encampment, while to the east the boggy ground between it and the Forth meant that an attack from that quarter was nigh-on impossible. That left the western perimeter, facing the Dryfield, and the Scottish army. In modern military terminology, that was the direction of the threat.

To safeguard the camp, a picket line of men would have been posted between the camp and the Dryfield, while further back more archers and spearmen would have been placed, ready to form up quickly if the alarm was sounded. As a final safeguard a detachment of cavalry from part of the army would have been deployed where it could attack anyone approaching the camp. The men-at-arms would have slept beside their horses and some might even have been bitted and probably saddled, just in case. From what transpired the next day it seems most likely that this security task would have been carried out by a detachment from the Earl of Gloucester's vanguard. Besides, in the morning the army expected to march off and seek out the Scots. That meant organising the encampment so the vanguard was closest to the Scots, and the rearguard deployed towards the eastern end of the camp. The main body would have occupied the centre, and within it would have stood the king's command tent. The English had a tried and trusted system for these encampments, and there is no reason to suspect it wasn't applied here.

If we expect the leading units – presumably the vanguard – to occupy their allotted places by 6 p.m. at the latest, then the rest of the army would have been settled well before nightfall. The carse would have been reasonably dry underfoot at that time of year, but small pools and burns would still have dotted the area. While the nobles enjoyed the comparative luxury of tents, the rest of the army endured more Spartan conditions, either sheltering inside a makeshift bivouac or sleeping under the stars. At least the men seem to have been fed, and some were able to bolster their courage with alcohol. According to Friar William Baston, who was there and later wrote a poem about the battle, the men drank and bragged during the long summer evening: 'While thus they vaunt themselves, as they drink and jest disdaining thee with boastful words.' They made themselves as comfortable as they could, in a place the *Scalacronica* describes as an 'evil, deep, wet marsh'. The likelihood is, though, that this ground lay further to the east of the carse – the ground chosen for the camp itself would have been dry enough to allow the wagons to be manoeuvred and the tents to be pitched.

Baston's account then described the mood in the English camp: 'The said English army unharnessed and remained all night, having sadly lost confidence and being too much disaffected by the events of the day.' This suggests the reverses that day had damaged English morale. While many English soldiers would have remained confident, others would have wondered if the army's misfortunes would continue. After all, if the Scots could defy the mounted might of the men-at-arms, what other misfortunes might befall the army in the morning? Friar Baston may have exaggerated the despair to appease his audience – he was a prisoner of the Scots when he wrote his poem – but he also mentioned the mood: 'Bewilderment is audible, bewilderment redoubling bewilderment, resistance is worn down, order losing order.'

In the Scots camp in the New Park the mood was much lighter. The morale of the army had been boosted by the day's successes, and a mood of optimism prevailed. According to Barbour, Bruce toured the camp, speaking to the men and assuring them that God was on their side, reminding them not only what they were fighting for but that the plunder would be theirs for the taking once the battle had been won. While this patriotic speech is all very stirring, the suspicion is that if Bruce addressed his men at all, his words would have had a more prosaic ring to them. Far more importantly, he would have called his senior commanders to the edge of the trees, where they could look out towards the English encampment. There King Robert would have briefed them on his plans for the following morning.

The short night was reasonably uneventful – no attack was launched across the carse, and the sentries of both armies were undisturbed. However, a mile and a half to the north of the English camp a band of soldiers led by a Scottish earl were about to launch their own nocturnal raid. The only place this is mentioned is in Barbour's *Bruce*. The poet claims that during the night David of Strathbogie, Earl of Atholl led a raid on a Scottish supply depot at Cambuskenneth, the priory sited on the north bank of the Forth. Atholl was an in-law of the Comyn family, and had aligned himself with King Edward since 1307. Although he made peace with King Robert, he switched sides again shortly before the campaign began after Edward, Earl of Carrick jilted his sister. While his raid had no impact on the coming battle, it might have had if the campaign continued. Elsewhere though, the soldiers rested as best they could, and wondered what the morning would bring.

16

Dawn Attack

It was obvious to everyone in both armies that dawn could bring a resumption of the battle, if the Scots didn't flee in the night. If there was to be a fight then this would be no mere skirmish – it would be the real thing. In those northern latitudes this meant some time after 4 a.m. Within an hour it would be fully light, by which time the soldiers of both sides would have risen, broken their nocturnal fast, donned their equipment and seen to their weapons. In the English encampment many might have hoped that King Robert's army would have marched away during the night. King Edward wasn't among them – this expedition had cost a fortune in time, effort and money, and he had no wish to see the Scottish army disappear like a will o' the wisp.

For King Robert's part he had pondered his dilemma the previous evening. A battle was an incredible gamble, as defeat would mean the potential unravelling of everything he had worked for since his coronation. The English army was much larger than his, and while the skirmishes of Sunday afternoon had been successful, there was no guarantee these successes could be repeated in a full-scale battle. He could slip his army away to safety and avoid any potential disaster, but the morale in the army had been buoyed by its two victories, and his men seemed eager for the fight. After what would have been much consideration he decided to fight. That decision was made the previous evening, after which he studied the ground, peered at the enemy camp, and drew up his plan of battle. Now that morning had come, King Robert was about to put that plan into action. It was certainly daring – rather than wait passively for the enemy to come to him, Bruce planned to take the fight to the enemy.

Opening moves

Before the Scots stirred, a defector was brought before the Scottish king. Sir Alexander Seton was a Scot, but he supported King Edward, largely because his lands in East Lothian were still in an area controlled by the English. According to the *Scalacronica* he defected during the night, and requested to speak to the king. Sir Thomas Grey claims he said to Bruce, 'Sir, this is the time if you ever intend, to undertake to reconquer Scotland. The English have lost heart and are discouraged, and expect nothing but a sudden, open attack.' King Robert intended to oblige them.

Barbour claims that the Scottish soldiers heard mass and then ate a frugal breakfast. Then they prepared for battle. It was probably some time between 4.30 and 5.30 a.m. The Scottish spearmen would have formed up in their mustering points among the trees of the New Park, and then moved off in their groups to emerge from the trees at the top of the Dryfield. There they were formed up into their three battles. As the *Scalacronica* confirms, the Scots 'marched out of the wood in three divisions of infantry'. Sir Thomas Grey adds that 'The aforesaid Scots came in line of shiltrons.' The same point is reinforced by the *Lanercost Chronicle*: 'They had so arranged their army that two columns went abreast in advance of the third, so that neither should be in advance of the other; and the third followed, in which was Robert.'

Today, the same ground – or at least the spot where this most likely happened – is occupied by Bannockburn High School, halfway between the modern Bannockburn Visitor Centre and the point where a railway line marks the foot of the Dryfield and the start of the carse.

At this location, when the Scottish spearmen began to form up, they would have been partially hidden from the English army thanks to the uneven terrain, but the English would have noted activity on the high ground. This would have removed any lingering doubts in English minds whether the Scots were actually going to fight.

King Robert was dismounted – as were his other senior commanders – a move explained by John of Trokelowe: 'so that danger being equalised between the nobility and the commoners, no one thought about flight.' The *Vita Edwardi Secundi* records how good the Scots spearmen looked that morning, as 'each was furnished with light armour, not easily penetrable by a sword. They had axes at their sides, and carried lances [spears] in their hands.' The three battles consisted of around 1500 or 2000 men apiece – spearmen for the most part, with a small number of dismounted men-at-arms, probably serving as contingent leaders. Then there were the three battle commanders, Edward Bruce, Earl of Carrick King Robert and Thomas Randolph, Earl of Moray – leaders of the vanguard, main body and rearguard respectively.

We don't know which order they appeared in, but the likelihood is that Moray was on the left, closest to his position the previous day, when Robert and Edward had formed up covering The Entry, behind the ford. The redeployment of the army involved what was effectively a ninety-degree turn, from a line parallel to the Bannockburn to one cresting the Dryfield, and at right angles to the burn. The easiest way that could be achieved without each battle marching through the others' encampments was for the Bruces to deploy to the right of Moray. Also, Edward, Earl of Carrick was senior to Thomas, Earl of Moray, so in accordance with medieval military protocol he would have deployed on the right of the army. When they moved forward, King Robert's battle would hang back slightly to become the reserve, while the other two battles formed the army's front line.

We can assume that these schiltrons would have been around five men deep. There was no standard depth for spear formations, but any more and the spears of the rear ranks would serve no defensive purpose. The men in the rear would therefore have no function apart from filling any gaps left by the fallen. Fewer men and the line would be too brittle, and might be unable to withstand the shock of impact, whether it came from mounted men-at-arms or other spearmen. Each man would have taken up roughly a yard of space. So, 1500 or 2000 spearmen formed up in five ranks would have held a line about 300 to 400 yards long. With two battles pushed forward and one held back in reserve, the front line of the Scottish army would therefore take up about 800 yards of ground. At the foot of the Dryfield there was roughly 1000 yards between the Bannockburn and the Pelstream. These would have anchored the Scottish flanks, and any gap in the Scottish line would most likely have been near the centre, where it was covered by the king's reserve battle.

Then, when everything was ready, the Scottish battle line slowly advanced down the hill. Most likely this was still done in columns, and the troops would deploy into line at the foot of the hill. The slope is a reasonably steep one, but still manageable – or rather it might be for a lean medieval spearman in his twenties, rather than for a portly and unfit modern historian, who found the descent rather difficult. It can be ridden up or down on horseback – at least an individual rider might be able to make the ascent – but a large body of mounted men-at-arms would have found it difficult. While a cautious equestrian descent could be made, particularly to the north where the ridge flattens out slightly, a full-scale charge up the slope would have to be made at the walk, and so was not a viable option.

Today the ground is occupied by school playing fields, a belt of trees and a jumble of modern housing, but in 1314 these slopes were open, and the area at their foot was used for the growing of cereal crops. The drop in height isn't particularly great – around forty feet – and 500 yards from the mustering point the slope levelled out as it reached the carse. Today a road and a railway run along the bottom of the slope, and possibly mark the place where the small road – The Way – ran along the bottom of the ridge, leading north through the crops towards

St Ninian's Church. That was where the Scots halted again, redressed their ranks, and then knelt down to pray.

In the English camp the appearance of the Scottish army on the ridge just three-quarters of a mile to the west would have caused an initial flurry of alarm. The English host was already up and about, and was busy assembling in its ranks. The trouble was, the battle King Edward and his advisors were expecting to fight was one where they did the attacking. The army was formed up ready to advance, which means it wasn't in the best tactical posture to deal with the Scots if they advanced onto the carse. It might take an hour or more to redeploy the army – time that Edward didn't have. Barbour claims that Sir Ingram de Umfraville recommended enticing the Scots down from the high ground by feigning flight, retreating behind the camp, and then falling on the Scots when they were busy plundering the camp. Edward dismissed this unchivalrous idea. Besides, the ground there was boggy. Instead he would advance to meet the enemy.

For a moment though, as the Scots knelt to pray, Edward – according to Barbour – took this as a sign that they were begging for mercy. If there is any truth in this then it speaks volumes about Edward's confidence that morning. Barbour's version of the tale – probably a literary invention – goes as follows:

> Short was the prayer to heaven they sent, as on their knees
>   they humbly bent,
> That God might aid them in the fight, now when the English
>   king caught sight,
> Of those who knelt their prayers to say, 'For mercy' he
>   exclaimed 'they pray',
> Sir Ingram said 'Your words are true, mercy they ask, but not
>   from you'.
> For God's forgiveness they implore, and hear for certain one
>   thing more,
> These men will either do or die, for fear of death they will not fly.

One doubts that Sir Ingram had the courage to speak to his king this way, or describe the Scots as fanatics. In fact, despite the disquiet reported by Sir Alexander Seton, that morning the mood in the English ranks was more determined – they wanted vengeance for the defeats the previous day. Grey claims the English cavalry were surprised by the appearance of the Scots: 'They mounted in great alarm, for they were not accustomed to dismount to fight on foot; whereas the Scots had taken a lesson from the Flemings, who before that at Courtrai defeated on foot the power of France.' Alarmed or not, the English hastily formed up into some semblance of a line of battle.

A lot of ink has been spilt on describing how and where the two armies deployed that morning. The problem lies in what appear to be discrepancies in the sources. This is hardly surprising – few were written by people who were there. Instead the authors were men – usually non-combatant clerics – who had little experience in the art of war. The best source was Sir Thomas Grey; not only was he a soldier, but his father fought in the battle, and both father and son had spent time as prisoners of the Scots. They would have undoubtedly talked to their captors about the battle: that is what old soldiers tend to do, particularly when given the chance to compare their experiences with those of their counterparts in the enemy ranks. This doesn't say we can ignore the descriptions of the fighting from other less professional sources – it just means we should use them with caution.

Sometimes, what they say makes perfect sense. Barbour writes, 'The English van, in martial pride, with fearless hearts came sweeping on', which suggests what we have already surmised – the English vanguard was at the front of Edward's army. The Earl of Gloucester's battle would have comprised the usual building blocks of men-at-arms, spearmen and archers. If the English army planned to advance that morning, then these troops would have been at the forefront, possibly with the same three building blocks of the main body – the largest battle – in the centre, followed by a similar division of troops in the rearguard. It therefore makes military sense – at least to a medieval commander – that the army was stacked up in this manner. However, these vanguards, main bodies and rearguards were administrative rather than tactical terms. Apart from the fact Gloucester was at its front, the exact way the army deployed may never be known.

We know from what happened next that a body of English cavalry under Gloucester's command were close to the front of the army, accompanied by a screen of archers. In the *Lanercost Chronicle*, these archers 'were thrown forward before the line'. That sounds like a protective screen of skirmishers, operating in advance of the cavalry and probably spearmen behind them. There must have been spearmen in the vanguard, because Barbour mentions them – in fact he specifically refers to schiltrons. He also adds that, thanks to the narrowness of the battlefield, they formed a solid mass, which appeared to Scottish eyes to form one great amorphous line of men.

According to Trokelowe, the English cavalry were deployed behind the infantry, but this is at odds with the other sources. Gloucester's men could hardly have pushed their way through the lines of spearmen, and then deployed ready for a charge, without causing the total disruption of the English line. Thinking about it, this also fits the profile of an army deployed ready to advance. The bulk of the cavalry would have been in the main body, in King Edward's battle, with possibly more cavalry belonging to the rearguard behind them. This deployment also explains why things developed the way they did when the two armies clashed.

The English archers sent forward were almost certainly the same men who had stood to during the night, to provide a protective screen for the camp. They would have had to advance to within 200 yards of the Scottish line for their arrows to have an impact on the Scottish schiltrons. At this stage the Scots would probably still have been at the foot of the Dryfield slope, and they countered this move by sending forward their own archers to meet the Englishmen. Effectively their job was to screen the Scottish schiltrons from enemy arrows. The two groups of archers, probably deployed in long skirmish lines, exchanged arrow fire, but the Scots were outnumbered, and eventually they were driven off, or more likely were recalled. The English archers had little chance to feel elated at their small victory. Once the remnants of the Scottish archer screen were ordered back behind the schiltrons, the Scottish spearmen began to advance.

It flies in the face of military logic that infantry should advance against cavalry. Convention dictated that their only hope of survival lay in bunching together to form a tight wall of spears, and this was best done at the halt. Advancing infantry were unlikely to do so in the tight formation required to fend off charging cavalry. However, at Bannockburn, it seems, that is exactly what they did. This said, the English cavalry facing them – the men-at-arms of Gloucester's vanguard – were only one element of the threat. Ahead of the advancing schiltrons was that screen of archers, while behind them the chances are that a solid line of English spearmen was waiting for them. Advancing in the face of the enemy was a bold move, but it had its advantages. The English army was already bunched up, deployed in the wrong formation in a constricted space. This advance would bunch them up even more, making it all but impossible for the English to bring their superiority in numbers to bear.

The English were certainly impressed by the move. The dramatic scene is described in the *Vita Edwardi Secundi*: 'They advanced like a thick-set hedge, and such a line could not easily be broken. When the situation was such that the two lines should meet, James Douglas, who commanded the first line of the Scots, vigorously attacked the Earl of Gloucester's line.' While the chronicler got it wrong about Douglas – he was too junior a commander to command the entire Scottish line – the sentiment is clear. The Scots initiated the action by advancing into the carse. This was a big gamble, one that depended on the Scottish spearmen being able to repeat their successes of the previous day, and repulse a powerful charge by English cavalry.

The English archers would have shot their arrows for as long as they could, and would then have withdrawn behind the waiting line of cavalry and spearmen. John of Trokelowe sets the time of this advance at the third hour – around 9 a.m. This, though, sounds unfeasibly late. If King Robert had decided his plan of battle was to form up and advance, thereby pinning the enemy in the carse, then he had to make sure he launched his attack before Edward did. It makes much more sense if the battle began earlier – probably around 5 or 6 a.m. In any event this was the moment when victory or defeat – when the fate of two nations – hung in the balance.

17

Gloucester's Death Ride

The unexpected advance of the Scottish spearmen must have caught the Earl of Gloucester by surprise. His men-at-arms had fought in the skirmish by the ford the previous afternoon, but most of his men hadn't got to grips with the enemy. This was their chance. They had spent the night with their horses 'bitted' and ready for battle. While this didn't necessarily mean a horse wore its bit – it couldn't eat or drink all night if it did – it was ready to be harnessed at a moment's notice. So, when they saw the Scots appear on the upper slopes of the Dryfield, they would have saddled their horses and donned their armour, ready for battle. Gloucester probably had around 600 men-at-arms with him, or possibly fewer, depending on how many riders had fallen the previous day. While Lord Clifford's men-at-arms were more badly blooded, the likelihood is that they were now deployed somewhere behind the front line. It was Gloucester's small vanguard who now had the chance to avenge their misfortunes of the previous day.

Gloucester's attack

The Scottish army was advancing in two long thin blocks of spearmen, with a third block advancing behind them. The first two blocks were led by Edward Bruce, Earl of Carrick and Thomas Randolph, Earl of Moray. Edward had gained his brother's old title after Robert was crowned, and while Barbour hints at a rivalry between the siblings, he may have lacked his elder brother's martial prowess. This, though, was a battle that called for courage and determination rather than initiative, and so in this instance Edward could be relied upon to do what was expected. Thomas Randolph had already proved his mettle the previous day, and his men would still have been buoyed up by their small victory. He was clearly a good man to have in a fight.

While the sources remain silent on exactly how the two battles were deployed, most historians – including this one – assume that the Earl of Carrick was on the right of the line and the Earl of Moray on the left. The reasoning for this is merely the location of both battles the previous day. However, Barbour suggests that when he charged, Gloucester attacked the Earl of Carrick's battle. By our logic that would place the scene of the action on the central or southern portion of the battlefield, closer to the Bannockburn than the Pelstream. King Robert's main body – probably as many as 2000 men strong – followed behind the leading two battles as a reserve. The gap between the two armies was now closing slowly, as the Scots spearmen advanced in good order. The sight would have been an impressive one. John of Trokelowe captured something of this when he wrote: 'The lines of both parties, approaching each other, showed a formidable sight to those who saw them. For the din of trumpets and clarions, the neighing of horses, the motion of standards, the calls of the leaders which sounded in their midst, could frighten the hearts of even the bravest men.' In fact Trokelowe was probably mistaken – at this stage only the Scots were advancing. No other source suggests that the whole of the English vanguard marched forward to meet them. The only movement in the front ranks of the English host would have been made by the archers as they scrambled to evade the advancing Scottish spearmen, and by Gloucester's men-at-arms as they readied themselves for action.

If the Scottish advance continued, then the constricting terrain would hamper any ability of the English army to deploy. Instead they would find themselves hemmed in between the two burns, with a marsh behind them. That would render the army largely impotent – the men-at-arms would be unable to charge, the archers would have too little space to deploy, and everyone would be forced into a tight mass of humanity, among the tents, wagons and detritus of the encampment. Clearly something had to be done. At that moment only one English commander was in a position to intervene. Gilbert de Clare, Earl of Gloucester had watched the Scots advance – a sight denied to most of the English army behind him, whose vision would have been obstructed by the men in front. He decided to buy time for the army by launching a charge against the Scottish spearmen.

Given the events of the previous day this was a rash move. Around 600 men-at-arms were about to charge a schiltron containing three times their number of spearmen. The way medieval cavalry worked is very straightforward. In an ideal world they would form *en haie* – in a long line – and launch their charge. Speed and momentum would be the key to victory. However, space and time often precluded this sort of clear-cut deployment on the battlefield. In practice this rarely seems to have happened, and tactical niceties were often abandoned in favour of huddled mass and momentum.

In order to defeat a schiltron the men-at-arms would have to find a way in amongst its ranks. This usually meant encouraging them to break formation, or by attacking it in the flank, or simply cutting a way in using whatever weapons came to hand. Charging horses would rarely plunge into a line of standing infantry. If mad with fear or in a frenzy of excitement, they would pull up short of the ranks of humans in front of them. There was nothing the riders could then do apart from slashing at the spearheads with axe or sword, in an effort to create a gap in the formation. For their part the spearmen would jab at the unprotected neck, belly and flanks of the horse, hoping to bring it down. Once that happened the unhorsed man-at-arms could either be finished off with a spear, sword or axe, or dragged through the Scottish ranks to become a prisoner.

Not only were the English men-at-arms less numerous than their opponents, a line of cavalry took up more space than the equivalent number of infantry. If we assume that the Earl of Carrick had 2000 men under his command, then a five-deep schiltron would stretch for about 400 yards, the same space taken up by around 150 cavalrymen riding abreast. This meant the horsemen were at a numerical disadvantage. What did work in their favour was psychology. Faced with a large horse bearing down on them at twenty miles an hour, most people would try to get out of the way. This is exactly what the men-at-arms wanted – to create a gap in the schiltron that they could ride into. Once past the line of spears they could then cut down the infantry with relative ease. It was all a matter of luck, intimidation and timing. What Edward Bruce's men had to do was hold their nerve.

When Gloucester gave the order to charge, the line of enemy spearmen could have been no more than a few hundred yards away. This was enough space to bring a horse up to a brisk trot or a canter. Contrary to popular belief, mounted men-at-arms didn't gallop – it was impossible to maintain any formation at that speed. Instead they trotted or sometimes cantered into battle. Most of the Earl of Gloucester's men would have been armed with lances, but after being used they were discarded, and the riders would wield swords or axes. The whole charge would have taken no more than half a minute to launch, barely time for Edward Bruce's men to brace themselves for the onslaught. They would most likely have paused in their advance and presented their spears to the enemy. The front rank – if it could – would have jammed the butt of their spears into the earth, to help absorb the impact if the horse actually charged home. Those behind would level their spears over their companions' shoulders, so that the riders faced a tiered wall of spears.

The clash of arms

When the clash came it would have been a dramatic moment, with horses shying and rearing, spears thrusting, and riders being thrown by their mounts. John of Trokelowe describes the scene:

On one side stood the magnates of England, advancing with their troops strongly against the Scots. On the other hand the leaders of the Scots stood defending themselves strongly, and their troops clashing against each other fought a most bloody battle. The crash of lances, the ringing of swords, the noise of hasty blows, the groan of the dying, the lamentation of the wounded, being heard in this conflict to split the air. For a long time it was fought at the front of the lines with the ringing of many swords and both armies fighting strongly against each other.

Inevitably Barbour paints an even more colourful picture. After confirming Gloucester's charge was launched against Edward Bruce's battle, he continues:

Straight as an arrow was their course, and each brave warrior
    spurred his horse,
Upon the Scots they fiercely set, and were with equal courage
    met,
When these two battles spear to spear, encountered, far off you
    might hear,
The clash of arms and captains shout, and then was stabbed
    without a doubt.
Full many a horse of gallant strain, and men were dashed to
    earth and slain,
Most gallant deeds of war were wrought, as hand to hand they
    stoutly fought.

Weapons of every kind they plied, steeds gored with gashes
　　deep and wide,
Rushed here and there all masterless, but the remainder,
　　through the press,
That might come to the shock of war, would not for combat
　　remain afar,
But boldly in the combat closed, and were right sturdily
　　opposed,
With lances that were sharp to wound, and axes that had been
　　well ground,
Wherewith much deadly harm was wrought.

As accounts of battles go this is heady stuff – medieval combat in the raw. What the poem fails to capture is the bigger picture. Gloucester's men-at-arms were making little or no headway. Unlike the fight with Moray's schiltron the previous day, the men of Carrick and Moray's battles were drawn up in line. With the king protecting their rear and the burns covering their flanks there was no need to stop, form circle and present a ring of spears at the English cavalry. That encounter near St Ninian's Church had been the exception to the rule. Except at Falkirk, schiltrons were deployed as lines of spears, and Gloucester's men soon discovered there was no way around them.

The *Lanercost Chronicle* paints a similar picture to the scene depicted by Barbour: 'When both armies engaged each other, and the great horses of the English charged the pikes of the Scots, as it were in a dense forest, there arose a great and terrible clash of spears broken and of destriers wounded to the death; and so they remained without movement for a while.' The image here is almost one of horses transfixed on the forest of Scottish spears. It was now becoming obvious that Gloucester's charge had failed, and however much his men wheeled their horses around, drew off and charged in, the outcome wasn't going to change.

This cycle – fall back, regroup and charge home again – would have been repeated until the men and horses wore themselves out, or were killed or injured. However, on the Earl of Carrick's left – if the battles deployed as we have suggested – the men of the Earl of Moray's schiltron continued to advance. Without the threat of enemy cavalry to face they engaged whoever they found in front of them – regrouping pockets of men-at-arms, fleeing archers, and probably the spearmen of Gloucester's vanguard. The confusion must have been incredible, and those behind the leading units would have had little idea what was going on. Those in the front rank weren't much better informed, as their attention was wholly taken up by the fighting that raged around them.

In front of Bruce's battle the fighting was reaching a climax. We might suspect that having repulsed the first wave of cavalry the spearmen edged forward again, stepping around the dead horses and men as best they could before the English cavalry launched another assault. Barbour describes the frenzy of the moment:

> Many a warrior strong and bold, headlong upon the earth was
>   rolled,
> Who never more should rise again, the Scottish men with
>   might and main,
> Were struggling to repulse the foe, and were prepared to
>   undergo,
> All pains and perils if they might prove victors in the doubtful
>   fight.

By now, though, the men of the English vanguard had begun to give up the struggle. They had fought as valiantly as they could, but as long as the Scots continued to stand firm there was nothing they could do. When they retired they would have tried to push their way past the men of the English main body behind them, clustered around the king. He had as many as 1200 fresh men-at-arms under his command, and from the sources it appears these men were divided into two divisions, presumably around 600-strong apiece. The trouble is that they were now hemmed in, and unable to charge. The whole situation was deteriorating rapidly for the English, thanks to the solidity of the Scottish formations and their ability to continue edging forward.

The schiltrons were slowly moving forward again, inch by bloody inch. Barbour describes the fighting in the Earl of Moray's portion of the battlefield:

> The Earl of Moray and his men, although they were not one in
> ten,
> From the hard conflict did not flinch, but drove the English
> inch by inch,
> Backwards before their spears; and yet, on every side by foes
> beset,
> They were so few they seemed to be, engulfed within a hostile
> sea.

Death of a firebrand

Clearly things were going badly for Edward. His men were being driven back, which would have created disorder, and this would in turn have spread to the ranks behind as men tried to push past them to escape from the fighting. Sir Thomas Grey claimed that the Scots 'attacked the English columns, which were jammed together and could not operate against them, so direfully were their horses impaled on the pikes'. The use of the word 'columns' is significant. The author of *Scalacronica* was a soldier, and didn't make mistakes when it came to things like troop formations. A unit of spearmen or even men-at-arms about to fight a battle would be deployed in line. If the same unit wanted to march, then it would form up in column, a long line of men of up to six or eight abreast.

This was a manoeuvrable formation, and to deploy it into line was simple. All the commander had to do was to wheel the head of the column through ninety degrees and march it off at right angles to the direction it had been marching in. The men would then be halted, and ordered to turn and face to the side. Then, if all went well, the column would have transformed itself into a line, ready for the coming battle. The problem here is evident. If the bulk of Edward's army was drawn up in column ready to march when the Scots attacked, then to fight effectively they had to change formation. This required space to wheel the column around, and in the carse that morning room to manoeuvre was in short supply. From Grey's account, it seems likely that most of the English army was in the wrong formation when the battle began, and never got the chance to do anything about it.

To increase the pressure King Robert now brought his battle forward, and placed it in line between those of his brother and the Earl of Moray. Not only did the Scots now present a long unbroken line of spears to the demoralised enemy, but the men in the centre of the line were still completely fresh and eager for the fight. Any gap that might have existed in the Scottish centre had now been filled, and the Scots continued to press forward, cutting their way through the increasingly disordered mass of troops in front of them.

By now the English vanguard had probably ceased to function as an effective battle, largely because it had been repulsed by the spearmen. With effective leadership the battle might still be able to regroup, and then launch itself back into the fray. This, though, was no longer possible, as the vanguard commander lay dead on the field. John of Trokelowe tells the story. After his first charge failed and after watching his casualties mount, the young and impetuous Earl of Gloucester decided to show his men how it should be done:

Wishing to win a name for himself, he presented an example to them as a bellicose boar. In the heat of anger he attacked the troops of the enemy, with their blood inebriating his sword. For whomever he struck with his sharp blade, he cut off a head, or some other limb. Finally, thirsting so for their deaths, the equilibrium of the battle was turned around to such a degree that the points of the lances being applied to each part of his body, stabbing several places, he was knocked to the ground, and his head was struck on all sides by the clubs of the enemy, until he breathed out his soul under the horse's feet.

Much of Trokelowe's bloodthirsty account might have been wishful thinking – a heroic warrior cut down after wreaking havoc in the Scottish ranks – and the suspicion is that the young nobleman's death came quickly, at the hands of a Scottish spear. The impact this had on Gloucester's men must nevertheless have been considerable. In an instant they had been deprived of their leader, the one man who could bring order out of the chaos they found themselves in. Trokelowe describes what happened next: 'Seeing him thus to be killed, all of the rest of his army [battle], gripped with fear, fled, alas, leaving their lord slaughtered on the battlefield.'

The trouble was, there was nowhere for these men to flee to. As the *Lanercost Chronicle* put it, 'Now the English in the rear could not reach the Scots because the leading division [the vanguard] was in the way, nor could they do anything to help themselves, wherefore there was nothing for it but to take to flight.' By way of authenticating his statement, the cleric then added: 'This account I heard from a trustworthy person who was present as an eye-witness.'

King Edward was losing the battle. By now – probably less than an hour after the Scots had begun their advance – the English found themselves in a near-hopeless position, and things were becoming steadily worse. The vanguard had been broken, and the English army had become a hopelessly entangled mass of troops. They were being forced back into their camp, which merely added to the chaotic mess. It was not too late to retrieve the situation. After all, the Scots were still heavily outnumbered, and Edward still had most of his men-at-arms at his disposal – men eager to prove their worth in battle. If only someone could halt the Scottish advance, that might buy enough time to turn the situation around. However, the remorseless step-by-step advance of the Scots continued. Only a miracle of some kind or a demonstration of inspirational leadership on the part of King Edward could now save the day. Neither would be forthcoming that morning.

18

Enter the Marischal

For King Edward the battle had now become desperate. He and his advisors – those who weren't elsewhere in the maelstrom of bodies – had to think quickly. They would have thought of the three building blocks of their army – spearmen, men-at-arms and archers, the rock, scissors and paper of fourteenth-century warfare. Clearly men-at-arms were unable to take on the Scottish schiltrons, however bravely the attacks were pressed home. The army's spearmen were barely holding their own against the Scots, as they were demoralised by the breaking of the English vanguard, and were standing in the wrong type of formation to take on an advancing enemy line. That left the archers. At Falkirk a decade and a half earlier English bow fire had carved great gaps in the Scottish schiltrons, allowing the men-at-arms to ride in and complete their destruction. With luck the same tactic would work again.

The archery gambit

Despite the rout of those attached to the vanguard there were still thousands of archers in the English army. While not the remorselessly efficient longbowmen of the mid-fourteenth century onwards, they still represented a potent force. If only they could work themselves free of the throng of soldiers, then they might still turn the battle around. Unfortunately, when the orders were issued the commanders of the various contingents of bowmen in the English main body found themselves unable to move. So, unwilling to disobey orders, it appears from Geoffrey le Baker's account that they gave the order to fire over the heads of their own men. With luck the arrow storm would fall on the ranks of the Scots schiltrons beyond.

One of the advantages of the bow compared to – say – the crossbow is that it can either be fired directly at a target in front of the bowman, or indirectly, a little like a round from a mortar. An arrow can thus be shot into the air, and if the archer has done his sums right it will fall almost vertically onto his chosen target. In this case the target was the heads, shoulders and backs of the Scottish spearmen.

Geoffrey le Baker claims however that the first volleys of arrows fell short, landing on the English troops fighting to hold the Scots at bay. Then, when the range was adjusted the arrows began falling beyond the English ranks. The problem here was that the schiltron was a fairly narrow formation. By now the three schiltrons might have been joined together into a line stretching for 800 to 1000 yards across the battlefield, but if they remained five men deep the whole Scottish line was a very shallow one. This meant that most of the arrows would have fallen beyond the spearmen, into the open carseland behind them, by this stage a landscape littered with the bodies of the dead and wounded.

The next option was to move the archers forward and have them fire directly into the faces of the Scottish spearmen. Unfortunately the English front line was no longer a cohesive formation. While most of the archers would have pulled away from the Scots, the front of the English line was now a mixture of spearmen, mounted men-at-arms and their companions whose horses had been killed beneath them. There was no clear line of sight. As a result the arrows struck 'few Scots in the breast, but [they were] striking more English in the back'. One can almost hear the howls of rage from the English combatants echoing down the centuries. If it happened then this 'friendly fire' incident was eventually stopped when the commanders of the archer contingents gave the order to cease fire. The likelihood, though, is the archers didn't waste their arrows without a clear target in front of them.

Whether this incident happened at all is open to question. Only Geoffrey le Baker mentions it, just as only John Barbour records the next attempt to use archery fire to stop the schiltrons. The fact that no other chroniclers mention either event, however, doesn't mean they didn't happen. The chroniclers relied on the testimony of others to supply details like this. Battles are often confusing, and the soldiers who took part might only be aware of what was happening immediately around them. Few would have had the 'big picture', unless they could view the battle from a suitable vantage point. Baker's description doesn't have a ring of truth to it, but it does sum up the desperation that was being felt behind the English front line.

The next incident is recounted by Barbour. Whether or not they were deployed somewhere behind the front line of the fight, someone had the idea of sending archers across the Pelstream burn. Once on its north bank they could shoot across the burn, directly into the flank and rear of the left-hand Scottish schiltron. While this mightn't have been a battle-winning gambit by itself, sufficient casualties might cause the schiltron commander – probably the Earl of Moray – to halt his advance. Once that happened the hard-pressed English might gain a breathing space, which would give them time to properly redeploy their army.

It is not recorded how many archers formed up across the Pelstream, or who commanded them, or whether they came from the English main body or rearguard, but the effect they had is described by Barbour:

> The arrows in such numbers fell, that whoso saw them might
> 	say well,
> That they a hideous shower did make, for where they fell I
> 	undertake,

They left behind them marks, which will severely test the
    leech's skill,
The English archers shot so fast, that, should the storm of
    arrows last,
The Scottish host would badly fare.

An interesting implication here is that arrows might not always kill a man outright. They were more likely to wound him, which given the medical practices of the time often amounted to the same thing. A man incapacitated through his wounds, was still one less spearman in the Scottish line. Either the arrow storm was stopped, or the left-hand Scottish schiltron would find itself falling apart like its predecessors at Falkirk.

Keith's charge

This, though, was a development that King Robert had already considered. He had a contingency plan in place – a small cavalry reserve under the command of Sir Robert Keith, the Marischal of Scotland. This was a hereditary title which had been bestowed on the Keith family since the late twelfth century. The job of the Marischal was to act as a senior military advisor – a chief of staff if you like – and Robert Keith had fulfilled the role since the death of his father in 1293. That means he served King John until his exile, and subsequently spent several years as a prisoner in Carlisle. On his release he returned to Scotland, and offered his support to Robert Bruce in 1308. He had remained a loyal supporter of King Robert ever since.

At Bannockburn Keith was given command of the Scottish reserve, a force of up to 500 mounted men-at-arms. They had remained hidden in the trees of the New Park during the first day of the battle and were still there now, while the fighting was raging in the carse. While this body of cavalry was too small to take on their English counterparts, they might be able to intervene in the battle if the odds were favourable. King Robert deemed that the moment had come.

In several accounts of the battle Keith's men are described as light cavalrymen. This almost certainly wasn't the case – they were probably every bit as well equipped and mounted as their English counterparts. The confusion comes from Barbour's use of the phrase (in the original medieval Scots), 'Fyve hunder armyt into stele, that on licht hors war horsyt welle.' The Macmillan translation of 1914 turns the phrase around, giving: 'Well mounted on their horses light, five hundred strong prepared to charge.' While this translation is excellent at maintaining the rhythm and timbre of the poem, it falls short when it comes to providing an exact translation.

Such a translation would read more like: 'Five hundred armed with steel, that on light horses were horsed well.' 'Armed with steel' means they were armoured, while 'horsed well' refers to the good quality of their horses and saddles. As we have seen, the word 'licht' can mean light, but it could just as easily mean 'nimble'. Light could refer to the size of the horses, or might simply be a poetic reference to their hue. Without more evidence than this one throwaway word by Barbour, the prudent course is to assume that Keith's men-at-arms were mounted on similar steeds to those ridden by their enemies.

As the battle developed Keith and his men had been watching from the safety of the wood, somewhere close to St Ninian's Church, or from behind King Robert's battle. Now he saw his chance to make a difference. He led his men out of the trees and across the Pelstream near the church, before riding down onto the carse on the north bank of the burn. There wasn't much room to deploy here, as Livilands Bog lay to their left and the burn to their right. Besides, there was no time for fancy manoeuvres. Keith's men-at-arms had probably moved down the slope in a long column. It was probably in this same formation that they launched themselves at the enemy archers.

The English bowmen would have been concentrating on the task in hand – shooting into the flank of the Scottish schiltron on the southern side of the burn. They probably failed to see Keith's cavalry coming until it was too late. The Scots men-at-arms barrelled into the exposed right flank of the enemy, and tore the formation apart. Those who could escape from the cavalry plunged back across the Pelstream into the packed throng of English troops beyond. Others weren't so lucky, and were cut down as they tried to flee. The whole action would have taken just a few minutes, but it dramatically altered the balance of the battle. The archery gambit had failed. Now the English commanders had no options left, or rather they had no ideas left that might help save the army.

Barbour paints a dramatic picture of the Marischal's attack:

Soon as he saw the battles go, in hostile strife together go,
And how the English arrows few, instantly, without more ado
Did forward to disperse them ride, and charged them fiercely
   from the side,
He and his men so rudely broke, the hostile ranks, with hostile
   stroke,
Of swords and lances laying low, the hapless wielders of the
   bow,
That in confusion every one, fled from the place, and there was
   none,
That dared again to bend his bow.

Sir Robert Keith's charge was a spectacular success, as it penned the English host inside the triangular confines of the Bannockburn and the Pelstream. While some historians suggest that Keith's men-at-arms then patrolled the north bank of the burn in order to deter a repeat of the English archery gambit, the likelihood is that they retired back the way they had come, and positioned themselves in reserve again, probably somewhere close to the small road at the foot of the Dryfield leading to St Ninian's Church. If they had remained facing the English army across the stream, the Scottish cavalry would probably have been shot at by any English archers who had the space to aim and loose their arrows. Nor were they in position to stop an important breakout attempt during the closing phase of the battle. The likelihood is, then, that they withdrew to reform, and to congratulate themselves on a job well done.

The only problem with Barbour's account is that he was the only chronicler to mention this important little action. Some historians have questioned whether the incident ever happened, and cite Barbour's desire to pander to Keith's important descendants. However, when he wrote the *Bruce* the course of the battle was still well known, particularly in court circles, and so it is unlikely he could simply fabricate such an important episode. The inference is, then, that not only did the charge take place, but it effectively sealed the fate of King Edward's army.

19

Slaughter in the Carse

The battle was now reaching a crescendo. The Scots were still pushing forward, bolstered by their reinforcement by King Robert's schiltron and by the end of the arrow storm. However, the battle was far from won. Victory and defeat still hung in the balance, although the odds were beginning to shift in favour of the Scots. In what was still a brutal meat-grinder of a battle the Scots were pushing the English back, but defeat for Edward's army was by no means inevitable. All Edward needed was a slackening of pressure, or a chance to alter the odds. The battle would continue, until it reached its sudden and dramatic conclusion.

Piling on the pressure

After the rout of their English counterparts the Scottish archers now returned to the fight. Having been forced back by the bowmen of the English vanguard at the start of the action, what remained of them moved up behind the Scottish line, and fired over the heads of their own spearmen. While the indirect fire by the English archers had been largely ineffective thanks to the thinness of the Scottish line, the Scottish bowmen were shooting into a tightly packed mass of men. It would have been almost impossible to miss. Barbour claims this return

to the action was inspired by the silencing of the English archers north
of the Pelstream:

> For when the English archers were cut down and scattered here
>   and there,
> Who, by their numbers ere they fled, inspired an overpowering
>   dread,
> The Scottish archers boldly thought, they might set all their
>   foes at nought.

While this shower of arrows wasn't a major part of the action, the
psychological impact must have been significant. If being packed into
a scrum of people with nowhere to move wasn't bad enough, waiting
for an arrow to fall from the sky would have been even worse. It helped
sap English morale at a time when the army was beginning to pull
itself apart. Still, whatever was happening behind them, the front of
the densely packed scrum of English troops continued to fight with
determination and bravery. What they lacked in organisation they
made up for in raw courage, and the fight raged on, with casualties
mounting on both sides. The danger for King Robert was that his men
might become too tired to continue the fight. As soon as the pressure
slackened on the English host it would be able to manoeuvre again,
and would uncoil itself before striking back with fresh energy.

After all, only a small proportion of the English army had actually
done any fighting – the rest were trapped behind them, without the
space to do anything other than stay where they were. The problem
of space was becoming even more acute. At the foot of the Dryfield
the gap between the Bannockburn and the Pelstream was about 1000
yards. A few hundred yards into the carse and that spear-shaped bend
in the Bannockburn reduced the width of the carse by more than 200
yards. Beyond that the carse narrowed further as the Bannockburn
looped north, until it merged with the Pelstream. From the centre
of this spear-headed bulge to the spot where the burns merged was

over 1000 yards, but after the Bannockburn began to flow north the carse became narrow. Now, given the likely place the Scottish line had reached – probably north of the spear-head – the eastern edge of the carse was just over 500 yards away. Beyond the burn lay the Skeoch bog, while to the north-east the flat, wet and increasingly boggy carseland ran down to the Forth.

In theory, 18,000 men wouldn't necessarily take up a lot of space. Just over half a mile north of the Pelstream burn stands the Forthbank Stadium, home of Stirling Albion FC. If you filled its pitch with soldiers, then you could fit 8140 men on it, giving them a square yard apiece. The ground's capacity is 3800, so a 12,000-strong army could just about fit itself into the space. The irregular quadrilateral of ground between the Scottish spearmen and the two burns was large enough to fit Forthbank Stadium into it twenty times over. While that suggests the English troops still had plenty of room, the truth was very different.

The same ground was occupied by hundreds of wagons, thousands of horses, several thousand camp followers and non-combatants, and probably the trampled remnants of tents, baggage, mobile workshops and sutler's stores, piles of provisions and personal possessions. There were also the occasional pools of water or small streams that dotted the carse. To fight effectively troops need to maintain a formation – anything which disrupted their cohesion would reduce their efficiency on the battlefield. Getting organised would have been impossible amongst all this clutter.

Most of the English army were in the wrong formation to start with, and the events of the morning would hardly have improved the situation. The conclusion is that space was now at a premium, and the Scottish spearmen were still pushing the English back. Every step backwards simply made the situation worse.

King Robert realised that his men seemed to be gaining the upper hand, and according to Barbour he called on them to redouble their efforts. The pace of battle was furious, and Barbour tried to capture the essence of it:

The Scotsmen, finding that the foe stoutly returned them blow
    for blow,
And did the struggle well maintain, laid on their blows with
    might and main,
Like men whose furious anger felt, such heavy strokes their
    weapons dealt,
As English armour could not brook, they cut all they overtook,
Beneath their battle axes' stroke, both head and iron headpiece
    broke.

This brutal exchange of blows and jabs, slashes and stabs was taking
place from one end of the battlefield to the other – some 800 yards of
violence, fear and death. While this wasn't a battle of attrition – Bruce
couldn't afford that – it had become a brutal grinding match, with
little finesse and even less glory.

A crumbling of resolve

Hand to hand combat with spear, axe and sword was exhausting
business, but while the Scots maintained their formation the English
did not – instead small groups of soldiers of various types formed the
front line, and therefore there was little overall control. At least
the Scottish junior commanders had the opportunity to rotate men
from the rear when they could, giving their men in the front some
relief from the fighting. While there is no evidence of this happening
at Bannockburn, it is a military technique used since antiquity. By
contrast the English soldiers in the front line had no such system in
place, and if they became too tired to fight their only option was to try
to slip back through the press of men behind them. Then it would be
the turn of someone else to stand and fight.

Some deliberately pushed forward to reach the front of the English
host. Men-at-arms in particular forced their way through in an attempt
to come to grips with the enemy. Others stayed where they were,

trapped in the carse by the men around them – it was later claimed that hundreds lacked the room they needed to even draw their sword. English men-at-arms who reached the front of the fight did so only to find themselves trapped there by the mass of humanity. Without the space they needed to manoeuvre or even turn their horse's head around they became easy prey for the Scottish spearmen.

Amongst these men-at-arms was Robert Clifford, the man who had been bested by the Earl of Moray the previous afternoon. Now he wanted to avenge that slight, even though he more than anyone would have known how deadly a Scottish schiltron could be. The *Vita Edwardi Secundi* records that Clifford 'was overcome by the Scots and died in the field'. When word of this was passed back, news of his death would have sent demoralising shockwaves through the packed ranks of English spearmen and men-at-arms. Clifford was the second of the army's senior commanders to fall within the space of an hour – and had been one of the few men with the ability to turn the tide.

While most of his men were still fighting as hard as they could, others began to push their way to the rear. Those little things – like being part of a unit, fighting alongside friends, the presence of leaders and the ability to hold fast – that determine the resolve of a soldier had been eroding steadily. Everything was beginning to unravel.

The Scots began to sense that the balance was tipping in their favour. Barbour summed up this new mood in a string of verses:

To see Sir Edward and his men, how they assailed the English
    then,
For well he led them to the fray, and warriors brave and strong
    were they,
The English army in the front, could not for long sustain the
    brunt,
Of such a furious attack,
But fearing for their lives, drew back.

A similar thing was happening in front of the Earl of Moray's schiltron:

> To watch Lord Randolph and his band engage in battle hand to
>   hand,
> Had seen them in that fierce turmoil, reckless of labour and of
>   toil,
> So that, where'er they turned their course, the English had to
>   yield perforce.
> Then many famous battle cries, rose bodily shouted to the
>   skies,
> 'On on', the Scotsmen cried, 'they fail', and once again they
>   did assail,
> More fiercely still and slew the foemen.

It was at that moment that a new battle of Scottish troops emerged out of the trees at the top of the Dryfield. At least that is what it looked like to many of the English soldiers. In fact these were the 'small folk' – the non-combatants and camp followers who accompanied the Scottish army, and who had remained in the New Park below Coxet Hill, a little rise above St Ninian's Church, a little to the east of the larger Gillies Hill. According to Barbour these men, women and children had been watching the battle from the safety of the wooded slopes, and like the soldiers in the carse they now sensed that the tide was turning. They decided to make their way down to the battlefield, where they could plunder what they could from the English dead.

If Barbour is to be believed these small folk carried improvised banners, in imitation of the soldiers they'd been watching. They also carried improvised weapons – knives, sticks, makeshift spears, whatever came to hand. During the past few days their job had been to keep out of the way, and to assist in the feeding of the army. Now they wanted to play a more important, and lucrative, role. Here, Barbour describes their advance:

'Twas thus that rabble rout appeared, as in great haste the field
    they neared,
And all at once began to cry, 'Slay, slay, upon them hastily'.

To English observers it appeared as if another Scottish battle had
appeared – fresh troops to add weight to the Scottish numbers, and to
finish off what their comrades had started.

According to Barbour, this was all too much for many of the English
combatants, who began to flee. Their only logical escape route was
across the Bannockburn, and so a slow but steady trickle of men –
almost certainly all infantry and non-combatants – began to push
their way through the mass of people and splash their way to safety.
Strangely, while Barbour makes much of the appearance of the 'small
folk', the other chroniclers don't mention the incident, and many
were looking for excuses to explain away the defeat. This, of course,
doesn't mean it didn't happen – just that it didn't have the impact on
the English army that Barbour claimed.

The rot, though, had most definitely set in. Still, the fight was
continuing, and still English men-at-arms and spearmen were working
their way to the front to play their part in the battle. One of these
reinforcements was none other than King Edward II. Accompanied by
his leading advisors, including Aymer de Valence, Earl of Pembroke,
he pushed his way through the throng of troops, and emerged in front
of the Scottish spearmen. This was a distinctly rash thing to do given
the circumstances, but it also conforms to the behaviour expected
of a medieval English king. He had to set an example to his men,
and conform to the high standards of chivalric honour and courage
expected of him.

By all accounts King Edward fought bravely. He had a horse killed
beneath him, and as he hacked at the Scottish spearmen his personal
shield bearer Sir Roger Northburgh was unhorsed and captured.
Now though, as the army began to waver, Aymer de Valence, Earl
of Pembroke decided to intervene. The death of the king would be

a national disaster, as it would greatly enhance the international standing of the Scots. However many of his nobles might have wished it, their king wasn't going to be put at risk. Worse still, he might be captured – an outcome that was looking increasingly likely. Not only would the Scots demand a king's ransom for his release, they would also be able to enforce peace on their terms – ones which included the safeguarding of their sovereignty and the recognition of their own king.

The Earl of Pembroke ordered his men to grasp the king's bridle and pull his horse away to safety. The *Scalacronica* describes the incident in detail:

> The English squadrons being thrown into confusion by the thrust of pike upon the horses, began to fly. Those who were appointed to the king's rein, perceiving the disaster, led the king by the rein off the field towards the castle, and off he went, though much against the grain. As the Scottish knights, who were on foot, laid hold of the housing of the king's charger in order to stop him, he struck out so vigorously behind him with his mace that there was none whom he touched that he did not fell to the ground.

His protests ignored, Edward was pulled back through the ranks and on towards the right flank, where most of the main body's men-at-arms were grouped. Placing the king in their midst Pembroke led them across the Pelstream burn, and then headed west along its northern bank. The king's escort consisted of half of the main body's men-at-arms, which – according to one source – had been divided into two groups. Each would have consisted of around 600 men, less those who had already forced their way to the front and died or been captured. It was a powerful force – one that could still make a difference in the battle.

Instead it regained the higher ground near St Ninian's Church, and then set off on the road towards Stirling. It is interesting that Sir

Robert Keith didn't try to intervene. Either he was somewhere else on the battlefield, or else he prudently thought the king's escort was too powerful to fight. Barbour – a great defender of the Marischal – is silent on the matter.

While the spiriting away of the king might have been the best thing for the long-term survival of the Plantagenet dynasty, it was a disaster for Edward's army. The flight of the king marked the end. Resistance collapsed as the English army ebbed away from the fight. For all practical purposes the battle was lost. Now it was a case of every man for himself.

20

Rout, Plunder and Capture

When the end came, it arrived quickly. The departure of King Edward had been noted by many of his troops, and those who hadn't witnessed his flight for themselves told those next to them. The presence of the king had bonded the army together, and despite the blows it suffered and the fact that it was being pressed back the army was still in the field, contesting every yard of ground. His sudden and very public departure from the field brought any sense of cohesion to an end. What had begun as a gradual trickle of people quitting the field gradually swelled into a flood. The lesser English commanders left on the field would have done their best to stem the tide and to organise some form of resistance, but it was now clear to everyone in the English army that the battle was lost.

After all, if the life of the king was considered in danger, then everyone else in the army was obviously at risk too. Worse still, when he departed he was accompanied by around a third of the remaining mounted men-at-arms. While this level of escort might have been considered necessary, it left a very big gap in the army's ranks. As long as the king remained on the field there was a clear chain of command. Now, with the death of two senior nobles and the departure of more who accompanied the king, the army was left without any evident commander. This came at a time when the remaining troops desperately needed good leadership.

The rout of an army

One of the few nobles to rejoin the fight was Sir Giles d'Argentan, who with the Earl of Pembroke had been responsible for getting the king to safety. His duty done, he decided to return to the battlefield. A warrior of such renown that he was regarded as the third greatest knight in Christendom behind Robert Bruce and the Holy Roman Emperor, d'Argentan had fought Bruce before at Methven, and had also won renown in Germany and the Holy Land. According to Sir Thomas Grey, before taking his leave he turned to Edward, saying, 'Sire, your rein was committed to me. You are now in safety. There is your castle where your person may be safe. I am not accustomed to fly, nor am I going to begin now.' With a final commendation of his king to God he turned his horse around and rode back into the fray. The *Scalacronica* continues: 'Then, setting spurs to his horse, he returned to the melee, where he was killed.' It was a heroic, glorious and futile end, one in keeping with the best traditions of honour and chivalry.

For almost everyone else that morning, self-preservation was uppermost in their minds. Now that the king had gone it was clearly acceptable to flee too – no accusations of desertion or cowardice could now be levelled at them. The problem facing these tens of thousands of English soldiers and non-combatants was how best to make their escape. The obvious direction was directly away from the enemy, but that was out of the question, as it led directly into boggy ground, and to the impassable waterway of the Forth. Escape to the north was a viable option – after all, that had been the route taken by the king. But he had done so escorted by a sizeable body of men-at-arms. Individuals taking the same route would either have to negotiate Livilands Bog, or else risk running past the flank of the Scottish army, to reach the road leading towards Stirling. That escape route was fraught with danger and could be blocked off at any time. Barbour agreed that neither of the two routes was viable:

> The English would no longer stay, by different paths they broke
> away,
> So hotly by the Scotsmen chased, that in their panic-stricken
> haste,
> They kept no order in their ranks, some, hurrying to the river
> banks,
> Threw themselves in the Forth, and there, most part of them
> drowned were.

The only remaining option was back across the Bannockburn. That had the advantage of being the most direct route to Falkirk, Edinburgh and the English border. The problem, though, was that just about everyone else in the English army had made the same calculation. Thousands of men and horses were pushing their way through to the burn and throwing themselves in. The burn was tidal, and there was no easy crossing point downstream of the ford where The Way crossed the burn near the start of the gully. Even today the Bannockburn might be just a sluggish stream, but it is still wide and deep – crossing it is a difficult proposition. It was even harder for panic-stricken soldiers trying to wade across it in such great numbers.

Inevitably men slipped and fell, and the banks would have become muddy and treacherous underfoot. Metal armour, helmets and padded brigantine jackets would have been cast aside, along with weapons and anything else that might slow the routees down. This same tidal wave of scared and desperate men would have fought to gain footholds on the far bank, and then haul themselves to safety. Barbour paints a grim picture of the scene:

> The burn of Bannock soon was filled, with all the men and
> horses killed,

Stepping on which, the waters broad, you may have passed
    with feet dryshod.

Meanwhile the victorious Scottish spearmen kept pressing into the
rear of the fleeing horde of English soldiers. While some would have
stopped to plunder what they could from the camp as they pushed
through it, most would have been caught up in the orgy of killing. The
rout of the English army may have caused a shift in the alignment of
the Scottish line. Before the English rout it had been advancing into
the carse, roughly in a north-easterly direction. There is a possibility
that when English resistance collapsed, most of the men in the
northern part of the field fell back towards the Bannockburn by fleeing
south-eastwards. The Earl of Moray's schiltron would have found itself
punching thin air, advancing into empty carseland. By wheeling the
line around towards the south-east it would be able to keep up the
pressure on the fugitives.

This ties in with a line in *Scalacronica*, which claims that 'The troops
in the English rear fell back upon the ditch of the Bannockburn.' If the
Bannockburn lay to their rear, then the English and Scottish lines
would have pivoted around as the English right wing collapsed. The
left wing was slower to follow, as the ground was thick with fleeing men.
John of Fordoun also mentions the chaotic scenes along the length of
the Bannockburn: 'A great many were drowned in the waters, and
slaughtered in pitfalls. A great many, of divers ranks, were cut off by
divers kinds of death, and many – a great many – nobles were taken.'

This reference to pitfalls has sometimes been taken as a reference
to the pits and ditches dug by Bruce's men, and therefore has been
seized on as a clue that these scenes were set further upstream. The
likelihood though is that the word here refers to the pools and small
rivulets which were found on the carse, or the boggy ground on its
southern bank. The suggestion here is also one of slaughter – the
English fugitives were slaughtered as they tried to cross the burn, or
when floundering through the ill-defined pitfalls. Barbour claimed

that many of the Scots doing the slaughtering were the 'small folk', who had reached the battlefield at the most lucrative possible moment for them:

> The rabble rout of striplings raw, ran to the Bannock, when
> they saw
> The English floundering in its bed, and without mercy smote
> them dead.
> It was indeed a piteous sight, of folk in such an evil plight,
> I never heard in any land, for on one side their foes did stand,
> Ready without remorse to slay, and on the other side there lay.
> The Bannock burn whose turbid course, was then so deep and
> full of force,
> That no one could across it ride, so they were forced there to
> abide.

For the Englishmen still trapped on the carse this was a grim development. With armed Scots on the banks of the Bannockburn their best avenue of escape was blocked. Their only hope now was to take their chances beyond the Pelstream burn, or else flee towards the Forth and hope to find a way to get across. Most men would have been unable to swim, but desperation and terror would have led many to try. Once more Barbour provides a vivid snapshot of the scene:

> And some were killed and some were drowned, none who fled
> thither safety found,
> However, as I heard men say, many escaped another way.

Their only other options were to surrender and throw themselves on the mercy of the Scots, or to fight and die where they stood. Surrendering was a sensible option for knights and noblemen: as prisoners they were extremely valuable, for they could be ransomed, even if their families paid heavily for their release. This usually meant leasing out lands or borrowing money, so when the prisoner returned home he would be considerably poorer and certainly no longer the proud warrior who had marched north under King Edward's banner. For the rest this option was a lot more dangerous. The Scots who captured them might decide to spare them, but it was more likely they would simply be slaughtered. Thousands were put to the sword as they tried to flee, or throw themselves on the mercy of the Scots.

One of the more fortunate prisoners was Sir Marmaduke Tweng, who had fought so valiantly at the Battle of Stirling Bridge. Finding himself trapped on the carse, he managed to wriggle out of his armour and hide himself somewhere on the battlefield. When, the following morning, he spotted King Robert, he rose from his hiding place and approached the Scottish king. Bruce greeted him, saying, 'Welcome, Sir Marmaduke – to what man art thou prisoner?' Tweng replied, 'To none – but here to you I yield, to be at your pleasure.' Bruce received his surrender, and not only gave Sir Marmaduke his freedom without any demand for ransom, but even gave him gifts to take south with him.

The battlefield secured, while some of the Scots pursued the men fleeing towards Stirling or Falkirk, others busied themselves looting the English camp, or stripping the corpses of the dead. The bodies of nobles, knights and men-at-arms provided rich pickings, particularly as most of the fallen had carried their money and valuables with them. The looters found gold and silver coins, jewellery and precious keepsakes, but the clothing, arms and armour of the dead were also extremely valuable, and would fetch a high price. By the end of the day thousands of corpses were lying naked in the midsummer sun, stripped of their dignity as well as their worldly possessions.

In the camp there was even more plunder to be found. Hundreds of wagons were ransacked, and a fortune in valuable gold and silver plate, clothing and ornamentation was found in the baggage of the English nobility. The *Vita Edwardi Secundi* claimed that goods in excess of £200,000 were taken – the equivalent of a minimum of £127 million today and probably much more, although the whole business of equating money then and now is fraught with problems. Many soldiers and 'small folk' established themselves for life on the basis of their Bannockburn plunder. For many fleeing Englishmen, though, this treasure was beyond worth. With so many Scottish soldiers and camp followers occupied in plundering the battlefield, the chances for these routed soldiers to escape were greatly increased. That is, of course, if they managed to escape through eighty miles of what had now become enemy territory, to reach the safety of Berwick.

The escape

When King Edward and his escort reached the walls of Stirling Castle they found that the drawbridge was raised and the gate closed to them. This was no act of treason by the Scottish-born garrison commander. Sir Philip Moubray was denying Edward entry for the king's own good. He knew that with the English defeat, the surrender of the castle was now inevitable. If the king insisted and took refuge inside its walls, then he would be captured by the Scots. It would have been a difficult few minutes for both King Edward and for Moubray, but eventually Edward turned and rode away. Before he did so, Sir Philip was able to give him some sage advice, suggesting that the king use the route he himself had taken when he rode out to meet Edward the previous day. After the events of that morning, this meeting must have seemed to have taken place half a lifetime ago, rather than the previous afternoon.

So, King Edward and his escort rode west, skirting around the New Park, Gillies Hill and the headwaters of the Bannockburn to avoid the Scottish army. Then they headed south, across the Sauchieburn to the Torwood, and then on to Falkirk. This though was only the start of the king's journey. By then a party of Scottish cavalry led by Sir James Douglas was on their trail, and it pursued the king's party as far as Linlithgow. Edward and his escort continued on to Winchburgh, a hamlet close to the modern site of Edinburgh Airport. After an hour's rest they pressed on, bypassing Edinburgh to reach Dunbar. It was an exhausting ride of about sixty-five miles, but the king completed it by nightfall. After being made welcome by Patrick, Earl of Dunbar the king sailed to Berwick, while his escort completed the journey overland. The life of the king was safe, even though his reputation was in tatters.

The *Lanercost Chronicle* is scaldingly critical of Edward's ignominious flight, saying:

> The king and Sir Hugh le Despenser and Sir Henry de Beaumont with many others, mounted and on foot, to their perpetual shame fled like miserable wretches to Dunbar Castle, guided by a certain knight of Scotland who knew through what districts they could escape. Some who were not so speedy in flight were killed by the Scots, who pursued them hotly, but these, holding bravely together, came safe and sound through the ambushes to England. At Dunbar the king escaped with some of his chosen followers in an open boat for Berwick, leaving all the others to their fate.

Then *Lanercost* records the fate of the remaining senior commanders in Edward's army:

> In like manner, as the king and his following fled in one direction to Berwick, so the earl of Hereford, the Earl of Angus, Sir John de Segrave, Sir Antony de Lucy and Sir Ingelram de Umfraville, with a great crowd of knights, six hundred other mounted men and one thousand foot fled in the other direction towards Carlisle.

The Englishmen decided to seek refuge in Bothwell Castle on the Clyde, and its governor Sir Walter Gilbertson welcomed them, but this was merely a ruse. He planned to switch his allegiance, and so he imprisoned the two earls and their party before handing them over to the Scots.

The chronicler goes on to report that Aymer de Valence, Earl of Pembroke – the man who spirited the king away to safety – collected a group of Welsh routees and marched them on foot all the way to Carlisle. Pembroke proved as competent a commander in defeat as he was in victory – one of the few English nobles to survive Bannockburn with their reputation intact. Other lesser nobles and knights were also taken prisoner as they tried to make their way south to the border. As the *Lanercost Chronicle* attests, 'Many were taken wandering around outside the castle and in the countryside and many were killed; it was said also that certain knights were taken by women. None of them got back to England unless in a miserable state.'

The great battle – the greatest of the Scottish Wars of Independence – was now over. Thousands of bodies were gathered up and thrown into burial pits – mass graves which so far have eluded the attention of archaeologists. It has been estimated that as much as a third of King Edward's army perished on the field – upwards of 6000 men. Of the rest, many more were captured or killed during the weeks following the battle as they attempted to flee southwards. Most, though, like Pembroke's Welshmen, formed themselves into large enough companies to dissuade local Scots from barring their retreat. In addition the army contained thousands of non-combatants and camp followers, very few of whom ever returned home alive.

Most of the foot soldiers came from Wales and the northern shires, so these counties would have felt the loss of life more than others. So too did the upper strata of English feudal society. The death toll of nobles and knights had been high, and the scars this left would take a decade or more to heal. As for the Scots, their casualties went unrecorded, save that Barbour mentioned the death of two Scottish knights during the battle. It had been a bloody affair, and the Scottish death toll would have been significant – possibly as high as 2000 men killed or seriously wounded. However, as no detailed records survive we will never know the true human cost of the Battle of Bannockburn.

It was clear to all who survived that something special had taken place over those two days of fighting. Before the battle began, King Edward II had been at the height of his power, having recruited one of the most powerful military forces ever seen in medieval Britain. By contrast King Robert I was a king, whose realm would only be united if he finally managed to remove Edward's men from Scottish soil. He was also a ruler whose subjects had still not fully united behind him. That all changed at Bannockburn. By the end of the fighting, Edward was the king on the run, while Robert was the monarch whose realm was united behind him. The amazing thing is that despite the brutal savagery of the battle in the carse, it probably took less than two hours to run its course, from Bruce's appearance on the summit of the Dryfield to the flight of the English king and the collapse of his army. It was not unknown at the time for a battle to continue for some hours, but there is nothing to suggest that this was the case at Bannockburn. Indeed, if the Scots took to the field at around 5 a.m., and the battle lasted just an hour or two, then it would have been over before the 'third hour' (9 a.m.) mentioned the chronicles. In that brief period the nature of Britain changed for ever, as the sovereignty of its two warring nations was defined in blood.

Understanding defeat or victory is seldom a simple matter of identifying one specific area of superiority or weakness, but there are several factors that we might consider crucial to the outcome of Bannockburn. There is no reason to assume that the English commanders were wilfully negligent or painfully ignorant, but they were over-confident. To some extent this was the confidence of a larger army faced by a weaker one, but the assumption that the Scots would fight a defensive battle along the lines of Falkirk and the success that Edward I had achieved there led the English commanders to believe that they were invincible. The Scots on the other hand, were confident because of their faith in King Robert and his subordinates, and they had been well trained. The English army fought because they owed service to their king, as did the Scots; but, crucially, the Englishmen didn't feel that their national sovereignty was at stake. They weren't fighting for their freedom.

21

A King in More than Name

The two-day Battle of Bannockburn was the most important battle of what became known as the Scottish Wars of Independence, and one of the most decisive in the combined history of the British Isles. Only the Battle of Hastings, fought two and a half centuries before, had a more dramatic impact on the geographical and political balance of British history. That said, King Robert's victory didn't end the war against England – that would rumble on intermittently for more than four decades. To steal the words of Sir Winston Churchill when he made a speech celebrating the victory at El Alamein in 1942: 'Now, this is not the end. It is not even the beginning of the end. But it is, perhaps, the end of the beginning.'

The forging of a kingdom

What Bannockburn really did was to alter the reason for the fighting. Before his victory, King Robert was a king in name alone, ruling much of but not his entire kingdom. The battle had been a huge gamble, as the stakes were so high. Defeat would mean the loss of much of what he had gained since 1306, in terms of the control of Scottish soil. He would probably have been forced back beyond the Forth, while King Edward re-established his grip on central and southern Scotland.

Victory meant that the situation was reversed. Within a year Edward would lose his last footholds in Scotland, with the exception of Berwick, which would remain in English hands for another four years. King Robert's control over his kingdom was secured at Bannockburn, or shortly afterwards.

This was thus no longer a struggle for Bruce's survival, or for the establishment of a Scottish nation. From Bannockburn on it was no longer a war of independence, but a struggle for recognition. Having secured their land, the Scots wanted their independence recognised by the world, and in particular by their English neighbours. Even more specifically, King Robert wanted the English to acknowledge his legal right to the throne. Everything that followed – the continuation of the war, the raids into England, the Declaration of Arbroath, the war between Edward and Robert's sons – it all centred on the formal recognition of what had been achieved at Bannockburn. That this took another fourteen years to achieve says as much about Scottish overconfidence as it does about English intransigence.

This, though, lay in the future. In the immediate aftermath of the battle the results appeared spectacular. First, the capture of the Earl of Hereford and his companions not only yielded a financial reward through ransom, but put King Robert in a position where he could negotiate for an exchange of prisoners. As a result Robert's wife Queen Elizabeth, his daughter Marjory and his sister Christina were all returned in exchange for Hereford, the brother-in-law of the English king. So too was Bruce's great supporter the elderly Robert Wishart, Bishop of Glasgow, who had gone blind during his long captivity. He would eventually die in Glasgow two years after his release. The Scottish king's teenage nephew Donald, Earl of Mar was also released, but during his captivity he had been well treated by Edward, and elected to remain in England. The return of King Robert's family and his loyal bishop must have been the sweetest fruits of his victory.

Other rewards included the surrender by Sir Philip Moubray of Stirling Castle, which was then slighted on the king's orders. A little over twenty miles to the south, Bothwell Castle was also handed over to the Scots, thanks to the opportunistic defection of Sir Walter Gilbertson. By year's end all of the remaining English strongholds in central and southern Scotland were under Bruce's control, including Jedburgh and Dunbar. Once Edward had fled, Patrick, Earl of Dunbar had acknowledged King Robert as his overlord, but while this saved his position and title, it didn't stop Bruce from slighting Dunbar Castle. Control of Scotland south of the Forth and Clyde gave King Robert a kingdom in more than name alone. He now had a realm, and controlled the full apparatus of government. While castles in themselves were of little use to him, the lands that surrounded them were vital if Scotland was to develop into a viable nation.

In England the shockwaves of King Edward's defeat reverberated through the realm. By the time Edward reached York he found that news of the great defeat had preceded him, and the countryside was seething with discontent. Bruce had proved magnanimous in victory, returning the English king's shield and privy seal, as well as the bodies of Lord Clifford and the Earl of Gloucester. This, though, did little to mollify the shock and indignation felt south of the border. When Edward held a parliament in York that September, King Robert sent a peace envoy to the gathering. He was rejected out of hand. Edward was still smarting from his defeat, but he also wanted vengeance. Besides, one of the criticisms levelled by the Ordainers was that he had lost the war in Scotland. Now that this had seemingly come true, Edward was in no position to make peace. To do so would play into the hands of his political enemies. So, for the sake of political expediency, the war would continue.

Now that he had secured Scotland, Bruce maintained pressure on the English king by invading the north of England. This invasion was a means of forcing Edward to the negotiating table, but it also reinforced the message that Scotland was secure – if the war was to continue, then it would be English lands that would bear the brunt of the conflict. The war would also be largely self-financing, thanks to the plunder and protection money the campaign would generate for the English coffers. These raids began in August, when the *Lanercost Chronicle* records that Bruce's men 'devastated almost all of Northumberland with fire', then extorted protection money from the bishopric of Durham, in return for sparing the bishop's lands.

The raids were repeated for several years, and Scottish raiding parties roamed as far south as Yorkshire. This, coupled with a long-lasting famine, caused utter devastation in England's northern counties. Carlisle was besieged, and in 1318 Berwick was recaptured, but still Edward refused to negotiate. Meanwhile Edward, Earl of Carrick had led an expedition to Ireland, hoping to carve out his own kingdom there. It ended badly for him – after defeat in the Battle of Faughart in 1318 his severed head was sent to King Edward as a present. Yet this was a sideshow. The real war was being fought in the north of England. In 1319 Edward led a fresh army north to recapture Berwick, but it dissolved without achieving anything when the northern nobles opted to protect their lands rather than serve their king. Finally in December 1319 the two sides agreed to a two-year truce. For the first time since his coronation, Bruce had brought peace to his realm.

A letter to the Pope

Having secured a temporary peace, King Robert had time to launch a diplomatic rather than a military initiative. It had the same objective – the recognition of his position and the sovereign independence of his kingdom – but this time the weapons were pens rather than swords. In April 1320 three letters were sent from Scotland to Pope John XXII in Avignon, all delivering a similar message. One came from King Robert, another from Scotland's senior clergy, and the third from the realm's nobles. Unfortunately only this third letter survives, so we have to assume the others were written in a similar vein. The letter sent by the nobles of Scotland is better known as the Declaration of Arbroath. Many modern Scots see this as a declaration of independence – a forerunner of the document signed by the American Founding Fathers in 1776. While it certainly emphasised that Scotland should be an independent country, there the similarities end.

For a start, it was a confirmation of Scottish independence, not a fresh declaration of it. Indeed it argued that Scotland had always been independent, that Edward I had attacked it, and that Scotland had the right to defend itself. It argued that King Robert was the country's rightful king and had delivered his kingdom from English domination. This document, signed by fifty-one Scottish noblemen, was in effect a piece of propaganda, aimed at bolstering Robert Bruce's status as the legitimate ruler of Scotland. What it didn't mention is how he had gained the throne. The Pope knew this – after all, Bruce had been excommunicated in 1306, on account of his murder of the Red Comyn inside a consecrated church. Now the Scots were not only trying to overturn this excommunication, but they wanted papal acknowledgement that Bruce was indeed their rightful king.

To justify this, the nobles claimed Bruce had been chosen as king by themselves – the representatives of the Scottish people – to protect the realm from English invasion. They also reserved the right to oust him if he failed to maintain the nation's sovereignty. This assertion was included because King John was not only still alive at the time of Bruce's coronation, but was a guest of the papacy. He had surrendered his sovereignty to King Edward I, so the inference was that Bruce was the man chosen to replace him. Even the stirring and oft-quoted passages about freedom and a refusal to be brought under English rule were intended to reinforce the same basic message – King Robert had defeated the English and won back the country's ability to govern itself. Now it was the job of the whole realm – king, nobles and prelates – to maintain that freedom.

This was heady stuff – and it still is today. While the document effectively justified the coronation of King Robert, and demanded papal recognition of his right to rule, it also contained a clear message about national identity. Scotland was more than just a land or a kingdom – it was a sovereign nation, with the strength to repel invaders and the skills to govern itself. This, of course, was a message that King Edward II refused to heed. While the long war between Scotland and England had begun over a claim of feudal overlordship, after almost quarter of a century it had evolved into a struggle for national identity – a war fought not for feudal rights but for national status.

An end in sight

Unfortunately the truce didn't last. In late 1321 the northern counties of England revolted against King Edward, encouraged by the earls of Lancaster and Hereford. The people were heartily sick of the war, and of a king who seemed unable to stop the Scottish raids. However, the rebellion was crushed, and both earls killed. Hereford fell in battle – a fate he had escaped at Bannockburn – while the Earl of Lancaster was beheaded. One of the worst charges levelled at Lancaster was that he had colluded with Bruce. Edward finally had his revenge on the cousin who had murdered his favourite.

Then, as he already had a powerful army at his back, King Edward marched into Scotland. The force that accompanied him was even larger than the one he led into battle at Bannockburn, but it achieved nothing, and eventually it withdrew back across the border. To add insult to injury the Earl of Moray and Sir James Douglas almost captured Edward during a lightning raid into Yorkshire, an attack that highlighted just how insecure the north of England had become. Lacking the resources and support to organise another campaign, Edward sent Aymer de Valence north to seek a further truce with the Scots. This would be Edward's last campaign in Scotland. It seemed his heart wasn't in it. However, he still steadfastly refused to recognise Robert Bruce as the Scottish king.

While the truce protected the north from Scottish raids, many saw it as a sign of weakness. Discontent continued to simmer, particularly when Edward recalled a new favourite from exile. As a knight, Hugh

Despenser the Younger had fought at Bannockburn and made his escape with the king. By 1321 the younger and elder Despensers had gained so much influence that the other nobles banded together to force Edward to banish them into exile. After the Earl of Lancaster's revolt was crushed the two Despensers were recalled, and this time there was no coterie of nobles to stand in their way. The only remaining royal advisor was the faithful Aymer de Valence, but when he died in France in June 1324 the last check on the Despensers was removed. Soon the duo would bring about King Edward's undoing.

In late 1325 Queen Isabella travelled to France, and the following October she and her lover Roger of Mortimer returned with an army. Her aim was nothing short of regime change. The nobles rallied to her, and the king and the Despensers were captured. While the father and son were executed, Hugh Despenser the Younger had been particularly detested by the Queen, and so he faced an especially grisly execution. King Edward was forced to watch, before his queen and her lover incarcerated him in Kenilworth Castle. The plan was to bring Edward to trial on a charge of incompetence – interestingly similar to the grounds the Scots barons cited if they ever wanted to get rid of King Robert. Edward though was spared a trial, as in January 1327 he abdicated the throne.

Isabella declared her son the royal successor, and he was duly anointed as King Edward III. He would prove a more competent king than his father, and one who was less willing to let the Scots live in peace. Edward was moved to Berkeley Castle in Gloucester, where on 21 September 1327 he died in mysterious circumstances. He was almost certainly murdered, but contrary to later claims he was probably strangled, rather than dying from having a red-hot poker rammed into his anus. The culprits – probably associates of Mortimer – went unpunished. The teenage king buried his father in Westminster Abbey, with full honours, and the long, unhappy saga that was King Edward's life came to its end.

In January 1327, as Edward III was being crowned, King Robert was leading an army across the border again. He knew that the young king's father had no appetite to continue the war, but the regent Roger of Mortimer needed to be discouraged from reviving the Anglo-Scottish conflict. So Bruce renewed it himself, in order to force the English to the negotiating table. After besieging enough castles to make his point he withdrew again. Mortimer responded that summer by sending Edward III north with an army, which failed to achieve anything in what became known as the Weardale campaign as the Scots refused to give battle. As soon as the English army disbanded Robert returned to besiege Norham Castle, the site of his grandfather's bid to become king.

It was there that the English peace envoys found him. Mortimer had realised that this costly war was achieving nothing apart from the financial ruin of England. So a peace treaty was negotiated, which gave King Robert everything he had asked for. For the first time since 1306 his right to sit on the Scottish throne was recognised by an English king. The English also abandoned any claims to Scotland, and the notion of English overlordship was abandoned. In return the Scots would pay a financial contribution of £20,000 over several years – a price Bruce could easily afford given what he had already plundered from England's northern counties.

The resulting Treaty of Edinburgh-Northampton was signed in Scotland on 17 March 1328. Six weeks later it was ratified by the English parliament in Northampton. A lasting peace had finally been achieved, as had everything King Robert had sought to achieve. It had taken fourteen years to bring about, after the great victory at Bannockburn. The road had been long and bloody, but for the Scottish king it had been worth the wait. This was a political victory on his terms – one whose groundwork had been laid at Bannockburn.

The final act of the new peace deal was a marriage – the union of Robert's heir David and Joan, the sister of the young English king. Although they were children of four and seven, the royal couple were duly married in Berwick in July 1328. Fourteen years before, the idea that the offspring of Robert and Edward would one day marry would have seemed utterly ludicrous. Now everyone who attended the wedding prayed that their union would finally draw a line under more than four decades of conflict.

Less than a year later the groom's father was dead. King Robert had been ill for some time. The *Lanercost Chronicle* claims he had contracted leprosy, but Barbour blames it on the effects of his time living in the hills, a fugitive in his own kingdom. He missed his son's wedding because of it – king or not, leprosy meant that you were treated like – well – a leper. Instead he retired to his new home at Cardross near Dumbarton, where he died on 7 June 1329. Like his old rival he was buried with due pomp and deference in Dunfermline Abbey, his body laid in a tomb of French marble. He left behind him a country at peace, one that was gradually recovering from the ravages of war. Unfortunately that peace wasn't destined to last.

A new-model army

It is sometimes said that armies only learn from their defeats. A long string of easy successes discourages military commanders from altering a winning formula, or even thinking too hard about other possibilities. A defeat, on the other hand, can have a silver lining to it. It encourages commanders to understand why they failed, and to devise ways to stop the same thing happening again. This certainly happened after Bannockburn. The two big developments in the years following the battle were the fall from grace of the mounted man-at-arms, and the rise of the bowman.

When the Anglo-Scottish War broke out again, the English would prove themselves a far more deadly force on the battlefield. Geoffrey le Baker claims that the English had been 'mostly accustomed to fighting on foot, imitating the Scots, ever since Stirling'. The *Lanercost Chronicle* says this development was first seen at the Battle of Boroughbridge in 1322, when the rebel Earl of Hereford was killed fighting a royal army. At the Battle of Dupplin Moor, which took place outside Perth in August 1332, the English men-at-arms fought dismounted, with their flanks protected by archers. This introduced the other big development. At Dupplin Moor the Scottish schiltrons were torn apart by English arrows – a result in stark contrast to that of Bannockburn.

The development of the longbow and the raising of men with the skill to use it effectively gave the English a distinct qualitative edge in missile power. Like the great bow of his father and grandfather's time, a longbow of the reign of Edward III was about six feet long, but the exact length varied to suit the height of the archer. Made from yew, hazel, ash or laburnum, these bows could produce a draw strength of around 80–100lb. While the effective range was similar to earlier bows – around 200 yards – the arrows they fired packed more of a punch. Modern tests show they could penetrate the mail armour of a man-at-arms at ranges up to 150 yards. What gave longbows their greatest edge was their rate of fire. A well-trained archer could loose a dozen arrows in a minute, and so a body of a few hundred archers could produce a deadly arrow storm which could stop any enemy in their tracks. This story was the key. The longbow wasn't so much about accuracy and penetration – it was about volume of fire.

Having first been tried out on the Scots at Dupplin Moor, these new weapons, skills and tactics were used again successfully the following year at the Battle of Halidon Hill outside Berwick. Thirteen years later the longbow proved its effectiveness once more at the Battle of Neville's Cross near Durham, fought in October 1346. During that battle not only were the Scottish schiltrons broken by arrow fire, but the English captured Robert Bruce's son, King David II. If this demonstration of the new efficiency of the English army wasn't enough, longbowmen mowed down the cream of French chivalry at the Battle of Crécy the same year. Ten years later the same thing happened at Poitiers. There is a good case for the argument that if the English hadn't lost Bannockburn, then they might well have gone on to lose the Hundred Years War before it had really begun.

Interestingly, after Halidon Hill the English not only recaptured Berwick, but went on to occupy Edinburgh and Stirling. The castles there were rebuilt, and once again central Scotland was occupied by an English army. It was almost as if Bannockburn had never happened. A contemporary English ditty captures the sentiment of vengeance the English must have felt:

Scottes out of Berwick and Aberdeen
At the Burn of Bannock ye were far too keen.
King Edward has avenged it now, and fully too, I ween.

The English eventually withdrew, and although the war would continue until 1357, for all their prowess on the battlefield the English were unable to summon the reserves of men, resources and will they needed to completely conquer Scotland. Through all those long years of defeat and national humiliation the Scots clung to one abiding memory. In 1314 they had inflicted a crushing defeat on an English army, and nothing could take that victory away from them. In theory, they felt they could do it again. That – the abiding collective memory of 'gubbing the English' – is perhaps Bannockburn's greatest legacy.

22

Bannockburn Remembered

Mel Gibson has a lot to answer for. *Braveheart* has been labelled one of the most historically inaccurate films of modern times, and the worst film to win an Oscar for Best Picture. Unfortunately it was a box-office success, and Gibson's portrayal of William Wallace as a kilt-wearing, woad-clad freedom fighter became the abiding image most people have of the period. It proved a great boost to Scottish tourism and created an upsurge of interest in Scottish history. Despite its numerous flaws, *Braveheart* was an emotive film, and tugged at the patriotic heartstrings. It is little wonder that Scottish Nationalist activists cashed in by leafleting audiences as they spilled out of Scottish cinemas. It has even been claimed that the film led to the establishment of a Scottish Parliament. This might be giving the outspoken and controversial actor-director more credit than he is due. Most Scots don't need an Australian to tell them about their own history, or how to interpret it.

North of the border, history seems to be more closely woven into the fabric of national identity than it is in England. Perhaps Robert Louis Stevenson made the point best when he said, 'For that is the mark of the Scot of all classes: that he stands in an attitude towards the past unthinkable to Englishmen, and remembers and cherishes the memory of his forebears, good or bad; and there burns alive in him a sense of identity with the dead even to the twentieth generation.'

There is more than an element of truth in this – it does seem easier to strike up a conversation about history in an Edinburgh or Glasgow pub than one in London or Manchester.

There is also an understandable resistance to accepting the 'Little England' approach to history. It's one that most modern historians have tried to avoid, but politicians – particularly Conservative ones – seem to regard it as the accepted view of the past. This blinkered approach to history is typified by former Prime Minister John Major, who once claimed, 'This British nation has a monarchy founded by the Kings of Wessex over eleven hundred years ago.' This displays the same arrogance that still regards Edward I as a good king, and holds that the Scots should have been more grateful he wanted to bring them into his realm.

Today this same viewpoint results in Conservative politicians espousing costly high-speed rail links designed to benefit London or to trumpet the end of a recession when anyone driving through Airdrie or Gateshead can see that isn't true. Sometimes it isn't only English historians who adopt this line. In an interview with the *Sunday Times* in 1992, historian Norman Stone argued that 'We Scots need [the English] because otherwise we would have slaughtered each other in a kind of ghastly turned-inward energy, which is after all the history of Scotland, pre unification.'

Fortunately historians are moving away from this approach. Historian Keith Stringer rightly claims that 'Thirteenth century Britain contained not one but two dominant states.' He argues that the pair of early medieval power blocs in Wessex and in Scotia – eastern Scotland north of the Forth – expanded in parallel, and ended up dividing the 'middle kingdom' of Northumbria (which once extended as far as the Forth) between them. This in turn made the full-scale conflict that became the Scottish Wars of Independence all but inevitable. He also argues that in terms of British history these wars ended in stalemate.

A similar welcome revision of history is reflected in the way the term 'English Civil War' has fallen out of favour, to be replaced by either the 'British Civil Wars' or 'The War of the Three Kingdoms'. Such terminology acknowledges that the conflict led to battles being fought from Sutherland down to Cornwall. Historians have been fighting back, and the Anglocentric tide is on the ebb.

When it comes to Bannockburn, there still seems to be a divide. You can usually tell the nationality of the author by their tone. From the fourteenth century on, one side has emphasised the battle as a heroic victory against the odds, while the other has struggled to explain why their army lost. Some English historians have even tried to justify Plantagenet aggression – for that's what it was – by portraying it as an attempt to create some form of benign and unified Edwardian realm, incorporating parts of France as well as the four nations of the British Isles. This flies in the face of the evidence that the period saw a steady increase in English domination over Ireland, Scotland and Wales, and that in some cases this developed into outright military conflict. It seemed as if the spread of English power throughout the British Isles was inexorable. In 1314 this Plantagenet juggernaut was stopped in its tracks.

If Edwardian aggression had succeeded, the history of Scotland, England and Britain might have taken a different path. In retrospect it seems hard to see how this could have happened. Not only did the Edwards balk at maintaining expensive garrisons throughout Scotland, but the geography of the country made it hard for them to exert a lasting influence much beyond the Forth and Clyde. Just as importantly, they failed to win the Scottish nobles over, largely because both Edwards essentially saw the Scots as rebels, resisting their rightful feudal overlordship. This whole overlordship argument is difficult to comprehend today, but at the time it was all-important.

Equally incomprehensible is the counter-argument given by the Scots, claiming that Scotland never had been subject to English overlordship. This argument was based on a mythical past, where Scotland had been founded by the Greek prince Gedyl-Glays, who married Scota, the daughter of the Egyptian pharaoh who was drowned when God parted the Red Sea for Moses, and then brought the waters crashing down on the pursuing Egyptians. The young royal couple travelled to Scotland by way of Spain and Ireland, bringing the 'Stone of Destiny' with them. Ludicrous as all this sounds today, in the late thirteenth and early fourteenth century it was the central pillar of the Scottish counterblast to Edward's claims.

For his part Edward claimed that Britain had been founded by Brutus, a Trojan warrior, who divided his realm between his two sons. The younger son was given Scotland, but owed fealty to his elder brother, who ruled England. This utter balderdash was actually trotted out as a justification for Edward I's claim of overlordship, and justified all that happened afterwards. Both English and Scottish clerics then linked these fables to the present, so that Edward Plantagenet and Robert Bruce were the latest in a long line of kings stretching back to these Greek and Trojan founding fathers. Even the Declaration of Arbroath of 1320 couldn't resist embellishing the tale, claiming that the Scots first came from Greater Scythia, and travelled to Scotland by way of Spain '1200 years after the setting forth of the people of Israel'. Medieval propaganda though it was, the point was clear – English claims are false, and we Scots have always been a free and independent people.

While, as we've argued, Bruce's victory at Bannockburn didn't end the war, it marked a historic turning point. After that King Robert's grip on Scotland was firm, even though its boundaries weren't the same as the Scotland we know today. Orkney and Shetland still belonged to Norway – something some islanders might wish was still the case – and much of the west coast and the Western Isles lay outside the authority of the Scottish king, and instead were governed by their own local rulers. Scotland, though, had survived its greatest period of trial, and would emerge as a reasonably stable and viable nation.

So Bannockburn was fought amid a propaganda war based on a mythical past. However shaky this bedrock of national sovereignty might be, there is little doubt that the period saw the clear emergence of a Scottish identity. Many have argued just how important such things were to the Scottish yeomen and farmers who made up the bulk of Bruce's army at Bannockburn. In 1992, in a study about Scottish identity, Andrew Marr made this point: 'It is impossible to analyse the nationalist feeling of the ordinary people, to pick over their nuances and discuss their quality. Unlike their shoes and cutlery, their unwritten thoughts cannot be excavated . . . All we can guess is that it had little to do with contemporary arguments about the nation-state.'

Marr's point is not that there wasn't a patriotic motive behind the willingness of Bruce's men to fight for him, and for their country. It was the fact that the Scottish kingdom they were fighting for wasn't an egalitarian place – it was a kingdom, organised on feudal lines, with the king, his nobles and his bishops dictating the agenda. This is in striking contrast with Robert Burns's vision of Bannockburn, and the strident communal patriotism of 'Scots Wha Hae', penned in 1793, just three years before the bard's death. It includes the lines

> Wha, for Scotland's king and law,
> Freedom's sword will strongly draw,
> Freeman stand, or Freeman fa,
> Let him on wi me.
>
> By Oppression's woes and pains,
> By your sons in servile chains!
> We will drain our dearest veins,
> But they shall be free
>
> Lay the proud usurpers low,
> Tyrants fall in every foe,
> Liberty's in every blow! –
> Let us do or dee.

While most Scots take this at face value – as a stirring patriotic call to arms – Burns was subtly linking Bannockburn to current events. The raging issues of the time were the proposed abolition of slavery and the French Revolution. Burns, a convinced Jacobin and radical, argues for universal liberty, while using the rhetoric of the Declaration of Arbroath, which first appeared in English translation fourteen years earlier. As Burns himself wrote, 'Scots Wha Hae' (originally entitled 'Robert Bruce's March to Bannockburn') was not just about Bannockburn, but was also 'associated with the glowing ideas of some other struggles of the same nature, not quite so ancient'.

The use of Bannockburn to underpin a more modern agenda isn't a new phenomenon, dreamed up by the Scottish government to celebrate the 2014 Year of Homecoming, a celebration designed to coincide with the independence referendum. In fact the various tourist agencies who serve the Scottish government have had great difficulty selling the idea of a 700th anniversary celebration of Bannockburn, complete with medieval re-enactors, new exhibits and patriotic pomp and ceremony. The trouble is, patriotism is easier when it's affordable – and this all-ticket event is priced too highly for most Scots, especially ones with families. This is in stark contrast to the 500th anniversary celebrations held in 1814 – the year Walter Scott's novel *Waverley* was published. Fifteen thousand people attended that commemoration, and it didn't cost them a penny.

It is no coincidence that the Scottish First Minister declared that the referendum on Scottish independence would be held in 2014, the 700th anniversary of Bannockburn. The Scottish National Party have used 'Scots Wha Hae' as their party song, to be sung at the end of every annual conference. While most of the time nationalist politicians studiously avoid direct references to the battle, other nationalist activists are less reticent – dozens of sites and videos available on the internet draw direct parallels, and some mix pictures of *Braveheart*-esque re-enactions with tirades against the iniquities of the English. For many Scots this is an unpalatably extreme form of tartan-clad patriotism, but the truth is that

Bannockburn and the events surrounding it have a special place in the Scottish psyche.

The celebrations in June allow these restraints to be lifted – for that brief window it is perfectly acceptable for First Ministers and Secretaries of State for Scotland to eulogise Robert Bruce, and to describe the emotional pull of Scotland's finest hour. Whether Scots will listen to a reborn Bruce in a suit and be stirred by a rallying cry for 'Freedom!' from the field of Bannockburn remains to be seen. They might also follow Roy Williamson's advice, slipped into the lines of 'Flower of Scotland': 'These days are past now, and in the past they must remain'.

The truth is, Bannockburn is not merely a historical backdrop for opportunistic electioneering and flag waving. Its impact on the complex relationship between Scotland and England has had a profound influence on the past seven centuries of national development, three centuries of which have seen the former protagonists stand together under a joint flag. In all probability it will continue to exert an influence for centuries to come. Whatever the outcome of the independence referendum, Bannockburn will still be seen as the defining moment of Scottish national identity long after the votes have been counted.

We all know that Bannockburn is an emotive battle – even more so than Flodden, the antithesis of Bannockburn as it was the Scots rather than the English on that occasion who had their dreams shattered on the battlefield. Bannockburn is more than just a battle, it is a national 'moment of destiny' – two days when the future of Scotland changed for ever. It is the centrepiece of our national epic – a story that encompasses Wallace, Bruce and this final climactic battle against the odds. Little wonder that politicians are keen to wrap themselves in Bruce's cloak, particularly when there's a referendum to fight.

Bannockburn, though – like all good battles – involved two sides. For the English, Bannockburn can be seen as a humiliating defeat, but in the popular consciousness it doesn't rank very highly – certainly less so than Agincourt, England's great medieval victory. However, just as it did in Scotland, Bannockburn had a profound influence on the course of history, both British and English.

It can be argued that without Bannockburn – or rather, without Scotland's survival during this period – then Britain would have been created four centuries too early, would have been a Plantagenet dictatorship where Scottish identity and culture were subsumed by an all-conquering English state. This didn't happen, and ultimately the English should be as happy about that as the Scots. Instead the two kingdoms were allowed to develop side by side, and when the time came to forge a union, it was one that was designed as a partnership of equals. That is perhaps the greatest lasting legacy of Bannockburn – the creation of two proud nations, rather than a flawed but unified superpower.

Today the existence of this union has been called into question, and the Scottish people – at least those who live within its borders – will get to vote on their political future. Politicians will use every weapon in their arsenal to convince you to vote for them, and this includes rewriting Scotland's past, in order to alter its future. Fortunately I agree with the sentiments of Robert Louis Stevenson, quoted at the start of the chapter. We Scots are a bloody-minded bunch, and are passionate about our past. Having read this book I hope you, the reader, will make your own mind up about what happened at Bannockburn seven centuries ago, and what these events mean to you. While Bannockburn may be the centrepiece of the Scottish national epic, we certainly don't need politicians to tell us what it means to us.

Scotland 1296–1314

- ✗ Battle sites
- ■ Principal Castles

0 _____ 50 miles
0 _____ 50km

N

ORKNEY

■ Skelbo

ROSS

Nairn ■

Tarradale ■ ■ Inverness ■ Elgin BUCHAN

Urquhart ■ MORAY ✗1307

LOCHABER ✗1308 ■ Aberdeen
  Kildrummy

■ Inverlochy

THE MEARNS

Forfar
■

Dunstaffnage Scone ■ Dundee
■ •
✗ 1308 1306 ✗ Perth
ARGYLL St Andrews

✗ 1297
Stirling ■
Dumbarton ■ 1314✗ Dunbar
ISLAY Rutherglen • ✗ ■ ✗
  1298 Edinburgh 1296

Bothwell ■ LOTHIAN Berwick ■

Irvine • ✗ 1307 Roxburgh ■
Rathlin ■ Ayr ■ Douglas ■ Jedburgh
  Dunaverty Selkirk Forest

■ Turnberry Dumfries
CARRICK ■
GALLOWAY ■ Caerlaverock Newcastle ■

IRELAND Wigtown ■ Buittle ■ Carlisle
  Burgh by Sands

ISLE OF MAN

For the sake of clarity this map omits the topography of medieval Scotland – for the most part the areas where castles aren't marked was rugged high ground, and largely impassable to medieval armies. That is why these castles were so important, not just for holding ground but to serve as administrative centres for Scotland's towns and rural communities.

Edward's Route to the Battlefield 17-23 June 1314

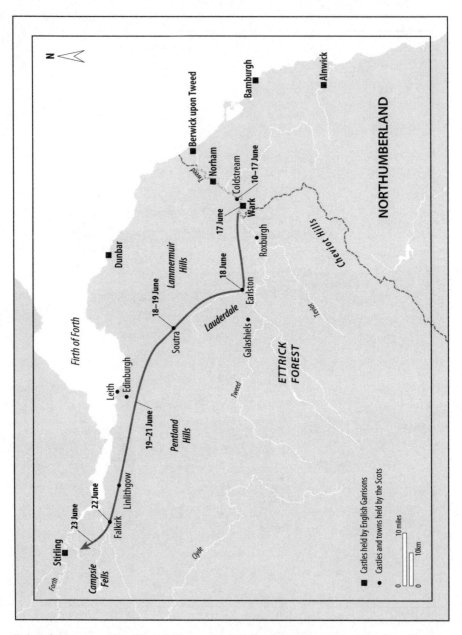

Before the invasion, King Edward II's army was clustered in a string of encampments along the southern bank of the Tweed. His choice of an inland route rather than a coastal one was made to accommodate the large convoy of supply wagons which followed the army as it marched into Scotland. As the Scots were likely to burn crops and destroy provisions in his line of march, Edward insisted that his army be entirely self-sufficient. A fleet of supply ships was sent ahead to Leith, to replenish these provisions when the army reached Edinburgh.

The Battlefield 23-24 June 1314

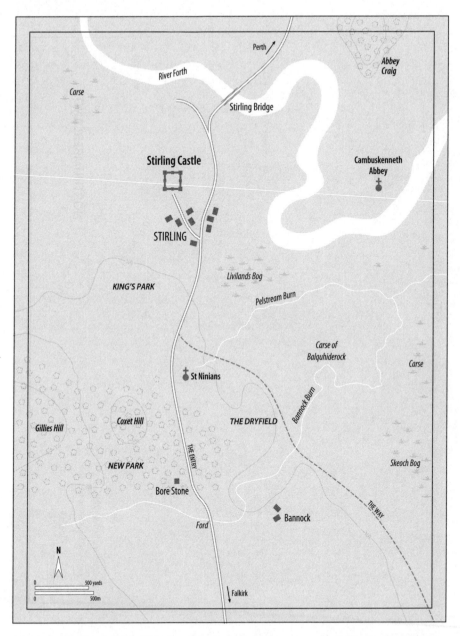

The lie of the land south of Stirling largely dictated the course of the battle. By deploying his army in the New Park, King Robert left King Edward with two choices – a frontal assault across the Bannockburn or a move to the right, onto the open carseland to the north of the burn. Effectively the battle was fought in three locations – the two skirmishes on 23 June took place near the Ford and St. Ninians, while the main battle of 24 June began on the slopes of the Dryfield, and reached its bloody conclusion in the Carse of Balquhiderock.

Notes

Prologue

p.xiii **Robert Clifford had met his match** This account of the action is based upon *Scalacronica* (Laing, 2000) and *The Bruce* (Mackenzie, 1912, Duncan, 1997)

p.xv **As he advanced** A more detailed description of the terrain can be found in Chapter 13 'The Field of Battle'

p.xvi **Sir Thomas wasn't so sure** *Scalacronica* iii, 73-75

p.xvi **The schiltron was a uniquely Scottish battle formation** For descriptions of the schiltron (also schiltrom) see Armstrong 29, Caldwell 33 and Brown (2008) 163-176

Chapter 1 Gubbing the English

p.4 **The long string of Scottish defeats** The battles of the Second Scottish War of Independence are described in DeVries (1996) 112-128, 176-187, Reid (2007) 114-144, Traquair (1998) 261-263, 269-271. The two 16th century battles are outlined in Caldwell (1998) 58-61, 71-72

Chapter 2 Interregnum

p.8 **This depressing train of events** *Scotichronicon* (Watt) 402-413, Traquair 15-17 p.9   According to the *Lanercost Chronicle*   *Lanercost* (Maitland) 106-108

p.11   **After the death of his son**   *Scottish Historical Documents* [SHD] (Donaldson) 37-38

p.12   **Bruce also strengthened his political hand**   *Documents* (Stevenson, 1870) i, no. 12

p.14   **The Scottish contingent**   Ibid i, no. 75

p.15   **In March 1290**   SHD 38-39

p.15   **The final version of the Treaty of Birgham**   Ibid 40-41, *Documents* i, 108

p.15   **While all this had been going on**   *Documents* i, no. 103, 107

Chapter 3 The Great Cause

p.18   **As a history graduate in Aberdeen**   My Scottish history tutor there was Dr Grant G. Simpson, an authority on this period. I owe the long-suffering chap a debt of gratitude

p.19   **The hearing was convened in Norham**   *Calendar of Documents relating to Scotland* [CDS] (Bain) ii, no. 470, Brown (2004) 166-168, Duncan (1975) 207-230

p.20   **This agreement became known**   SHD 43-44

p.20   **He immediately set about**   Watson (1998) 16-17

p.20   **When the court reconvened**   Traquair 27-28

p.22   **Of the remaining six**   Stones & Simpson (1979) covers the legal development of the Great Cause in detail, and its argument forms the basis of this chapter

p.23   **That was followed by a vote**   Stones & Simpson (1979) i, 21-23, Barrow (2013) 65-66

Chapter 4   Toom Tabard

p.25   **John Balliol was crowned king**   Brown (2004) 169, Barrow 66

p.26   **After 'The Great Cause'**   APS (Thomson & Innes, 1814-75) i, 449, Barrow 63 p.27   **In September 1293**   *Documents* i, 317, 319-320

p.28   **In the autumn of 1295**   Macdougall (2001) 19-20

p.28   **The resulting Treaty of Paris**   SHD 45-46, *Lanercost* 115-116

p.29   **Pope Celestine V**   *Chronicle* (Rothwell, 1957) 243, 270, Barrow 83

p.30   **In fact John did respond**   Traquair 48-49

p.30   **Edward's army crossed the Tweed**   *Documents* ii, 25-32   For details of the Bruces' involvement see CDS ii, 718, 723

p.31   **Berwick fell in a matter of minutes**   *Scalacronica* (Maxwell, 1907) iii, 18, Traquair 46-47

p.32   **The Lanercost chronicler recorded a ditty**   *Lanercost* 136, CDS ii, 742, *Fordun* (Laing, 1872) ii, 318

p.33   **The final humiliation came the following day**   *Lanercost* 138-145, *Fordun* ii, 317-320, *Documents* ii, no. 152

Chapter 5   The Wallace

p.34   **In fact even Blind Harry accepts**   Blind Harry incorrectly gives Wallace's father as Sir Malcolm Wallace of Elderslie. A surviving seal on a letter from Wallace sent to Lübeck in 1297 cites his father as Alan Wallace. A copy now resides in the Mitchell Library, Glasgow. For a detailed discussion of this evidence see Mackay (1995) 13-23, Brown (2005) 48-49. Also see *Fordun* ii, 321

p.35   **In the account given by Sir Thomas Grey**   *Scalacronica* iii, 219

p.35   **Moray at the time**   CD ii, 922. Also see Traquair 65

p.36   **These two experienced commanders marched north** *Documents* ii, 198-200, 202

p.37   **By mid-July they were in Aberdeenshire** CDS ii, 742, *Chronicle* 297, *Documents* ii, 175

p.38   **When the Scots arrived**   This account of the Battle of Stirling Bridge is based on *Chronicle*, 299-306, CDS ii, nos. 1462, 1470, *Lanercost* 163-165, *Fordun* ii, 322. Also see Barrow 114-115, Traquair 74-77, Mackay 139-153, Watson 48-49 p.41   **He had about 25,000 foot soldiers**   Traquair 81-82

p.41   **On 22 July 1298 Wallace was encamped**   This account of the battle of Falkirk is based on *Scotichronicon* vi, 86-89. Also see Brown (2004) 186-187, Watson 61-67, Barrow 99-103, Traquair 83-84

p.43   **The victorious Edward continued on to Stirling Castle** *Chronicle* 328-329

Chapter 6   Rivals and Guardians

p.45   **In August the Scottish nobles and prelates met again** *Documents* ii, 301-305, 431, CDS ii, 1978.

p.46   **Pope Boniface VIIII issued a papal bull**   Traquair 97

p.46   **In May Bruce resigned**   Barrow 150

p.0   **King Edward passed through Selkirk and Peebles**   CDS ii, 1047-1148, 1159

p.47   **Philip IV had his own problems**   The account of the Battle of Courtrai is drawn from DeVries 9-22

p.48   **Alarmed by the notion that**   Barrow 160

p.49   **In late February Segrave was attacked near Roslin**   *Documents* ii, 448, *Fordun* ii, 326-328

p.49   **He then marched to Perth**   Details of Edward's campaign can be found in *Lanercost* 171-172, *Fordun* ii, 325-328. Also Watson 120-133, Brown (2004) 194-195, Traquair

p.51   **The surrender talks began on 19 January**   Barrow 127, Watson 181-194

p.51   **No fewer than thirteen great trebuchets**   CDS ii, 1475, 1498-1500

p.53   **Wallace was taken to London**   Brown (2004) 197, Traquair 193-195, Mackay 260-266

Chapter 7   From Murderer to Monarch

p.54   **We don't know exactly what happened**   *The Bruce* (Duncan, 1997) v, 78-81, *Chronicle* 367, *Scalacronica* 28. Also Barrow 146-148, Traquair 126-127 p.55   **Bruce used the opportunity to lobby**   *The Bruce* v, 70, Watson 215-216, Brown (2004) 199

p.56   **In September 1305**   *Documents* ii, 1588, 1604

p.58   **He called upon his supporters and followers**   CD ii, no. 1834, Barrow 191-192

p.59   **So, over a number of meetings**   *Documents and Records* (Palgrave, 1837) 335-336, *The Bruce*, 21

p.60   **The inauguration was held on 23 March 1306**   *Chronicle* 367, *Documents and Records* 319, *Scalacronica* 130, *Flores Historiarum* (Luard, 1890) iii, 324. Also Barrow 195-196, Traquair 133

p.61   **It was claimed that when his fury**   This version of Edward I's reaction is one of several versions – it is also claimed it was his son Prince Edward who made the vow about not sleeping two nights in the same place. See Penman 66, Barrow 198 for a less dramatic version of Edward's response

Chapter 8   The King in the Heather

p.62   **De Valence raised a small force**   CDS iii, 1756, 1782, 1787, Duncan (1975) 125-151

p.64   **The so-called Battle of Methven**   CDS ii, 1807. Also Barrow 150-161, Duncan 130-138, Brown (2004) 201

p.64   **In the fight that followed**   CDS iii, 1810, *Fordun* i, 342, *The Bruce* vii, 35, Barrow 207-208

p.65   **Edward shipped them south to Berwick**   *Chronicle* 367, *Documents and Records* 358-359, *Scalacronica* 130, *Flores Historiarum* iii, 324. Also Barrow 195-196, Traquair 133

p.66   **Two months later John, Earl of Atholl was hanged**   *Chronicle* 309, *Scalacronica* 131, *Flores Historiarum* iii, 134-135.

p.66   **By that time Bruce was either on little Rathlin Island**   CDS ii, 1833, iii, 502, Barrow 212. In fact there is no clear evidence where Bruce and his followers spent the winter. Rathlin is the most likely candidate, but other suggestions include Islay, Orkney and even Norway p.67   **They sailed into Loch Ryan on 9 February**   Traquair 144-145

p.67   **Unfortunately for Bruce the local village**   CDS ii, 1896

p.68   **In March 1307**   *The Bruce* vii, 488-635, Duncan 138, Traquair 145-146

p.70   **There, on 10 May**   *The Bruce* 161-201, 282-309, *Chronicle* 378, Duncan 138

p.70   **Edward died at Burgh-on-Sands**   CDS iii, no. 1926

p.70   **At the end of July Edward marched**   Traquair 150

Chapter 9   King Hobbe's War

p.72   **In the chronicle known as the *Vita Edwardi Secundi*** Denholm-Young (1957) 12-13

p.73   **His appearance in Kintyre**   *The Bruce* viii, 310-335, Duncan 142-144, Barrow 174-178

p.74   **Before Christmas he signed a truce**   Barrow 175-177

p.75   **Barbour claimed the sickness**   *The Bruce* ix, 57-59, *Fordun* iii, 336

p.76   **He had been reinforced by a contingent**   *The Bruce* ix, 231-232. For a detailed account of the battle see Marren (1990) 70-74

p.76   **John Barbour, an almost sycophantic admirer**   *The Bruce*, ix, 294-300

p.78   **As Bruce approached the head of Loch Awe**   *The Bruce* ix, 360-367, *Scotichronicon* vi, 244, Barrow 178-181

p.78   **So, when King Philip of France**   CDS iii, 114, 138

p.79   **The relief force was led by Edward's new commander**   *Lanercost* 189

p.80   **By September a large army had gathered**   CDS iii, 177

p.82   **So, between his raids into England**   Traquair 169

p.82   **In January 1313 it was the turn of Perth**   *The Bruce* ix, 348-351, 390-400, CDS iii, 299, 339, v, 566, *Lanercost* 202, *Fordun* ii, 338

Chapter 10   In the Shadow of Longshanks

p.85   **The scene was a crowded Westminster Abbey**   This account of the coronation is drawn from Jones (2012) 362-366, supported by *Vita Edwardi Secundi* 4-6

p.86 **Piers Gaveston had first appeared at court as a teenager** *Vita Edwardi Secundi* 3, Jones 359

p.87 **As Edward's chronicler put it** *Vita Edwardi Secundi* 1-2

p.88 **Described as a strong, handsome and athletic youth** *Vita Edwardi Secundi* 2, Traquair 158

p.89 **In July though, he reached an agreement** *Vita Edwardi Secundi* 6-7, *Scalacronica* iii, 457

p.91 **The Ordainers rose in rebellion** *Vita Edwardi Secundi* 20-22, Jones 370-373, Traquair 160-161

p.91 **On 19 June 1312 he was dragged to a nearby hill** *Lanercost* 219, Jones 374-378

p.92 **Parliament also agreed to the funding of a new campaign** CDS iii, 337, *The Bruce* ix, 376-404, Duncan 131, Barrow 267-268

Chapter 11 The March on Stirling

p.93 **In 1250 the monk Matthew Paris** Paris was a monk in the Abbey of St Albans, whose magnum opus was the *Chronica Major*, a history of the world from the creation onwards. His map of Britain was designed to accompany this work, and is now in the collection of the British Library (British Library Cotton MS Claudius D.vi, f.12v)

p.94 **Linlithgow fell by trickery** *Lanercost* 204, *The Bruce* x, 182-90. For the fall of Roxburgh see *The Bruce* x, 196-258

p.95 **Three weeks later it was the turn of Edinburgh Castle** *Scalacronica* iii, 458, Traquair 175

p.97 **He proposed a deal** Fordun ii, 339, *The Bruce* x, 377-403, Duncan 149-150, Traquair 175

p.97 **In November Edward set the whole thing in motion** Barrow 267, Duncan 131, Traquair 174

p.99 **The expedition finally crossed the border** CDS iii, 365, *The Bruce* x, 410-519, *Vita Edwardi Secundi* 50, Brown (2004) 208, Barrow 203-232 p.99   **According to the chronicler** *Vita Edwardi Secundi* 50-52. Also see *The Bruce* xi, 201-204

p.100   **Robert had used the time wisely**   *The Bruce* xi, 195-197

Chapter 12   Raising an Army

p.105   **John Barbour's epic poem** *Bruce*   *The Bruce* (Mackenzie, 1912) xi, 159-164. Also see xi, 105-117 for an even more colourful description of the size of Edward's army. The Scottish numbers are given in xi, 240-244. Also see Andrew of Wyntoun (Laing, 1872-79) iii, 336, *Liber Pluscardensis* (Skene, 1877) i, 183, *Vita Edwardi Secundi* 50

p.106   **The** *Vita Edwardi Secundi* **beefs up the Scottish numbers** *Vita Edwardi Secundi* 50

p.107   **A battle was a medieval term**   DeVries 1-8, Armstrong (2002) 26-27, Brown (2008) 181-184

p.107   **In fact two more divisions**   *The Bruce* xi, 425-431, 460-464, xiii, 48-57, 228-246

p.109   **The most important troop type**   Reese (2000) 61-62, Brown (2008) 152-162, Cornell (2009) 143-144. Also see Coss (1993) and Strickland (1998) for a detailed study of 14th century men-at-arms.

p.111   **The evidence for this stems**   *The Bruce* xiii, 54

p.111   **At Bannockburn, most of the men**   Brown (2008) 163-176, Reese (2000) 63-64. See also Prestwich (1999) for a detailed examination of the capabilities of medieval infantry

p.113   **After all, archers had proved highly effective**   Reid (2007) 145-170, 191-215. See also Brown (2008) 176-179

p.114   **But we do know rank structures existed**   Brown (2008) 179-180

Chapter 13   Field of Battle

p.118   **Its late as 1924, the deeply respected military historian** Oman (1924) was actually a reprint of an earlier study of 1905, reprinted in 1913, but it was his amended 1924 account that exerted the greatest influence on the popular perception of the battle

p.119 **Written by Mackay Mackenzie** Mackenzie (1913) and Miller (1914) continued the argument over the site of the battle for the best part of two decades. However, they were unable to alter the general perception that Oman was right and they were not

p.119 **In 1959 Sir Philip Christison** As a military man Christison was given great credence, and was influential in the way the National Trust for Scotland interpreted and sited the battle. He argued that while the main battle on the 24th June was fought to the north-east of the proposed visitor centre, the land around the Bore Stone where this was sited was close to The Entry – the road leading into the trees of the New Park from the ford. This therefore places it in the approximate vicinity of the fighting on 23rd June

p.119 **The next big development** This report – Watson & Anderson (2001) was commissioned to solve Stirling Council's problems – by selecting one of the rival battlefield sites the council would be free to develop other potential building sites in the area. While the report favoured the Dryfield, it was unable to rule out the possibility that other locations were also viable

p.121 **In Geoffrey le Baker's *Chronicon*** (Thompson, E.M. (ed.), Oxford, 1889) 7-8, cited in DeVries 72-73. Also see *The Bruce* xi, 365-378

p.122 **That was just how Walter Bower** *Scotichronicon* vi, 370-373. Morris (1914) describes 19th century excavation of these obstacles

Chapter 14   Clash of Vanguards

p.124 **As Barbour put it** *The Bruce* ix, 361-364

p.125 **The *Vita Edwardi Secundi* mentions** *Vita Edwardi Secundi* 51

p.125 **James Douglas and Robert Keith** *The Bruce* ix, 459-464

p.125 **The English host soon met their sight** *The Bruce* (Mackenzie, 1912) ix, 465-474

p.125 **According to Barbour** Ibid ix, 487-490

p.126   **The said King of England**   *Scalacronica*, reprinted in Brown (2004) 23

p.127   **The sources are a little unclear**   Ibid 23, *Lanercost*, reprinted in Brown (2003) 64

p.127   **If we agree with the evidence**   A copy of the relevant William Roy map can be found in the collection of the National Library of Scotland. An original is in the collection of the British Library

p.128   **According to the *Vita Edwardi Secundi***   *Vita Edwardi Secundi* 51

p.128   **According to Barbour others followed him**   *The Bruce* xii, 34

p.129   **Now when Sir Henry was aware**   *The Bruce* (Mackenzie, 1912) xii, 43-60

p.130   **In the *Scalacronica,* this attack is described**   *Scalacronica*, reprinted in Brown (2004) 23

p.131   **The Scottish warriors glad to see**   *The Bruce* (Mackenzie, 1912) xii, 75-84

Chapter 15   Beyond the Bannockburn

p.134   **Two sources mention the way Clifford**   *Scalacronica, Lanercost* (both Brown, 2004) 23, 64

p.135   **The battle that followed**   *Scalacronica* (Brown, 2004) 23-24

p.136   **The Scots did not interfere until they**   *Lanercost* (Brown, 2004) 64

p.136   **Barbour implies the Earl of Moray**   *The Bruce* xii, 544-551

p.140   **According to Friar William Baston who was there**   *Scotichronicon* vi, 367-375

p.140   **They themselves as comfortable as they could**   *Scalacronica* (Brown, 2004) 24

p.140   **Friar Baston may have exaggerated**   *Scotichronicon* vi, 368

p.140   **The only place this is mentioned is in Barbour's *Bruce***   *The Bruce* xiii, 488-500. Also see Brown (2008) 259-260

Chapter 16 Dawn Attack

p.143 **Sir Thomas Grey claims he said** *Scalacronica* 142

p.143 **Then they prepared for battle** *The Bruce* xii, 407-409

p.143 **As the *Scalacronica* confirms** *Scalacronica* 142

p.144 **King Robert was dismounted** *Chronica et Annales* (Riley, 1866) 84

p.144 **The *Vita Edwardi Secundi* records how good** *Vita Edwardi Secundi* 52

p.144 **The three battles consisted** Several modern accounts of the battle claim there were four Scottish battles, adding the one Barbour claims was commanded by Walter Stewart and Sir James Douglas during the battle (*The Bruce* xi, 326-340). However, this is at odds with the other sources, including *Lanercost* 225 and *Chronica et Annales* 84

p.146 **Barbour claims that Sir Ingram de Umfraville** *The Bruce* xii, 445-476

p.146 **For a moment though, as the Scots knelt to pray** Ibid xii, 477-490

p.147 **Grey claims the English cavalry** *Scalacronica* (Brown, 2004) 24

p.147 **Barbour writes, 'The English van, in martial pride'** *The Bruce* (Mackenzie, 1912) xii, 498-499

p.148 **In the *Lanercost Chronicle*, these archers** *Lanercost* (Brown, 2004) 64

p.148 **According to Trokelowe** *Chronica et Annales* 84

p.149 **They advanced like a thick-set hedge** *Vita Edwardi Secundi* 52

p.150 **John of Trokelowe sets the time of this advance** *Chronica et Annales* 84. What he actually says is 'at about the third hour of the day' (*et circa horam diei tertiam*), which equates to 9 a.m. in the contemporary monastic daily cycle. This, as we have noted, is unfeasibly late, as dawn was five hours earlier, and it is unlikely either army would have remained inactive for so long

Chapter 17   Gloucester's Death Ride

p.152   While the sources remain silent   This general arrangement was favoured by the National Trust for Scotland in their official interpretation of the battle (see Taylor, 1984) based on Christison (1959), and followed by Traquair (1998), Reese (2000), Armstrong (2002), Nusbacher (2005) and Sadler (2005). Incidentally, all but Traquair and Armstrong divided the Scottish army into four spear-armed battles

p.152   John of Trokelowe captured something of this   *Chronica et Annales* 84

p.155   On one side stood the magnates of England   Ibid 84-85

p.155   Straight as an arrow was their course   *The Bruce* (Mackenzie, 1912) xii, 501-511

p.156   The *Lanercost Chronicle* paints a similar picture   *Lanercost* 225

p.157   Many a warrior strong and bold   *The Bruce* (Mackenzie, 1912) xii, 525-532

p.158   The Earl of Moray and his men   Ibid xii, 563-570

p.158   Sir Thomas Grey claimed that the Scots   *Scalacronica* (Brown, 2004) 24

p.159   Wishing to win a name for himself   *Chronica et Annales* 85

p.160   As the *Lanercost Chronicle* put it   *Lanercost* 226

Chapter 18   Enter the Marischal

p.163   As a result the arrows struck   *Chronicon Galfredi de Baker* (Thomson, 1881) 8

p.164   The arrows in such numbers fell   *The Bruce* (Mackenzie, 1912) xiii, 39-47

p.166   The confusion comes from Barbour's use of the phrase   *The Bruce* 53-56 in the original Scots, compared to the translation in *The Bruce* (Mackenzie, 1912) xiii, 53-56. The definition of 'lycht' from *Chambers Scots Dictionary* (Edinburgh, 1987) 329-330

p.167   Soon as he saw the battles go   *The Bruce* (Mackenzie, 1912) xiii, 61-73

Chapter 19   Slaughter in the Carse

p.170   **For when the English archers were cut down**   *The Bruce* (Mackenzie, 1912) xiii, 81-86

p.172   **The Scotsmen, finding that the foe**   Ibid xiii, 135-144

p.173   **The *Vita Edwardi Secundi* records that**   *Vita Edwardi Secundi* 54

p.173   **To see Sir Edward and his men**   *The Bruce* (Mackenzie, 1912) xiii, 161-168

p.174   **To watch Lord Randolph and his band**   Ibid xiii, 162-173

p.174   **In fact these were the 'small folk'**   See *The Bruce* xiii, 225-235

p.174   **Here Barbour describes their advance**   *The Bruce* (Mackenzie, 1912) xiii, 243-246

p.175   **By all accounts King Edward fought bravely**   *Scalacronica* 77, *Vita Edwardi Secundi* 54, *Chronica et Annales* 86

p.174   **The English squadrons being thrown into confusion** *Scalacronica* (Brown, 2004) 24-25

Chapter 20   Rout, Plunder and Capture

p.179   **According to Sir Thomas Grey**   *Scalacronica* 77. Also described in *The Bruce* xiii, 295-323

p.180   **The English would no longer stay**   *The Bruce* (Mackenzie, 1912) xiii, 325-332

p.180   **Barbour paints a grim picture**   Ibid xiii, 333-336

p.181   **This ties in with a line from *Scalacronica***   *Scalacronica* 77. Also *Fordun* i, 339

p.182   **The rabble rout of striplings raw**   *The Bruce* (Mackenzie, 1912) xiii, 337-350

p.182   **And Once more Barbour provided a vivid snapshot**   Ibid xiii, 351-354

p.183   **Bruce greeted him**   *The Bruce* xiii, 514-536

p.183   The *Vita Edwardi Secundi* claimed that   *Vita Edwardi Secundi* 56

p.185   The *Lanercost Chronicle* is scathingly critical   *Lanercost* (Brown, 2004) 65

p.185   In like manner, as the king and his following fled   Ibid 65-66

p.196   Many were taken wandering around outside the castle   Ibid 66

Chapter 21   A King in More than Name

p.189   **First, the capture of the Earl of Hereford**   *The Bruce* xiii, 680-696, *Lanercost* 211, CDS iii, 402, Barrow 343, Traquair 202

p.190   **Bruce had proved magnanimous in victory**   *The Bruce* xiii, 686-688, Traquair 202

p.191   **These raids began in August**   *Lanercost* (Brown, 2004) 66, CDS iii, 470. Also Barrow 305-308, Traquair 210-11

p.191   **The raids were repeated for several years**   *Lanercost* (Brown, 2004) 67-72, *Vita Edwardi Secundi* 70-72, CDS iii, 128, 384, 543. In the *Vita Edwardi Secundi* 70 it claims that in Northumbria during these years the inhabitants were reduced to eating horses and dogs

p.191   **It ended badly for him**   Barrow 382, Brown (2004) 212-213, Traquair 203-206

p.191   **In April 1320 three letters were sent**   SHD 55-58. Also Brown (2004) 217-219, Traquair 223-224

p.193   **However, the rebellion was crushed**   *Lanercost* 234-244, *Vita Edwardi Secundi* 122-126, *Chonicon Galfredi* 13-14. *Chronicles of the Reign* (Stubbs, 1882-83) 302. Also Jones 398-401, DeVries 86-99, Traquair 226-228, 252

p.193   **The force that accompanied him was even larger**   *Vita Edwardi Secundi* 126, CDS iii, 747. Also Jones 404, Brown (2004) 220-221

p.194   **Her aim was nothing short of regime change** Jones 412-421, Cornell 247-248 p.194   **In January 1327, as Edward III was being crowned**   Reid 108-112, Jones 422-425, Traquair 242-247, 253

p.195   **The resulting Treaty of Edinburgh-Northampton**   SHD 61-62. Also Brown (2004) 229, Traquair 249. Some English commentators described the treaty as 'a shameful peace', as the defeat at Bannockburn had not been avenged

p.195   **The final act of this new peace deal was a marriage**   Brown (2004) 229

p.196   **Less than a year later the groom's father was dead**   Barrow 418-419, Brown (2004) 229-220, Cornell 251

p.196   **Geoffrey le Baker claims that the English**   *Chonicon Galfredi* 13, *Lanercost* 242-243. Also Jones 445-446, Reid 114-144, Traquair 253, 261-27, Cornell 253, DeVries 112-128, 176-187

Chapter 22   Bannockburn Remembered

p.200   **This blinkered approach**   Quoted in *The Times*, 24 May 1994. Also see Grant & Stringer (1995) 12

p.200   **In an interview with the *Sunday Times***   Quoted in the *Sunday Times*, February 1992

p.200   **Historian Keith Stringer rightly claims**   Grant & Stringer 199

p.201   **This argument was based on a mythical past**   Ferguson (1998) 36-55, Trevor-Roper (2008) 11-13, Marr (2013) 10-11

p.203   **In 1992, in a study about Scottish identity**   Marr 13-14

p.203   **It includes the lines**   Quoted in Crawford (2014) 92, together with a discussion about Burns's egalitarian agenda

Bibliography

Published Primary Sources
Note: All these published sources are available in either the National Library of Scotland in Edinburgh or the British Library in London

Bain, J. et al. (eds); *Calendar of Documents Relating to Scotland* [CDS] (London, 1881-82, Edinburgh, 1887) 2 volumes
Bartholomaei de Cotton; *Historia Anglicana* (London, 1859)
Denholm-Young, N. (ed.); *Vita Edwardi Secundi* (London, 1957)
Donaldson, Gordon; *Scottish Historical Documents* (Edinburgh, 1974) Scottish Academic Press
Duncan, A.A.M. (ed.); John Barbour: *The Bruce* (Edinburgh, 1997)
Laing, D. (ed.); *The Chronicle of John of Fordun* (Edinburgh, 1872)
—— *Scalacronica of Sir Thomas Grey* (Llanerch, 2000)
—— *The Original Chronicle of Andrew of Wyntoun* (Edinburgh, 1872-79)
Luard Lord, H.R.; Matthew Paris: *Flores Historiarum* (London, 1890)
Mackenzie, W. (ed.); *The Bruce* (Glasgow, 1912)
Maitland, J. (ed.); *Chronicon de Lanercost* (Edinburgh, 1839)
Maxwell, Sir Herbert (ed.); *Scalacronica of Sir Thomas Gray of Heton* (Glasgow, 1907)
—— *Chronicle of Lanercost* (Glasgow, 1913)

Palgrave, F. (ed.); *Documents and Records Illustrating the History of Scotland* (London, 1837)

Riley, H.T. (ed.); Thomas Walsingham: *Historia Anglicana* (London, 1863-64)

—— Johannis de Trokelowe et Henrici de Blaneforde: *Chronica et Annales* (London, 1866) Rolls Series

Rothwell, H. (ed.); *The Chronicle of Walter of Guisborough* (London, 1957) Camden Society

Skene, F.S.H.; *Liber Pluscardensis* (Edinburgh, 1877)

Stevenson, J.; *Documents Illustrative of the History of Scotland* (Edinburgh, 1870) 2 volumes

Stubbs, W. (ed.); *Chronicles of the Reign of Edward I and Edward II* (London, 1882-83) Rolls Series

Thomson, E.M.; *Chronicon Galfredi le Baker de Swynebroke* (Oxford, 1881)

Thomson, T. & Innes, C. (eds); *The Acts of the Parliament of Scotland* [APS] (Edinburgh, 1814-75) 12 volumes

Watt, D.E.R. et al. (eds); *Scotichronicon of Walter Bower* (Aberdeen, 1991, 1996)

Secondary Works

Armstrong, Pete; *Bannockburn, 1314: Robert Bruce's Greatest Victory* (Oxford, 2002) Osprey Publishing

Barron, Evan Macleod; *The Scottish War of Independence* (Inverness, 1934) Robert Carruthers

Barrow, G.W.S.; *Robert Bruce and the Community of the Realm of Scotland* (London, 1965) Eyre & Spottiswoode, reprinted Edinburgh University Press 2013

Bradbury, Jim; *The Medieval Archer* (Woodbridge, 1985) Boydell

Brown, Chris; *Robert the Bruce: A Life Chronicled* (Stroud, 2004) Tempus

—— *William Wallace: The True Story of Braveheart* (Stroud, 2005) The History Press

—— *Bannockburn 1314: A New History* (Stroud, 2008) The History Press

Brown, Michael; *The Wars of Scotland, 1214-1371* (Edinburgh, 2004) Edinburgh University Press

Caldwell, David; *Scotland's Wars and Warriors: Winning Against the Odds* (Edinburgh, 1998) The Stationery Office

Chaplais, Pierre; *Piers Gaveston: Edward II's Adoptive Brother* (Oxford, 1994) Clarendon Press

Christison, P.; *Bannockburn – 23rd and 24th June, 1314: A Study in Military History* in *Proceedings of the Society of Antiquaries in Scotland*, xc (1959)

Clark, David; *Battlefield Walks: Scotland* (Stroud, 1996) Sutton Publishing

Cornell, David; *Bannockburn: The Triumph of Robert the Bruce* (London, 2009) Yale University Press

Coss, Peter; *The Knight in Medieval England, 1000-1400* (Stroud, 1993) Alan Sutton

Crawford, Robert: *Bannockburns: Scottish Independence and Literary Imagination, 1314-2014* (Edinburgh, 2014) Edinburgh University Press

Crum, Frederick Laurence; *Bannockburn* (Stirling, 1927) Learmonth

DeVries, Kelly; *Infantry Warfare in the Early Fourteenth Century* (Woodbridge, 1996) Boydell Press

Duncan, A.A.M.; *Scotland: The Making of a Kingdom* (Edinburgh, 1975) Mercat Press

Ferguson, William; *The Identity of the Scottish Nation: An Historic Quest* (Edinburgh, 1998) Edinburgh University Press

Forbes, George; *Scottish Battles: 86 AD to 1746* (Glasgow, 1996) Lang Syne

Fryde, Natalie; *The Tyranny and Fall of Edward II, 1321-26* (Cambridge, 1979) Cambridge University Press

Du Garde Peach, L.; *Robert the Bruce* (Loughborough, 1964) Wills & Hepworth (Ladybird)

Grant, Alexander; *Independence and Nationhood: Scotland, 1306-1469* (London, 1984) Edward Arnold

Grant, Alexander & Stringer, Keith J. (eds); *Uniting the Kingdom? The Making of British History* (London, 1995) Routledge

Hardy, Robert; *Longbow: A Social and Military History* (Yeovil, 1976) Patrick Stephens

Hardy, Robert & Strickland, Matthew; *The Great Warbow: From Hastings to the Mary Rose* (Stroud, 2005) Alan Sutton

Jones, Dan; *The Plantagenets: The Kings who Made England* (London, 2012) Harper Press

Keen, Maurice; *Medieval Warfare: A History* (Oxford, 1999) Oxford University Press

Macdougall, Norman; *An Antidote to the English: The Auld Alliance, 1295-1560* (East Linton, 2001) Tuckwell Press

Mackay, James; *William Wallace: Braveheart* (Edinburgh, 1995) Mainstream

Mackenzie, William Mackay; *The Battle of Bannockburn: A Study in Mediaeval Warfare* (Glasgow, 1913) Grant & Murray

—— *The Bannockburn Myth* (Edinburgh, 1932) Grant & Murray

McNamee, Colm; *Robert Bruce: Our Most Valiant Prince, King and Lord* (Edinburgh, 2006) Birlinn Ltd

—— *The Wars of the Bruces: Scotland, England and Ireland, 1306-28* (Edinburgh, 2006) John Donald

MacPhee, Andy; *The Scottish Wars of Independence, 1286-1328* (Paisley, 2010) Hodder & Gibson

Marr, Andrew; *The Battle of Scotland* (London, 1992, augmented and reissued 2013) Penguin

Marren, Peter; *Grampian Battlefields* (Edinburgh, 1993) Mercat Press

Miller, Thomas; *The site of the New Park in relation to the Battle of Bannockburn*, published in *Scottish Historical Review* XII, No. 45 (1914)

   The Site of the Battle of Bannockburn (London, 1931) Historical Association (leaflet)

The Battle of Bannockburn was won beside Skeoch Hill (Stirling, 1938) self-published

Morris, John E.; *Bannockburn* (Cambridge, 1914) Cambridge University Press

Morrison, Dorothy; *The Wars of Independence: A Sense of History* (Harlow, 1996) Longman

Nicholson, Ranald; *Scotland in the Later Middle Ages* (Edinburgh, 1974) Edinburgh University Press

Norman, A.V.B. & Pottinger, Don; *The Medieval Soldier* (Barnsley, 2005) Leo Cooper

Nusbacher, Aryeh; *1314: Bannockburn* (Stroud, 2005) Tempus

Oman, Charles; *The Art of War in the Middle Ages, 1278-1485* Vol. II (1924, reprinted London, 1991) Greenhill

Penman, Michael; *The Scottish Civil War: The Bruce & the Balliols, & the War for Control of Scotland* (Stroud, 2002) Tempus

Phillips, J.R.S.; *Aymer de Valence, Earl of Pembroke* (Oxford, 1972) Oxford University Press

Pollard, Tony & Oliver, Neil; *Two Men in a Trench II: Uncovering the Secrets of British Battlefields* (London, 2003) Michael Joseph

Prestwich, Michael; *Edward I* (London, 1988) Guild Publishing, reprinted Yale University Press 1997

—— *Armies and Warfare in the Middle Ages: The English Experience* (London, 1999) Yale University Press

Reese, Peter; *Bannockburn: Scotland's Greatest Victory* (Edinburgh, 2000) Canongate Books

Reid, Peter; *By Fire and Sword: The Rise and Fall of English Supremacy at Arms, 1314-1385* (London, 2007) Constable

Sadler, John; *Scottish Battles: From Mons Graupius to Culloden* (Edinburgh, 1996) Canongate Books

—— *Bannockburn: Battle for Liberty* (Barnsley, 2008) Pen & Sword

Scott, William; *Bannockburn Revealed: A reappraisal* (Rothesay, 2000) Elenkus

—— *The Genius of Bannockburn* (Rothesay, 2012) Elenkus

Shearer, John E.; *Fact and Fiction in the Story of Bannockburn* (Stirling, 1909) R.S. Shearer

—— *The Battle of Bannockburn, 1314: The Reputed Sites and the Mythical Carse Site Reviewed* (Stirling, 1914) R.A.

Stones, E.L.G. & Simpson, Grant G.; *Edward I and the Throne of Scotland* (Oxford, 1979) 2 volumes, Oxford University Press

Strickland, Matthew (ed.); *Armies, Chivalry and Warfare in Medieval Britain and France* (Stamford, 1998) Paul Watkins

Taylor, Cameron; *Bannockburn* (Edinburgh, 1984) National Trust for Scotland

Traquair, Peter; *Freedom's Sword: Scotland's Wars of Independence* (London, 1998) HarperCollins

Trevor-Roper, Hugh; *The Invention of Scotland: Myth and History* (London, 2009) Yale University Press

Watson, Fiona; *Under the Hammer: Edward I and Scotland, 1286-1307* (East Linton, 1998) Tuckwell Press

Watson, Fiona & Anderson, Maggie; *The Battle of Bannockburn: A Study for Stirling Council* (Stirling, 2001)

White, Robert; *A History of the Battle of Bannockburn* (Edinburgh, 1871) Edmonston & Douglas

Young, Alan; *Robert Bruce's Rivals: The Comyns, 1212-1314* (Edinburgh, 1997) Tuckwell Press

Index